BE BLESSED...

DOING GOD'S WORK

WITH BROTHERS AND SISTERS IN CHRIST
SERVING IN MILWAUKEE.

ARN QUAKKELAAR

Published by White Blackbird Books, an imprint of Storied Publishing

Permission requests and other questions may be directed to the Contact page at www.storied.pub.

Printed in the United States of America

ISBN: 978-1-7340181-9-6

Printed in USA

Cover design by Sean Benesh

ALSO BY WHITE BLACKBIRD BOOKS

All Are Welcome: Toward a Multi-Everything Church

The Almost Dancer

Birth of Joy: Philippians

Choosing a Church: A Biblical and Practical Guide

Co-Laborers, Co-Heirs: A Family Conversation

EmBRACE: A Biblical Study on Justice and Race

Ever Light and Dark: Telling Secrets, Telling the Truth

Everything Is Meaningless? Ecclesiastes

Heal Us Emmanuel: A Call for Racial Reconciliation, Representation, and Unity in the Church

The Organized Pastor: Systems to Care for People Well

Rooted: The Apostles' Creed

A Sometimes Stumbling Life

Urban Hinterlands: Planting the Gospel in Uncool Places

Follow whiteblackbirdbooks.pub for upcoming titles and releases.

PRAISE FOR DOING GOD'S WORK

Arn Quakkelaar's missional commitment and curiosity about Milwaukee unfolds into a life-giving and city-changing experience. God uses Arn to unite urban and suburban, to lift the lives of the impoverished and oppressed, to bridge racial divides, and to rebuild broken lives, families, and neighborhoods. In this book readers will find a new kind of church, a citywide church being revealed that fits our time and reflects the vision of God's heavenly Jerusalem. Take the journey with him in *Doing God's Work*.

Glenn Barth
President, GoodCities

How do we get past individual incremental programs and posturing to get to the needed redeemed changes and transformed places, lives, families, neighborhoods, and cities?
Arn Quakkelaar did this by casting the visions, calling the meetings, catalyzing the resources, convening and coordinating the efforts, and helping to define and produce the outcomes?
It has taken a lifetime, but he has pulled together the top leaders—and the least, lost, last, and left out—to produce multiple metrics of grace.
He shares in this book how it *has* happened and how it *can* happen.
He also earned ten words essential to this happening:
Competent/Rooted/Longevity/Transformational/Persistent/Resilient/Relevant/Trusted/Focused/Incarnational.
He built the teams, completed the outcomes, and finishes well.
The mark of a serving leader!
Are you a leader with a broken heart for your city, and wanting to learn how to invest your life intelligently?
Read this book so you can envision your city, train your people on

what to do and how to think, and then equip them with the necessary tools.

This is a book for every city - anywhere!

Art Erickson
Founder, Urban Ventures
Director, StudiOne-Eighty

Would that more individuals who have the gifts and experience of Arn in the world of leading successful companies would demonstrate the power of the Word of God in other cities. May this be the book that not only makes Milwaukee famous in the cause of the Gospel, but is used by God to show a seismic movement of his grace and power in these momentous days.

Walter C. Kaiser, Jr.
President Emeritus, Gordon-Conwell Theological Seminary

In 1999 I met my good friend Arn Quakkelaar in New York City. He is the founding leader of BASICS in Milwaukee. I had a heart to energize and develop leaders and so did Arn. He knew everyone in Milwaukee, and I knew no one there. Arn loaned me his hard-earned leadership equity and personal credibility. Because of that partnership, thousands of leaders were equipped and inspired. If anyone knows about *Doing God's Work*, it is Arn Quakkelaar. Following my meeting in NYC with Arn, I wrote him a letter. One of the sentences says, "You have such a gentle, yet strong spirit about you. It was a blessing just to be with you." That was true in 1999, and it is still true today. It is my distinct honor to call Arn Quakkelaar my partner, friend and brother.

Sam Chand
Leadership Consultant
Author, *Leadership Pain*

ABOUT THE AUTHOR

Arnold "Arn" J. Quakkelaar attended Calvin University and earned a BS in engineering physics and mathematics. He began his career in 1955 with Johnson Controls and finished with Rockwell International as the International Vice President of The Global Technical Support Division. His team established ninety-one technical centers located in twenty-eight countries.

Arn was married in 1959 and raised five sons with his wife, Norma. Arn has served as deacon, elder, and chairman of the Council of Elders in his home church. When Arn felt a call into full-time ministry, he spent a year on the streets of Milwaukee, meeting and talking with hundreds of people. He experienced first-hand the dreadful conditions in the city. Arn visited with community leaders, organizations, pastors, deacons, gang leaders, and Christians, building relationships in preparation for the work God had for him to do.

In 1997 Arn started BASICS (Brothers And Sisters In Christ Serving), a nonprofit organization ministering to the underserved in the inner city of Milwaukee. BASICS has worked with over 400 churches and ministries. In 2005 Arn also founded GENESIS, a prison reentry ministry serving hundreds of "returning citizens" to assist them in recovery. Arn is currently serving as emeritus with BASICS and GENESIS.

DEDICATION

This book is lovingly dedicated to our many faithful
brothers and sisters in Jesus Christ who have faithfully
served our Lord together to bring the good news of
Jesus Christ to our city of Milwaukee:

*Arthur Riemer, Ed Edwards, Lamar Beverly – Davis, Arnold
Brownstein, Paul Merriken. Jack Brown, Paul Kjenvet, Ron Koepke,
Suzanne Hull, Fred Sindorf, Scott Martin, Fred and Jinny
Schneider, Ron Knox, Clarence Hill, Bridgett Sheehan, Jerome
Spencer, Bill and Jan Godfrey, Mary Kay Meeker, Cary Bogue,
Carol Jeffries, Michael J. Hayden, Bud Ipema*

My inspiration to *serve* comes from God's Word:

But as for me, I will always have hope;
I will praise you more and more.
My mouth will tell of your righteousness, of your salvation all day
long, though I know not its measure.
I will come and proclaim your mighty acts, O Sovereign Lord;
I will proclaim your righteousness, yours alone.
Since my youth, O God, you have taught me,
and to this day I declare your marvelous deeds.
Even when I am old and gray, do not forsake me, O God,
till I declare your power to the next generation,
your might to all who are to come.
Psalm 71: 14–18

Blessed are all who fear the Lord, who walk in His ways.
You will eat the fruit of your labor;
blessings and prosperity will be yours.
Your wife will be like a fruitful vine within your house;
your sons will be like olive shoots around your table.

Thus is the man blessed who fears the Lord.
May the Lord bless you from Zion all the days of your life;
May you see the prosperity of Jerusalem,
and may you live to see your children's children.
Peace be upon Israel.
Psalm 128: 1–6

ACKNOWLEDGMENTS

Writing this book has been an awesome experience of witnessing God's presence in guiding my life to see and remember the many stories of his people doing his work to bring his kingdom to his city. This book is truly God's story, and the telling of this story gives God the glory for what he has and is doing for you and me.

All the stories in this book are true to the best of my memory. In some cases I've made minor changes to protect individuals from embarrassment or criticism, and in a few stories I've taken editorial liberties to provide illustration or clarity in certain events. I've researched background details as thoroughly as I could, although at times inferences were made from limited facts available.

I praise God for blessing me with a wonderful friend and wife, Norma, who has been a loving and caring wife, mother, grandmother, and great-grandmother to our family while making it possible for me to write this story. Her love and faithfulness for over sixty years of marriage is a blessing and gift far beyond anything I deserve. Our family history gives testimony to God's goodness with over six generations of both Norma and I having God-fearing parents and grandparents.

My dear friends and pastors, Stuart and Jill Briscoe have been my inspiration and guide for over a half century with their life examples of servant leadership, humility, wisdom, three-point sermons, and living insights that were truly God-given. I praise God for their magnificent examples.

I also praise God for the gifts of the many individuals who have generously given their precious time, talents, treasures, touch, and tears to make this book a reality:

- Mark Mallwitz, project manager
- Todd Svanoe, writing coach
- Alaina Mallwitz, editor
- Deana Ratz, editor
- Claire Berger, editor
- BASICS Prayer Team
- BASICS Ministers to Milwaukee
- Milwaukee pastors and ministry leaders
- Volunteers and donors
- Storied Publishing and Doug Serven

CONTENTS

FOREWORD BY DR. STUART BRISCOE

This is a book about a man, his vision, and his city.

Like many of his contemporaries facing midlife, Arn Quakkelaar sat down and took stock of his life. As he sought the Lord, something stirred inside him, a vision for what things could be if God would bless a work. The result was the kindling of a work which is still unfolding in the streets, storefronts, drug dives, prisons, boardrooms, safe houses, and churches of his adopted city of Milwaukee, Wisconsin.

Arn was a successful professional engineer. He had risen to International Vice President of his company. A devout Christian, he had also immersed himself in the life of his church including serving as Board Chairman and managing the building of a twelve million dollar facility.

So it was not surprising that he, with the support of his loyal wife Norma, responded positively to what they believed was God's call to take an early retirement and devote themselves to taking the Christian Gospel wherever needed. That turned out to be the inner city of Milwaukee, once described by the renowned American evangelist, Dwight L. Moody as the "graveyard of evangelists."

Arn was advised to spend at least one year on the streets learning everything about the city, which he began to do. By day he introduced himself to anyone he met. Then he listened to everyone who would talk to him. By night he studied everything he could find about Milwaukee's history—its founding and development; its politics, religion, and demographics. He met the city's leadership and the many pastors of small storefront churches, who were rich in faith but poor in resources.

Two things became clear to him: the crushing realities of poverty and the presence of many believers in difficult and often dangerous living circumstances.

He went back to the churches in the suburbs where he was well-respected and began to speak about fellowship and partnership with his new friends, the people of the inner city. Through this vision and these conversations, Arn founded BASICS, "Brothers and Sisters in Christ Serving." Its mission is to be a Christian organization supporting community development by integrating spiritual, social, and physical aspects into a change process.

More than twenty-five years later this "change process" is taking place wherever change is called for—derelict buildings are being restored and occupied, drug dens are closing down, churches are being planted, ex-offenders are being recognized as returning citizens, runaway kids are coming home, trafficked girls are being delivered, jobs are being created, drop-outs are being trained, and families are being restored.

We rejoice to witness the biggest, best change of all—men and women and boys and girls are being born again into the company of the redeemed, the community of faith, the disciples of Jesus, the Kingdom of God!

If I may, I would like to summarize my reading of this book by utilizing one of Arn's favorite methods of taking voluminous notes (of everything)—bullet points.

- Information—all that you may not know about Milwaukee, and all that God is doing there through devoted followers of Jesus.
- Inspiration—to sense the ache of recognizing need, the excitement of being called to meet the need, and the joy of being part of the answer.

- Invitation—to wish in some way to model the prophet Isaiah who when he was challenged by God, replied, *"Lord here am I. Send me."*

Stuart Briscoe
Pastor Emeritus, Elmbrook Church.

INTRODUCTION

As a believer in Jesus Christ, have you ever been accused of being a hypocrite because you didn't do what someone thought you should have done? Or, have you lost your desire to go to church because you just didn't like the people there, or the pastor always made you feel inadequate because you were not doing what God says you should do? Maybe you believe you're a fairly decent person and doing well, but there's something lacking and you just can't understand what God wants you to do? Life is filled with so many complications and pressures, you'd like to stop and start over. Don't feel alone!

My life has had its ups and downs. At times, I thought things were going well, but I didn't feel there was a purpose or direction that aligned with God's plan. My story may be just what you need to put your life together God's way—doing your work as worship and watching him build his kingdom with the resources he gives you.

My first twenty years of life were quite normal, I thought, followed by forty years in the corporate world, and then only to find out that God was always preparing me to do his work in far greater ways than I could ever have imagined. The next twenty-two years in full-time ministry work for God were blessed far beyond anything I could have dreamt and were the most exhilarating years I could ever have anticipated. God put me in places throughout the world I could never have imagined or arranged. He showed his miracles in ways that changed my life and the lives of many others who I'll only know about if God tells me in his eternal home.

The basic themes you'll find in reading this book will help you build a closer walk with the God who created you for specific functions together with other Brothers and Sisters in Christ Serving (BASICS) together in unity, harmony, and peace. Some practical lessons I've learned along this path are based on reading and studying God's Word, which is the foundation of everything in this book. The second foundation is a strong prayer life.

God created the heavens, the earth, me, and you for his purposes and with the ability to make choices to obey or disobey his commands to believe him or deny him. What an awesome responsibility we have for our life or death! These are the absolute truths of life.

Over the past century, the US government and society has assumed much of the responsibility for taking care of the impoverished citizens in the United States. At the beginning of the twentieth century, the faith community (largely those from Catholic, Jewish, and Lutheran traditions) assumed the role of providing compassion to those who needed help.

During the 1960s, government systems unknowingly began to encourage the fathers of families to leave so the mothers could receive government welfare support. During the nineties, the government changed the ground rules requiring mothers to go to work in order to qualify for W-2 financial support. This created a new industry of social services relating to employment, training, childcare, transportation, etc., which took mothers out of the home and forcing their children to be taken care of by grand-mamas, aunts, friends, or childcare agencies.

Poverty in America continues to grow even though the numbers don't show it. The threshold of poverty income keeps rising to make the data look better. Misery among those who have the ability and desire to work must overcome tremendous obstacles. These obstacles are not always recognized by society, and sadly not even recognized by faith communities who have ignored areas of extreme poverty. An increasing number of citizens have consequently fallen into the category of the invisible, abandoned working poor.

Agencies compete intensely with each other for tax funds that become increasingly difficult to win and often require increasing amounts of administrative costs resulting in less money available to reduce the poverty it was intended to impact. Collaboration, cooperation, and coordination among social service organizations have been difficult to achieve when attempting to provide holistic services for the needy. This presents a unique opportunity for the faith community to demonstrate the value of partnerships that build an infrastructure of solutions to reduce poverty and bring unity within neighborhoods.

My hope is to give you real-life stories to show and tell God's love to disenfranchised citizens in Milwaukee. The resulting miracles serve as signs of God's work, using us as vehicles, to bring his love to our neighbors.

It occurs to me that the churches in Milwaukee could be like producing "Milorganite," a process of collecting all the human waste and returning it into the city "purified by God's mercy and grace." Milorganite is fertilizer produced in Milwaukee through its hi-tech waste-water process of dehydration and fermentation. It causes a horrible smell when changing waste into purified water funneled back into Lake Michigan at the Milwaukee's Sewage Treatment Plant on Jones Island. God washes away our sins when we believe that Jesus Christ is his son, and through the power of the Holy Spirit, he transforms us to be his children and heirs to the Kingdom of God.

My prayer for you is that God will show you his love and how you can choose to overcome the waste in your life and have it lead to showing and telling his love through the power of his Holy Spirit to change and transform lives of your family, friends, neighbors, and yourself.

May God bless you as you worship him doing his work his way.

MILWAUKEE MIRACLES

Have you ever been moved with compassion by news of the suffering poor, life lost to violent crime, or lust-driven human trafficking in Milwaukee? Have you ever wondered where people of faith or hope, with talents and resources, could be found to help feed a deserving family, mentor a fatherless child, or improve living conditions for vulnerable fellow humans? What will move us? What moved me out of the salt shaker and into the world?

For years, as a successful engineer raising five sons, I conveniently drove the highway around these problems and ignored them. They were out-of-sight and, therefore, out-of-mind. But something missing in my life began to eat away at me. I professed to follow Jesus, who walked toward, not around, these people. He said, *"To whom much is given, much is required."* I knew I had been given a lot.

Have you ever asked, as I did, "God, what more do you want from my life?" When I followed his answer, got out of my comfort zone, and introduced myself to my disenfranchised Milwaukee neighbors, my assumptions were reversed, my faith came alive, and my life was changed.

What I saw on the news had seemed overwhelming and impersonal until, in the late '90s, I prayed with gangsters Tommy Gun and Fat Boy and helped the Madam of Milwaukee start a ministry to prostitutes. News of Milwaukee's dilapidated buildings, about to be condemned, seemed hopeless until we developed new relationships with African American, Latino, and Asian pastors who heard about their code violations. They recruited over a thousand volunteers, along with building-material donors, and restored more than fifty centers of worship!

In the following pages, you'll hear dozens of stories of how God responded to our prayers when we faced our fears, resulting in Milwaukee Miracles on a scale we could not have imagined. These experiences have led me to ask, "Are our city's problems too big, or is our faith too small?" Little by little over the last sixty years of my adult life, God has built my faith, often through my urban brothers and sisters. He has taken me from living my own life my own way at the limits of my resources, to living the love-laced life God opens to me doing things his way. I am now tapping his unlimited resources, *"immeasurably more than all we ask or imagine"* (Eph. 3:20).

We Wisconsinites, looking at our urban problems, are no different from Moses. He was afraid to confront Pharaoh and the grand scale of deep misery tied up with the slavery of God's people in Egypt. We're no different from Noah who people scoffed at for what seemed a delusional big-boat dream to save people and animals from extinction.

Can we scratch the surface of these mammoth troubles in our own power? Of course not! That's why the prophets say, *"Ah, Sovereign LORD, you have made the heavens and the earth by your great power and outstretched arm. Nothing is too difficult for you"* (Jer. 32:17, NIV).

Maybe I've been called the Moses of Milwaukee because I listened to the question God asked Moses, *"Is the Lord's arm too short?"* (Num. 11:23, NIV) and had the audacity to say *no!* (OK, it may also have something to do with my grey hair and beard!).

In 1996, I took a challenge from Chicago urban minister and former classmate Bud Ipema to spend a year hoofing it through the toughest neighborhoods of Milwaukee to meet movers and shakers there, gang leaders to pastors, to have listening sessions, and get up front and personal.

I felt the painful stories, brokenness and despair of our city, which is still the most racially segregated city in the US. And I wept, like Jesus wept, overlooking Jerusalem.

Yet I cried not so much at the poverty, evil, and hatred on our doorstep, but at my own misconceptions and at the fact that people in the suburbs had no idea what was going on in Milwaukee. My expectation was that I would bring them Jesus. It was just the reverse.

They taught me. They had deeper faith than I had as they relied on God for their very survival. I could buy anything I wanted. Wealthy people just don't know the brand of faith, hope, or love that sustains so many marginalized people.

I was shocked to learn of an association called Pastors United. It consisted of nearly five hundred inner-city pastors and leaders who were up against things I had never experienced. They were relying on God's Word and praying with greater fervency than most of my best friends. Unity for them does not come easy, but the depth of shared needs bonds them like soldiers in danger before an enemy as they risk their lives and depend on one another.

Meanwhile God had shown me, in both the church and the corporate world, his greater capacity and willingness, as we asked him, to meet wide-scale human needs in unexpected and miraculous ways:

• When he gave me wisdom to create the Global Technical Support Division of Rockwell International, growing a $110 million start-up from one to 1,100 employees in twenty-eight countries, with a 10 percent return-on-investment over three years.

• When he allowed me to plan and supervise the building of a new Elmbrook Church, making it the largest place of worship in Wisconsin.

• When my wife Norma and I joined an American business delegation that created a symposium with atheistic communist Tajikistan leaders. Despite falling prey to our worst fear, being kidnapped by rebels, by God's grace we were still allowed to share God's Ten Commandments with the entire delegation, seven boxes of Bibles with the community, and televised faith testimonies with the entire nation!

● Before entering Tajikistan, our host transported us for a divinely timed visit to Red Square in front of the Kremlin, where Mikael Gorbachev oversaw the historic transition of the Russian state from Soviet Union to the Commonwealth of Independent States.

All of this prepared me to believe in a God big enough for Milwaukee, or any other city! Again, can we scratch the surface in our own power? No chance! But is it in his heart to heal and redeem us, and will he act if we ask and trust him? Absolutely!

This book shares (mostly chronological) stories of what God has done, meant to inspire you to pray as a vessel of faith, hope, and service, and to offer not only time, talent, and treasures, but your tears and touch.

Read on and you will hear how God has blessed dozens of ministers to Milwaukee, people just like you, with their own visions, mentored and supported by the organization I started in 1996, BASICS, (Brothers And Sisters In Christ Serving).

Ask yourself, what can you do to help heal Milwaukee or your city? You may have read the Bible's Acts of the Apostles, stories from Jesus' earliest followers of love-in-action done through Jesus' resurrection power. Be inspired by modern stories of what God has done and continues to do in our city.

Then I challenge you to look honestly at what may be missing in your own blessed life, and pray, "Here I am, Lord. Send me!"

As I always say, "*Straight ahead!*" (Prov. 4:25, NIV).

IN THE BEGINNING

1937

In the beginning God created the heavens and the earth.
Genesis 1:1

O Lord, you have searched me and you know me.
Psalm 139:1

For you created my inmost being, you knit me together in my mother's womb. I praise you because I am fearfully and wonderfully made.... All the days ordained for me were written in your book before one of them came to be.
Psalm 139:13–16

What:
A testimony of how God created me for his purposes.
So What:
To encourage readers to reflect on their own early years to recognize God's work in creating their own unique personal characteristics for life.
Now What:
Apply the principles to your life.

My life began as a blessing to my parents and grandparents as a third-generation first-born son of a devout Dutch Christian heritage of righteous, disciplined living. There was no swearing, drinking, smoking, movies, dancing, or riding our bikes on Sundays. I had no idea how families who were not Christians lived until I joined the US Army at the age of seventeen. Loving my dad, mom, two brothers, and three sisters was our family's way of life with virtually no fights and no abuse other than having my mouth washed out with soap for saying "Gosh," not knowing that was using God's name in vain.

At birth, I was found to have a large cyst in my left chest. Surgery successfully corrected the problem. My life almost ended when I swallowed a quarter and couldn't breathe. My Gramma Koster slapped my back and saved my life. As a toddler I wandered into a pasture with cows. Our dog Tippy got my mom and led her to where I was and brought me home to safety. I think many of us have had similar experiences for which we can say, "God was with us." I learned very early that God loved me and took care of me.

My earliest memory was at the age of five in 1941 when the attack on Pearl Harbor was announced on the radio Sunday morning while our family was getting ready to go to Franklin Street Christian Reformed Church on the Southwest Side in Grand Rapids, Michigan. A gripping fear entered my life, but I saw that mom and dad had a deep sense of trust in God.

At the age of eight in 1945 when the Second World War ended, I vividly remember celebrating the victory being carried on my dad's shoulders to see the Victory Parade in downtown Grand Rapids, Michigan. The shouting, flag-waving men, women, and children like me were stretching our necks to see the soldiers and military vehicles representing the power of America along with the exhilarating feeling of freedom from the fear of war.

Prayer was the foundation of our family life starting with prayer at every breakfast meal together with my brother and two sisters. During the war, dad was eager to serve in the army but was not allowed to go because his job was considered critical as part of the food supply industry delivering baked goods for Farm Crest

Bakeries, and because he was valued as the father of a family of four young children. He eagerly volunteered as a Civil Defense Captain and was assigned to the Naylor Street neighborhood. After quickly being trained and supplied with a uniform, gas mask, and helmet, he was given the responsibility to instruct the neighbors to follow government directives for obtaining food stamps and instruct them as to what they should do when the air-raid sirens sounded. I remember being very frightened when we were told to hurry into the basement to be protected from gas attacks by either German or Japanese bombers. This caused everyone to become very alert and fearful of the dangers during warfare.

During this war time period, our family became very close with a strong spirit of love and care. Every breakfast, lunch, and dinner were started with prayer, and then we had Bible reading after supper. Mom was an outstanding gospel music piano player and taught us many Christian songs with the harmony, rhythm, and words that were to impact my life forever. We learned that praying and singing together gave us a "peace that passes all understanding."

In our home, there were absolutely no dirty words, swearing, drinking, drugs, or sexual promiscuity. We also were very poor and could afford no vacations. We enjoyed a very stable Christian lifestyle and didn't realize how poor we really were.

Our family lifestyle changed dramatically on October 31, 1946, on my dad's thirty-sixth birthday. Mom received an urgent call from Mr. Story, dad's boss at Farm Crest Bakeries, informing her that there was a terrible accident involving dad and he was critically injured. He came to pick up mom and bring her to the emergency room at Blodgett Memorial Hospital in Grand Rapids. Virtually every part of dad's body was broken: a skull fracture, both arms and legs broken, one hand and one foot almost severed, eight ribs broken. He was in critical condition within moments of death.

Prayer was immediately initiated throughout our family and church family for God's healing mercies. We witnessed God's plan miraculously demonstrated by arranging a medical team of army doctors having just returned from Europe to be available to put my

3

dad back to life during the next nine months in the hospital. I remember being told by my dad that I would now have to be the man of our family because I was the oldest; I would have to take good care of mom, Rog, Grace, and Joyce.

During the next three years our family became very poor with an income of only twenty-one dollars per month. God enabled me to learn the importance of work very early in life. My first introduction to a formal job occurred when I was nine years old. I was hired to plant onion sets on my hands and knees on a muck farm in Wyoming, Michigan for twenty-five cents per hour. This gave me a little money to be able to buy milk in school during the lunch hour in the fall.

The next three summers from 1947 to 1949, I was able to work picking strawberries with my brother Rog at the Versluis Fruit Farms in Standale, Michigan. Our day started early with a five-mile ride on our old bikes from southwest Grand Rapids to Standale. We would get back home just before dark every day of the week except Sunday.

Work became our way of life. We worked collecting and selling newspapers and magazines to recycle, going door-to-door selling cookies and greeting cards my dad would get for us from a wholesale distributor he knew. Rog and I also worked cutting lawns and shoveling snow, doing whatever we could to help pay the bills and buy our own clothes. Early in our lives, God was preparing me to learn the value of money and work and how to spend money wisely.

My relationship with God and knowing Jesus was real and present through my loving family and neighbors. Dad's recovery was slow and painful, leaving him a cripple for the rest of his long life of eighty-seven years. Mom stayed close to his side as a marvelous example of faithfulness in marriage. Divorce was never ever mentioned and would never be an option—a great model for me to follow in my life living God's way.

My teen years involved mostly work: delivering newspapers for the Grand Rapids Press, working as a grocery packer and shelf-stacker in Lenger's supermarket, doing artwork on card tables for a

Catholic charity, earning enough money to pay for my own clothes and expenses while attending Grand Rapids Christian High School. One night while riding my bike home after work with another friend, he swerved in front of me causing me to wipe-out. I landed on the back of my head causing a severe brain concussion and a skull fracture. God was with me the last mile home in the dark without my glasses, bleeding and in severe pain. Dad took me to the hospital where I couldn't move for two weeks and learned more about only being able to look up to God for healing. These were formative years in preparing me for life.

FIRST CALL
1950–53

As a child, I always felt God was real and I was to fear him. It was in 1944 at a summer Bible school near our home, I confirmed my belief in Jesus and vowed to obey his commandments for the rest of my life. He chose me and appointed me to go and bear fruit —*"fruit that will last. Then the Father will give you whatever you ask in my name"* (Jn. 15:16). It was a formative decision that gave direction to the many decisions, for good or evil, for the rest of my life.

When I was thirteen, my pastor preached a powerful message that brought God directly into my soul. I couldn't sleep that night. I experienced God's presence like I had never experienced before. That night I was convinced God called me to become his servant as a pastor, minister, missionary, or whatever he wanted me to be. My personal prayers focused on asking God to show and lead me into his way. From that point on, I felt led to focus on learning and developing skills related to ministry such as music, the arts, social sciences, English, history, etc. in preparation for college at our denomination's Calvin College and Seminary in Grand Rapids.

During high school at Grand Rapids Christian, I worked part-time and summers for the Kent Home Improvement Company owned by my Uncle Gabe Quakkelaar. This introduced me to home improvement construction trades and hardware store sales, a very practical and comfortable working environment I enjoyed and learned a lot from. My extracurricular activities and spare time were spent in the arts and music. I won local and state awards, which seemed to confirm my direction into ministry.

At graduation from high school, I decided to join the United States Army Active Reserve (since I was classified by the draft board as "A-1" to be drafted into the military upon graduation). There were openings in the 70th Infantry Division Army Band so I auditioned and was accepted as a clarinet and baritone saxophone player. I felt this eight-year experience and income would be helpful for me while attending college and preparing for my career in ministry.

I was convinced that God was in control of my life.

THE CORPORATE WORLD
1960–1990

In November of 1955 Johnson Service Company (now Johnson Controls, Inc.) offered me a part-time position as draftsman of schematics for Johnson Control systems. One of my high school drafting teachers referred Johnson Controls to me because of my art skills in his class. I saw this as a direct message from God. I knew God says, *"I know the plans I have for you, declares the Lord, plans to prosper you and not harm you, plans to give you hope and a future"* (Jer. 29:11). I immediately started working in their engineering department.

My first day on the job, my boss's boss informed me that to be successful and keep my employment with the company, I would have to get an engineering degree. I enrolled in the pre-engineering curriculum at Calvin College in the midterm session February, 1956. I wondering why God would direct me to go in a different direction than ministry. How could engineering be a ministry?

Entering college with an intensive science emphasis requires prerequisite courses in high school math, physics, chemistry, etc. I had none of these courses in high school. I was put on academic probation and assigned to an academic advisor. Another challenge was registering mid-semester. There was a limited selection of classes and I was assigned to two second semester courses in Chemistry 101 and Economics 302. I had not completed the prerequisites; both led to failing grades. My academic advisor called me into his office at the end of that first semester to suggest my college experience had ended, and I would be much better suited to a career in construction. But I didn't quit.

I knew God called me to do what he directed, and not go my way. So I worked hard with my school studies, served in the Army Reserve, stayed active in my church, worked for Johnson Service Company as a part-time draftsman and technician, and dated my future wife. I seldom got more than four hours of sleep at night, which was a good preparation for a future in ministry.

Upon graduation, I was hired by Johnson Service Company as its first graduate Application Engineer to begin a career I had never expected would lead to world-wide experiences I would never have expected. God certainly was in control.

MARRIAGE TO NORMA AND
A BLESSED FAMILY
1956–PRESENT

Shortly after graduating from Grand Rapids Christian High School, I met a beautiful girl at a church youth group gathering of the West Leonard Christian Reformed Church. Norma Flietstra became the love of my life. We dated for three-and-a-half years and were married on August 28, 1959. She helped me financially to complete my final year at Calvin College and I graduated in June, 1960 debt-free. God's plan for my life was under his control, *"Many are the plans in a man's heart, but it is the Lord's purpose that prevails"* (Prov. 19:21).

During the first twelve years of our marriage, God blessed us with six wonderful children: Daniel Jay, David Jon, Douglas James, Luanne Joy, Dale Jeffrey and Dean Joseph who have given us wonderful daughters in love, fifteen grandchildren and one great grandson.[1] God has blessed us far beyond what we deserve.

Being a husband and father was the most challenging and fulfilling experience of my life during the 1960s and '70s. I changed diapers, picked up toys, washed and dried dishes, got groceries and milk (twelve gallons per week), and taught the boys how to play sports (football, soccer, baseball, basketball, golf, mini-golf, and driving). We were blessed that Norma could be an at-home mom. She was an expert at anticipating what mischief the boys would get into before the boys did it until they figured out how to look innocent. When they became adults at twenty-five years old, we were shocked when they told us of schemes they got away with. Fortunately, they never ended up in jail (but did have a few close calls). I learned later my boys were not as perfect as we thought they were.

For some strange reason having five boys qualified us to be invited to give seminars in churches on marriage, romance, and parenting. These sessions would be totally unrealistic in today's world where respect for marriage, life, family, education, abstinence, authority, celibacy, and seniors has almost disappeared. May heaven help us!

During the 1960s and '70s, Norma and I led a very active life-style that prepared us for an intensive life of ministry. We played and coached sports; organized and sang in various productions; had major surgery and learned to play the guitar while in recovery. I completed my time in the active Army Reserve duty with an honorable discharge. I became a deacon and served with Norma as co-presidents of church organizations. I continued living with very little sleep, rising-up early and staying up late. This was a busy decade of raising a family and helped prepare us for ministry.

A FAMILY LEGACY
1995– PRESENT

God blessed us with a large family that has grown far beyond our blood relations to brothers (and sisters) by other mothers (and fathers). Each life is precious in his sight and he loves them very much, "*Sons are a heritage from the Lord, children a reward from* him. *Like arrows in the hands of a warrior are sons born in one's youth. Blessed is the man whose quiver is full of them. They will not be put to shame when they contend with their enemies*" (Ps. 127:3–5).

Our boys always seemed eager to bring home their friends, especially those in distress who had no place to go, "*When a stranger sojourns with you in your land, you shall not do him wrong. You shall treat the stranger who sojourns with you as the native among you, and you shall love him as yourself, for you were strangers in the land of Egypt: I am the LORD*" (Lev. 19:33–34). Our home is always open to family at any time whether we are home or not through the front door or garage door if the front door isn't open. Be aware! We are a hugging family, unless we are sick!

Our home has always been open to strangers also, and we have entertained many overnight guests and others for weeks, months, and even years. God has blessed us to be a blessing to those he sent to us from many unique and difficult situations. The blessings of our large family continue today through the Q Group Donut Quality Testing (DQT) Team.

Communication with Grampa Q (Arn) has become a family legacy on Saturday mornings, when available. The QGDQTT sessions are precious! We meet one-on-one or in groups depending on who is available on Saturday mornings, and we go to the donut shop of their choice. I believe every person loves an occasional donut whether they are on a diet or not. Norma says I can have a donut if I only eat the "hole" of it. I interpret that to mean the "whole" of it. Each of us can have two donuts of their choice unless the donut shop (Krispy Kreme) has the red light on, then everyone gets an extra free donut just made and still warm.

God has blessed me far beyond what I deserve with a new generation of young people and millennials who are much wiser than I am on the ways of the world. It's critical for me to know and understand their values and concerns, so "listening sessions" are very important to me. I love the spirit and enthusiasm they have for their future in a world I often see as falling apart. They give me my "attitude adjustments," often when I need them the most.

The discussion that follows is usually something they talk about in the car while we are driving to the donut shop, or a simple question I have that I'm curious about. The responses are "fantabulous," and I just listen until they seem to be interested in what I might have to say. My desire is to give them respect for their opinions that other adults often don't give them. We have no age limit, young or old, for our donut outings. Even the adults in their twenties still enjoy our time together.

Here are some comments from the DQT team:

"I always looked forward to those trips. I knew that when you and Grandma would come to visit us in Columbus, or St. Louis, or wherever we were living, it would be a part of the trip. I would usually take time to think about some sort of subject we could discuss during our time at the donut shops. I really enjoyed passing thoughts and ideas around with everyone who was there. It felt like a special meeting only few were invited to. I really appreciated the time you took to listen to our thoughts and observations about the world. I felt respected and valued."
–Kezia

"I have so many fond memories of the Saturday morning donut runs to Krispy Kreme or Dunkin Donuts with grandpa. As a kid, it was special to know that our grandpa wanted to spend quality time with us and that he cared for us. I know that those outings have fostered the close relationship that we have with him, but they also allowed us to learn and mature from knowing him. He would always make a point to have intentional conversations to get to know us better, and he would share stories with us from his past experiences. As we stuffed our mouths with donuts (always one too many), we shared our interests, ideas, memories, and many laughs together. My grandpa became an inspiration and example to me, and I am convinced the example he set influenced me as I grew in my personal faith in Jesus Christ, pursued a rewarding career, chose a loving spouse, and so much more. I am blessed to have a grandfather who has been invested in the lives and futures of his grandchildren."

–Sarah

The gifts of my time, talents, treasure, touch, and tears built the legacy that binds us together whether urban or suburban, whether in our "blood" family or family of faith. This legacy goes on to today, but in 1971 God provided a major change I would never have dreamed possible.

---

1. Luanne passed into heaven eleven hours after birth with a rare case of pneumonia.

LEADERSHIP PREPARATION IN MY CAREER

1971

This is what the Lord says—your Redeemer, the Holy One of Israel: 'I am the Lord who teaches you what is best for you, who directs you in the way you should go."
Isaiah 48:17

What: Show how life's circumstances prepared me to lead God's people to do his work.
So what: To help the reader relate to God's work in his/her life to develop leadership skills.
Now what: Assess where skills align with circumstances God's way.

In 1971 I was offered and accepted a position with Johnson Service Company at their International Headquarters in Milwaukee, Wisconsin as the manager of Central Engineering for North America. This required moving our family to Milwaukee, the milk and beer capital of America. Our boys grew up on the milk—nine to ten gallons per week—so this put us closer to the source.

Many doors of opportunity opened up that prepared me for servant leadership, which caused me to pursue a much deeper study of the Scriptures and an intense daily prayer life and devotional book reading, always seeking God's guidance. The model and example of Jesus Christ and blessings of the Holy Spirit were my constant reminder of how to live in a very demanding period of my life.

Being promoted to a national position of leadership was an overwhelming opportunity. I searched for and learned every possible concept of leadership and management I could find. The source that gave me the greatest overview of secular leadership styles and strategies was the book by Auren Uris called, *The Mastery of Management.* But the greatest insights to management and leadership came from studying the Bible and searching what God's design was and is for servant leadership; to follow the example of the Good Shepherd—Jesus Christ.

WORLDVIEW AND CHURCH WORK
1975–79

During the 1970s, God led me into many significant experiences that expanded my worldview and my understanding of global poverty.

We attended Elmbrook Church where our entire family became actively involved in classes, Bible studies, and committees, which led to being elected to the board of deacons, council of elders, and chairperson. Spare time was spent on community service work, coaching sports teams, serving on community boards, and school meetings as president of the PTA. Spare time was spent growing in awareness of community organization, and my time at work grew other skills as well.

My career with Johnson Controls took off when I designed and developed an extensive Branch Engineering And Installation Management System (BEIMS) for environmental control systems. This led to extensive speaking tours throughout North America to introduce the new business operations strategy. This led me to the design and implementation of a computer-based Project Planning and Control System (PPCS) for construction project management, scheduling, estimating, and cost control. All this gained a lot of attention in the industry and was recognized by the United States

Government. This led to an appointment by the American National Standards Institute (ANSI) and the National Fire Protection Association (NFPA) to serve as the United States Chief Delegate for fire safety with the International Standards Organization.

The attention given to the work at Johnson Controls qualified me to become a registered Professional Engineer in the State of Wisconsin and certified as a Customer Service Executive by the National Association of Service Management. This recognition came with enormous responsibilities and commitment to a servant leadership attitude of helping others willing and eager to follow.

At the same time, the church home we selected to attend when we moved to Milwaukee was the Brookfield Christian Reformed Church, which was part of the same denomination we were part of since birth. They were meeting in the school facility because they chose to build a school facility before a church sanctuary to honor their faith promise to educate their children in God's ways. In 1993 they decided it was time to build a church sanctuary, and because of my background in construction management, I was asked to be the building chairperson.

The sanctuary project was completed in 1975. At the time, our three oldest boys had become involved in the youth program at Elmbrook Church and for about a year, we attended both churches. Eventually we decided to join Elmbrook Church. Elmbrook quickly wanted us to get involved, and they asked me to organize a kitchen committee and set rules of operation for the newly completed facility (the most unlikely desire of my heart because I'm not comfortable in the kitchen). Soon after completing that task, I was asked to design a fire and security system for the church. That led to being nominated and elected to the role of a deacon.

The involvement in leadership at Elmbrook church expanded my understanding of the challenges of operating a local church. God used it in a significant way to open my eyes so I could better understand his work through people willing to serve as volunteers. That lesson stuck with me.

BILLY GRAHAM CRUSADE
AND THE BARNABI BROTHERS
1979–87

During the 1970s, a woman in her eighties had been praying for twenty-five years that a major revival would occur in Milwaukee. She sent a letter to the Billy Graham Association asking Billy Graham to come to Milwaukee for a Crusade. It was due to this letter that Billy Graham decided to have a campaign and Crusade in Milwaukee.

The Billy Graham Association contacted John Fisco, president of ProBuCols and publisher of the *Christian Courier* Newspaper, to organize a leadership team to organize the event to be held in Milwaukee County Stadium. John chose Arthur "Art" Riemer, president of Chicago Bridge and Iron Company and Richard "Dick" Leep, president of Leep Development to co-chair the event that would occur in 1979. They Immediately began to organize teams of church leaders throughout Milwaukee to follow the guidelines established by the Billy Graham Association to conduct the event.

A significant outcome of the 1979 Billy Graham Crusade was the creation of The Barnabi Brothers. Art Riemer and Dick Leep, co-chairs of the Crusade, wanted to continue the Spirit God planted in the city that hopefully could start a revival. They invited a group of eight Christian business executives to meet monthly to encourage each other as Barnabas did in the early church, thus the name of the group became The Barnabi Brothers.

The goal of The Barnabi Brothers was to develop ways to solve the major moral and ethical issues facing our city using God's way and the truth taught by Jesus Christ. We met quite regularly throughout the 1980s until one of the members declared we must do something rather than just meet and talk. That challenge caused us to pray for God's guidance in discerning what he would want us to do. The seed was planted, but God didn't answer our prayers until 1987.

GOD'S CALLS INTO FULLTIME MINISTRY

1987–95

For God is not unjust so as to overlook your work and the love that you have shown for his name in serving the saints, as you still do.
Hebrews 6:10

What: Discuss the nature of God's calls and how to watch/listen for God's call and direction.
So what: Observe God's work in giving purpose to life.
Now what: Apply these truths to his/her own life.

In 1980 my work at Johnson Controls appeared to have gone as far as it could. God amazingly opened the door at the corporate headquarters of the Allen-Bradley Company to use my skills and experience to move their corporate culture.

I was employed as the Allen-Bradley's National Support Services Manager and was challenged to build a new service division from scratch. Over the next eleven years the management team of Allen Bradley amazingly worked together to establish a Global Technical Support Division involving ninety-one technical support centers in twenty-eight countries worldwide. I was appointed its first international vice president.

In 1987 Rockwell International acquired Allen-Bradley Automation Systems, which required that I establish my office anywhere in the world that would facilitate effective communication and logistical functions. I chose to relocate from Milwaukee to the Netherlands (my family's country of origin). I moved my wife Norma and our youngest son Dean to a small village called Heemstede. The reason for selecting the Netherlands was primarily due to the Dutch people having strong technical knowledge and also communication ability to speak fluently in as many as five languages. It was also at a time when the Iron Curtain came down in Germany which was part of opening the doors to the European Community enabling us to expand our business activities not only in Europe but also in the Soviet Union and in the Middle East.

God was working far beyond anything I could imagine in opening the doors for me to serve him and expand my worldview.

ELMBROOK CHURCH SAID YES!
1987–89

To walk with God as Enoch did in the Old Testament has always been my prayer and dream in serving my Lord. But how do I do that? This question is often the response in the minds and hearts of many people in the pew after a powerful message from the pastor in the pulpit. The practical questions rarely get answered and so little action is taken. Could it be that God's Holy Spirit stirs us into God's work as people of faith, hope, and love with our work as worship? Faith with work can be a life of serving God as worship and praise for what God has done for us.

Norma and I have attended many missions festivals in our lives, but in October of 1987, the event at Elmbrook Church was special. God's Holy Spirit was there. The guest missionary speaker was John Bechtel, a missionary/field worker from China who gave a powerful challenge. At the end of his story, he asked the people in the pew if we felt the Lord's Holy Spirit calling us to serve him somewhere in the world, and to stand up and pray that God would show and tell us what, when, where, how, and why we should serve him, his way. Both Norma and I immediately rose to our feet and committed our lives to work for God as he would lead us. We were ready to go without talking to each other beforehand and together said *yes*! But God was still molding our lives to fit his plan.

The 1980s were the golden years of Elmbrook Church with significant increases in attendance and at outreach events, which brought people to the church in large numbers. The Spirit of God was certainly moving in his Church not only at Elmbrook, but throughout Milwaukee. Elmbrook Church was functioning as a resource center supporting God's work with as many as 17,000 people entering the church during a week to attend the many services offered.

It became evident that the sanctuary and building facilities were inadequate to serve the number of people attending. This caused some people to leave Elmbrook and others to fill their vacant seats, but the need for a larger facility became a major concern. Preliminary plans were formed and presented to the members of Elmbrook church for a decision to expand the facilities and utilize the entire forty-acre property to maximize our facility. In 1989 the proposal was given to the church membership, a vote was taken, and a resounding *yes* was made by the church to expand the facilities and begin a fundraising effort to raise $12,500,000 for Project Expand.

At this time, Norma and I were living in the Netherlands, but the chairman of the council of elders had asked me several months before this if I would be involved in the Project Expand. I said *yes*. I would consider and pray about it, which I did.

A RENEWED VOW ON A STORMY NIGHT
1990–1995

It was in August of 1990 during a stormy night on the North Sea when Norma and Dean were back in Milwaukee getting ready for my son Doug and Liane's wedding, and I was alone in the Netherlands. The Spirit of God was moving in that storm and I decided to walk on the nearby sand dunes of the North Sea to pray. As I was standing on the sand dunes facing the United Kingdom and beyond to America, God was saying to me: "I have new plans for you!"

I had no idea what God had in store for us, but my response was *yes!* I was ready to go wherever and whenever God wanted me to go!

I called Norma that night and told her we are being called by God to move! Norma wanted to know when, where, and what will you do? My answer was, "I don't know yet. God hasn't told me. We must just watch and pray!"

That November I was at home in the Netherlands with Norma and received a call late at night from Lowell Argue, the chair of the council of elders, to tell me the church had just voted *yes!* on expanding the facilities and asked if I would be willing to serve as the building chairman to manage the entire project with a budget of $12.5 million. I immediately answered *yes!* That was the new direction from God I was looking for. It was a tremendous honor that God would choose me to be a part of building his Church in Southeast Wisconsin.

Leaving the corporate world was like a graduation commencement ending my wilderness training of forty years to enter a new world of serving God, which was awesome. My urgent desire was to show my love for him and to express how thankful I was to be blessed with gifts to be used as he wanted.

When I informed my boss that I was leaving to build a church, he asked, "And how much will you be paid for doing that?" My answer was, "Lots of zeros and that's all." The separation package he presented to me was a clear indication of God's faithfulness in all the details leading into the next phase of my life. The company granted me a one-year continuation of my salary, an eighteen-month continuation of health care insurance, and a bonus of corporate stock which gave me adequate funds to start the BASICS ministry in 1996.

In addition to all this, they paid for management consulting services to start my own business resulting in the Quakkelaar Group, Inc. (Q Group), a consulting firm to assist corporations in establishing customer support services. The Q Group flourished with an impressive staff of seven people during the three years of construction with contracts to serve many major corporations in both the US and Europe.

The Q Group consulting services were also used by Johnson Controls, Inc. and eventually led to my being rehired by them as Director of the Johnson Controls Institute to expand their training services to include employees and customers worldwide using the developing vocational training tools being designed to enable online training. This was a five-year project that was completed in two and a half years 1993 through 1995. This assignment provided income but more importantly, gave me an opportunity to learn more about adult vocational training, which became an urgent need in Milwaukee's urban communities. I saw later how this uniquely aligned with God's plan for prisoner reentry in Milwaukee.

The Q group put bread on our table while leading the construction project of Elmbrook Church for three years—truly a miracle of God's doing.

OPERATION MERCY
1993–95

In 1993, through Elmbrook Church's Foreign Missions Outreach, I became involved with the International Ministries of Operation Mobilization/Operation Mercy and was asked to lead a delegation of US business leaders to present government leaders of Tajikistan in the new Commonwealth of Independent States (CIS) to conduct the Tajik-American Symposium in September of 1993. Our primary role was to present the American way of doing business to the top government, business, education, and medical leaders of the country.

On our trip to Tajikistan, we went through Moscow for a three day layover to stay with a Christian woman who was eager to show us a big event in Red Square. It was the celebration of the change from the Soviet Union to the Commonwealth of Independent States (CIS), a solemn occasion for the people who did not know what the future would hold. She invited us to take the subway train into Red Square where both the old regime's troops and the new troops gathered on opposite ends of the Square with thousands of people gathered in between.

With our hostess, Norma and I were able to stand about fifty feet in front of the stage where the American National Symphony Orchestra was playing, fifty feet from the Kremlin main gate on our right, and Saint Peter's Cathedral to the left of us about two blocks away. It was awesome to be in such a place in history. It was totally unplanned by us but in God's plan.

Mikhail Gorbachev, his wife, and his daughter were on the stage along with many dignitaries from the US and CIS. It was beyond overwhelming when the orchestra played Tchaikovsky's "Overture of 1812" with two cannons: one on each side of the stage pointed horizontally over our heads. With the bells of Saint Peter's Cathedral ringing for the first time in fifty years and the last changing of the guard at the Kremlin on our right, I felt we were in a God-ordained moment.

The lyrics of the "Overture of 1812" are:

Mighty Lord, preserve us from jeopardy. Take thee now our faith and loud crying in penitence. Grant victory o'er our treacherous and cruel enemies, and to our land bring peace. O Mighty Lord, hear our lowly prayer, and by shining holy light. Grant us, O Lord, peace again. O Mighty Lord hear our prayer and save our people forever, forever.[1]

That night, our host's son drove us through the city to show us the capital building, a beautiful stately white building lit up with bright lights that was attacked and burned the next day. I believe God gave us a divine appointment to show that he was with us on this mission endeavor. There was much more to come, and we knew God was with us!

The US Ambassador to Tajikistan was our host along with Chairman Rusalov of the Government of Tajikistan. The primary goal of the leaders of Tajikistan was to build relationships with

America. The plenary session was televised nationally and was the first such event between Tajikistan and America.

Our delegation decided the first presentation of the general session should be an introduction to the Ten Commandments since our audience was mostly non-Christian and may never have heard about our country's godly heritage. Our delegation prayed fervently that our presentation of God would not get us expelled from the country or worse. The presentation was given and translated into both Tajik and Russian languages.

At the conclusion of our first presentation, our government host, Chairman Rusalov responded to the audience with what appeared to be an emotional angry tirade with shaking fist and shouts. Shoista (the interpreter assigned to me) refused to translate his response. We were concerned our worst fears were becoming reality, and we'd be sent to Siberia. Chairman Rusalov then pointed to me as the chief delegate and made a very intense statement which Shoista then had to translate. She said: "Chairman Rusalov is asking if you would be willing to put this presentation into writing in both Tajik and Russian so we could send this throughout our country?"

Later, Shoista told me in private that chairman Rusalov was reprimanding the leaders in the audience for never having told that message before. God miraculously answered our prayers. We were overwhelmed with joy and praised God with silent elation for his faithfulness. The TV interviews that followed were all about our God and produced a greater outcome than we were even praying for.

A significant side note: Our delegation had brought with us seven boxes of Bibles in the Russian language that went through customs in Moscow and arrived unopened in Tajikistan. These were made available to the people of Tajikistan to fulfill God's plan. During the next two weeks after the symposium, we met with the Tajik national leaders from the government, businesses, universities, and hospitals who gave us a tremendous opportunity to learn what leadership in a communist world was like. This significantly expanded our view of the world we live in.

Before leaving Dushanbe on the last weekend of our visit, our delegation was kidnapped by the rebel military and brought to their camp in the mountains as a political move to gain attention. We were not harmed. We were treated as royalty. God blessed us all with a fantastic eye-opening experience as part of his preparation for what was to come next.

After the Tajik-American Symposium experience, I was elected to serve on the board of Operation Mercy's Central Asia Development Agency (OM-CADA) and became its Chairman for five years (1994–1998), which led to a return visit to Tajikistan and a trip into Northern Afghanistan in 1997. God takes funny routes when calling us to serve him. Although my path to full-time ministry was not a direct path, God fulfilled many of his purposes through my winding journey of a life of ministry.

BUILDING A CHURCH SANCTUARY
1990–93

My prayer became, "Lord, help me to build your church of bricks and mortar into your sanctuary at Elmbrook Church. Then please let me be a part of building your church to bring your kingdom to the City of Milwaukee with your people united and guided by your Holy Spirit to bring the truth of Jesus Christ to Milwaukee and Southeast Wisconsin."

God has answered my prayers far beyond anything I could have ever imagined! Praise the Lord for his marvelous works!

Elmbrook Church's Project Expand began in 1990 with a budget of $12.5 million. The goal was to redesign the entire forty acre site at 777 South Barker Road into a new facility to accommodate the expanding fellowship. The project was completed in 1993 with 3,200 seats, and it came in $50,000 under budget. The fifteen-year loan was paid off in seven and a half years .Praise our Lord for his goodness to us.

But God still had more to teach me before he would answer my prayer to build his kingdom in Milwaukee.

MY WINDOW TO THE WORLD
1992

Why did God put me in engineering, church leadership, and community involvement? Why did he give me national and global exposure? Why did he have me serve as the Rotary President and in an International Standards Organization? And why did he bless me with a beautiful wife and family? What was his plan? I couldn't wait to find out! My prayers became urgent requests for God to lead me where he wanted me to go and to give me discernment and wisdom to accomplish his plan, his way. Was God calling me to Milwaukee?

In 1992 my pastor and dear friend Stuart Briscoe wrote his sermon, "Window On My World." Hearing this sermon was an aha moment for me. His words not only touched my heart but inspired my soul like a starting pistol at the beginning of a race. I was more convinced than ever before that God was preparing me for an exciting future doing his work, his way.

Stuart Briscoe's "Window On My World"

In short, my windows look onto a world that is full of the most incredible diversity, the most appalling need, the most glorious opportunities, and the most aggravating contradictions: famine, poverty, crime, disease, helplessness, hopelessness, and powerlessness in one direction; and plenty, abundance, excess, and the heady triumvirate of money, sex, and power in the other. A schizophrenic society.

I see a society whose economy refuses to respond as it always has, leaving many hard-working people frustrated and bewildered and not a little frightened. A society suffering from anorexia of the soul.

I want to step through my window and under the sill and begin to reach more and more people with the ever relevant and powerful message of the risen Christ to believe in the necessity of prayer and compassion and involvement at a thousand-and-one levels. Five or six thousand points of light plugged into the throne through worship, empowered by fellowship, and shining in discipleship.

It is his world and he intends to get it back and establish his eternal kingdom. I cannot draw the drapes. There will be a polishing of the windows and a rolling up of the sleeves. Will you join me?[2]

Stuart's perspective coincided with the international recognition by Rev. Billy Graham of marketplace ministry as the next major people group for world evangelism at the 1989 Lausanne Conference in Manila. This seemed to confirm my sense of calling to serve in outreach ministry to use my experiences in the marketplace to bring God's truth to Milwaukee. I didn't know how this could be a part of my life, but I was eager to trust God to show me his way. I was committed to letting God lead me to work in the city God put me in—Milwaukee, Wisconsin.

Marketplace workers are among the greatest forgotten and invisible people in the world, especially in urban communities. This presents a great opportunity to mobilize believers in church on Sundays to become active in the marketplace 24-7 to show and tell their neighbors the truth of God's love. What a great way of responding to the challenges given by pastors in the pulpits to engage the people in the pews to worship God by serving in their place of employment as Christians disguised as examples of Jesus Christ at work.

This insight inspired me to look at Milwaukee's social life from a different perspective. At the time, the characteristics I observed in Milwaukee entailed disrespectful attitudes, abusive addictions leading to displaced people, victims of abuse, an entitlement mentality, fear and anger, horrible living conditions, political unrest, and inadequate education. May God help us!

But I asked myself: What on earth am I doing for heaven's sake to transform our society to God's way? I just can't do nothing!

1. "Overture 1812 Lyrics," Flash Lyrics, originally written in 1880 by Pyotr Ilyich Tchaikovsky, https://www.flashlyrics.com/lyrics/tchaikovsky/overture-1812-58.
2. Stuart Briscoe, "My Window to the World," sermon at Elmbrook Church, Milwaukee, Wisconsin, February 1992.

TRANSFORMATION FROM THE
MARKETPLACE INTO GOD'S WORK

1995

As he (Jesus) approached Jerusalem and saw the city, he wept over it.
Luke 19:41

What: Describe how God works in life to change passions and life direction to fulfill his plan.
So what: Evaluate how history and life experiences (good and bad) are God's way of testing and teaching us.
Now what: Understand that man's ways don't always align with God's ways.

A PLAN TO BUILD A BRIDGE
TO CHRIST'S CHURCH IN MILWAUKEE
1995–96

In January 1995, I was reelected to the council of elders at Elmbrook Church. This was a year of prayer and searching for God's direction to my growing passion to build God's kingdom in Milwaukee. In November of 1995, the formation of a vision and mission statement for outreach to Milwaukee was completed and presented to Elmbrook's council of elders, the Barnabi Brothers, and several dear friends, including my pastors Stuart and Jill Briscoe.

A side note: Many of our friends continuously kept asking, "What are you doing these days?" One day while driving east to Milwaukee on I-94, it occurred to me that I was working on building bridges for brothers and sisters in Christ to serve in the city.

Hey, that's an acronym for "basics," and what I'm doing is getting "back to the basics" of serving God in Milwaukee. That could be a name for our ministry: BASICS in Milwaukee, Inc. So in 1996, we applied to the IRS under the BASICS name for the designation as a 501(c)(3) nonprofit organization which was granted in 1997.

There is a town in the Netherlands named Kwakkel that I traveled through to get to work in Uithoorn where my European office was located in the Netherlands. I asked one of my Dutch colleagues the meaning of the name and he said it means a bridge over a canal. Knowing that the originality of my name came from France where the "Q" became "Kw" in Dutch, and adding "aar" to Quakkel would become "Quakkelaar," "a builder of bridges over canals." Thus, the name "Quakkelaar" could be translated as a "bridge builder." Hey! That's what I'm doing! And the canal could be the Menominee River.

BASICS in Milwaukee is a Christian organization supporting community development by integrating spiritual, social, and physical aspects into a change process. Its primary beneficiaries are leaders in church and urban ministries whose missions are based upon Christian values and a commitment to improve the spiritual well-being and quality of life for residents in the central city. BASICS is committed to encourage and facilitate activities in the Christian community that are united in focusing on the love of Christ in practical and powerful ways.

The intended purpose for BASICS was to support urban ministries by providing:

- Facility restoration
- 501(c)(3) application assistance
- Financial planning
- Leadership development
- Ministry startup classes
- Funding consultation
- Partnerships

BASICS serves urban ministries by connecting them with resources available from the faith and wealth communities of greater Milwaukee. Our goal is to assure that the resources and contributions provided are used effectively and with accountability.

Our vision is that people served by faith-based ministries in Milwaukee will realize lasting improvements in quality of life by following a Christian lifestyle. The foundation for our ministry is the statement of faith: For the Lord Jesus Christ, God's son, redeems us through his death and resurrection and empowers us by the Holy Spirit. The Bible is God's Word, and through it we are called to live out justice, reconciliation, and redemption. The Church nurtures God's people, who are gathered in community to carry out God's Word.[1]

The purpose and passion of BASICS is to assist sustainable faith-based ministries dedicated to heal our community's problems of poverty, hunger, lack of clothing, violence, drugs, unplanned pregnancy, etc. to show that true healing will come only when well-managed, cost-effective programs that help the community are accompanied by spiritual regeneration of the soul through relationships with Jesus Christ. Because, *"there will always be poor people in the land. Therefore, I command you to be openhanded toward your brothers and toward the poor and needy in your land"* (Deut. 15:11).

A critical component of urban ministry is to build relationships of trust and respect along with networks of resource partners working together in harmony. This was evident in the people God led us to partner with in creating the BASICS ministry during the first five years of operation.[2]

COMMISSIONING AND COMMENCEMENT 1996

The response to the BASICS plan was overwhelmingly supportive resulting in a commissioning and anointing of Norma and me as Elmbrook Missionaries to urban Milwaukee. God's blessing was on us and we were energized and eager to get started. We considered our proposal as an action plan to serve God as our act of worship. The Barnabi Brothers became the Board of Advisors for BASICS in Milwaukee, Inc. with Art Riemer as its Chairman and me as Founder and President/Executive Director. Doing God's work through Brothers And Sisters In Christ Serving (BASICS) in Milwaukee was started.

The Mustard Seed Foundation and a dear friend in our neighborhood Bible study donated the first $15,000 to demonstrate God's affirmation of our plan. Elmbrook Church also committed to a monthly support contribution and encouraged the other churches to do the same.

My transfer from a corporate executive in the marketplace to an urban missionary was consummated, confirming in our hearts that our direction aligned with God's will.

MILWAUKEE LEADERSHIP FOUNDATION, LEADERSHIP FOUNDATIONS OF AMERICA, MISSION AMERICA, AND CCDA 1996–PRESENT

In my search to find churches and nonprofit organizations involved in serving the disenfranchised people of Milwaukee, I learned about the Milwaukee Leadership Foundation (MLF). This was primarily a small group of women who were functioning as an agency serving the poor with minimal funding. They found donations from people of faith willing to give their time, talents, and treasures.

Social services organizations were frequently using the services of the MLF, stretching their resources far beyond their ability to meet the demand, but God always answered their prayers for the specific items needed to help those with urgent needs. Food, clothing, furniture, appliances, and various kinds of help were given in the miraculous ways only a loving God could provide.

I asked God, "If you are already working through many servants like these women in the city, why do you want me to do the same kind of things? It would make much more sense to build networks of people who are called and gifted to work together. They just need to know how to connect and work together."

God's answer became more and more clear as I studied his word and listened to his pastors: keep building your relationships of love with me, your neighbors, and yourself. God told me to let him lead me in the way I should go: *"Jesus replied: Love the Lord your God with all your heart and all your soul and with all your mind. This is the first and greatest command. And the second is like it: Love your neighbor as yourself. All the Law and the Prophets hang on these two commandments"* (Matt. 22:37–40).

The psalmist writes, *"Search me, O God, and know my heart; test me and know my anxious thoughts. See if there is any offensive way in me, and lead me in the way everlasting"* (Ps. 139:23–24)

Through my connections with MLF, I met a fellow classmate from Calvin College, Bud Ipema, who was president of the Midwest Leadership Foundation in Chicago. When Bud learned of my vision for Milwaukee, he strongly urged me to spend at least one year on the streets of the city learning everything I could, especially the religious configurations and cultures. This turned out to be brilliant counsel. I accepted it as a direction from God, so 1996 became my year of research in Milwaukee.

I first studied the 1990 US Census of Milwaukee and its suburbs. I was quickly drawn to one question that was asked at the time but which is no longer asked: "Are you Bible-reading and devotional?" The answers to that question helped me in my quest to find out where the Christians were located. I had thought that most of the Christians would be in the suburbs, but the census facts were the opposite. The people who answered yes to that question were in the inner city of Milwaukee.

This information had a major impact on my understanding of people in the city. They were my brothers and sisters in Christ, and they already know about Jesus. I found that many of the believers I met during that year and the following years could teach me a lot about faith, hope, and love because they had to learn how to live in poverty without the financial means to overcome their problems. Even the poorest could testify to God's goodness because they had to trust in God for the basic things in life such as food, clothing, shelter, and health care. My attitude changed from thinking I was bringing the Gospel to receiving the Gospel by understanding their practical lives and circumstances.

While spending most of my day in the city, my evenings were spent reading as many books I could find about urban living. The Leadership Foundations of America, Mission America, The Lausanne Conferences, and the Christian Community Development Agency were great sources of information, but I learned the most by building relationships with the people.

In driving through the major areas of poverty and crime, I found a significant number of storefront churches either empty or in very bad condition. Those where a car was parked in front of the church usually meant the pastor was there studying his Bible, preparing his sermon, and praying.

I decided to stop and meet with them when I could. My visits were during the week. I knocked and waited there for a few minutes while the pastor unlocked the doors and visually checked me out before letting me in. I would give my name, saying I just wanted to get to know him or her and pray for them and their ministry. Most pastors were shocked that this tall, White, bearded guy would come to see them, but all of them were warm, friendly, and eager to talk and become friends. Many of these pastors are still loving friends. I will always remember and value our time together. I've learned so much from them and respect them for what God was leading them to do for him.

Over the years that followed, I was invited to meet the leaders of urban ministries throughout America to learn what others were doing to address the problems of poverty and crime in urban areas. God led me to attend national conferences with Reid Carpenter of the Leadership Foundations, Paul Cedar of Mission America, John Perkins and Wayne Gordan of Christian Community Development Agency, Glen Barth of Good Cities, and many other leaders who had significant passions for the disenfranchised people of America. I learned much from these wise individuals who have been doing the work of urban ministry for years. John wrote, *"Whoever wants to enter my service, must follow the way; and where I am, my servant will also be. And my father will honor every person who enters my service"* (Jn. 12:26). Urban ministry theology mixed with praxeology (practical studies) became my focus while walking with God in Milwaukee without fear.

MILWAUKEE'S FAITH HISTORY
1400–PRESENT

A military or ministry maneuver always begins with a study of all the characteristics of the territory to be occupied. Just as the ten spies were sent into the Promised Land by Moses, I spent a year studying Milwaukee and found some interesting details. During the fifteenth century, Native Americans migrated into the Milwaukee area mostly from the Green Bay area. The tribes were Menomonee, Fox, Mascouten, Sauk, Potawatomi, Ojibwe (Algic/Algonquian), and Ho-Chunk (Winnebago). They had various names for the area:

- *Millioke*: an Algonquin word for "good, beautiful and pleasant land."
- *Minwaking*: a Potawatomi word with similar meanings.

- *Ominowakiing*: an Ojibwe word for "gathering place by the water."
- *Manawaukee*: where the "Great Spirit" wanted peace.

The tribes often fought over hunting and trapping lands, but the swamp land in the delta of three rivers coming together was considered sacred land and was dedicated to burying their dead. It is claimed that there were over five hundred burial mounds in that area of which virtually none can be found today. Some have been unearthed during construction projects in the downtown area but rarely preserved.

Competition was intense between the Juneau and Kilbourn families, resulting in cannon balls being shot at each other over the River and roads not aligning with each other, so eventually, when bridges were required by the State, they were built on a diagonal, as they still do.

Milwaukee became a city of immigrants with many escaping revolutions in Europe—Germany during the 1840s, and Poland during the 1850s. These people were searching for hope and a better life in America. This continues to this day but from other parts of a world in distress.

Over the years as immigrants moved into the area, the early East Side was dominated by the Jewish community—later by internationals. The West Side was mostly occupied by German Lutherans and later by people from the Southern States—mostly Protestants/Baptists. The South Side was settled by Italian and Polish Catholics, and later by Hispanics who were mostly Catholic. The first churches in Milwaukee were:

- Catholic—1830
- Methodist—1835
- Baptist—1837
- Dutch Reformed—1846

A major migration of Blacks from the South during the 1960s resulted in the White Flight to the suburbs. They were at the bottom of the industrial ladder and faced historic race discrimination. Many formed their own churches such as the Church of God in Christ (COGIC) and the Missionary Baptist Churches (MBC).

Many Hispanic/Latino migrants began moving into Milwaukee in 1925 and have come from nearly every Spanish speaking country around the world.

Several major religious denominational headquarters were established in Milwaukee such as the Roman Catholic Church Archdiocese, Episcopal Diocese, Evangelical Lutheran Church of America (ELCA), and others with a current total of over 1200 churches in Milwaukee County and 1200 in the surrounding suburbs. There are also now over 150 Catholic and Christian outreach ministries in Milwaukee.

UNIQUE FACTS AND
PEOPLE OF MILWAUKEE
1840–PRESENT

Milwaukee is known as a land overflowing with milk and honey, beer, cheese, baseball, bowling, festivals, and food. In 1840 the first American brewery was established in Milwaukee where German immigrants mixed beer with whisky and vinegar dusted with limestone to give it a head. Beers made Milwaukee famous. The best known were Pabst (1844), Schultz (1849), Miller (1879), Blatz (1851) and Schlitz (1859). Bowling and beer are very popular "sports" in Milwaukee where the oldest certified bowling alley, the Holler House (1908), is still operating.

Downtown Milwaukee is built on swampland and creates unique foundational problems: City hall (the tallest building in the United States between 1855–1899) is slowly sinking, and the Northwestern Mutual Insurance building is built on Lake Emily. Thousands of wood pilings in water must be constantly maintained at a certain level to stop the building from sinking.

There have been many dynamic religious leaders in the history of Milwaukee. Some achieved national and international fame, while others have had significant impact on the local culture with very limited recognition. Those who have worked tirelessly while impacting the heart and soul of the city deserve mention. This section will give a brief summary of these individuals.

The Glover Event and Underground Railroad in Wisconsin

Joshua Glover was a run-away slave from Saint Louis who escaped from his slave master and was able to take the Underground Railroad to a way station in Racine where he sought asylum in the early part of 1852. He got a job in a sawmill and lived in a small cabin about four miles from Racine where the abolition sentiment of the people was sympathetic.

His slave master from Missouri, B. S. Garland, found a way in the United States District court to capture Joshua. US deputy marshals found his small shanty, and while he was playing cards, surprised him, knocked him down with a club, pointed a pistol at his head and handcuffed him, mangled and bleeding. They dumped him into a wagon and brought him to the Milwaukee County Jail. Joshua's dream of creating a new life in the North was thwarted. He thought.

In Milwaukee, an alarm was sounded that a negro accused of fleeing from his slave pen in Missouri was caught in Racine and was being held in the Milwaukee County jail. Over a hundred men gathered shouting, "Freemen to the rescue!" They used a battering ram, rescued Joshua, and then hid him for a short time in Prairieville (now Waukesha). When safe travel could be arranged, he eventually was put on a ship to Canada where he was able to start his new life as a free man. This story was given national attention and impacted great emotional support for the antislavery movement throughout America.

Father James Edmund Groppi and the 16th Street Viaduct

Father Groppi was a Roman Catholic priest and noted civil rights activist in Milwaukee who aggressively fought for housing equity and social justice in the inner city. He was born to Italian immigrant parents and was raised in Bay View with his eleven siblings. He attended Immaculate Conception Grade School, Bay View High School, Mount Calvary Seminary, and St. Francis Seminary. He was ordained to the Roman Catholic priesthood in 1959. He was assigned to the St. Veronica Parish on Milwaukee's South Side, then transferred to St. Boniface Parish in the heart of Milwaukee's inner city core, a largely African American community.

He participated in the 1963 March on Washington and the Freedom Summer Project in Jackson, Mississippi. In his growing passion for the civil rights movement, he then traveled to Selma, Alabama, in 1965 where he marched beside Martin Luther King Jr. and became very concerned about racism, hypocrisy, and prejudice in Milwaukee.

Returning to Milwaukee, he actively protested busing and overcrowding in inner-city schools, became an advisor to the Milwaukee NAACP Youth Council, and led young Black youths in civil rights protests in a 200-day campaign to secure a city-wide open-housing ordinance. His many arrests and marches on Martin Luther King Jr. Drive on the North Side and across the 16th Street Viaduct over the Menomonee River Valley into the predominantly White South Side involved effigies, yelling insults, stone and bottle-throwing, tear-gas and violence. The Associated Press voted Groppi Religious Newsmaker of the Year.

Groppi had been a long-time thorn in the side of authorities leading to a Poor People's March to Madison, Wisconsin, where crowds forcibly entered the floor of the Assembly in the capitol building for eleven hours to protest welfare reductions. The protest resulted in an increase in the Capitol security force and disunity between Milwaukee and State legislators. His ecclesiastical superiors did not always agree with his decisions, and he eventually became disenchanted with the priesthood.

Father Groppi left the priesthood in 1976. He married a fellow activist, had three children, lived in poverty, became a bus driver in Milwaukee, and passed away from cancer in 1985. His life certainly had a major impact on the life and culture of Milwaukee, and he became known as the most famous priest in the history of Milwaukee.

Creation of The Socialist Party of America

Victor L. Berger, an Austrian Jewish immigrant, became the first of two Socialists elected in 1910 to the US House of Representatives. He was a primary initiator of Sewer Socialism, a name that came from the unique sewer system built in Milwaukee. He was barred from the House in his second term after his trial and conviction under the 1917 Espionage Act for opposing the US intervention in World War I. He introduced programs that were adopted such as old age pensions, unemployment insurance, and public housing.

In 1910, the Milwaukee City Council and County Board was made up mostly of Socialists, and Emil Seidel was elected its mayor. He was the first socialist mayor in the United States.

In 1916, Daniel Hoan was elected mayor and served until 1940. He continued to have a major impact on the city and its socialistic culture.

The last socialistic mayor, Frank Zeidler, served three terms (1948–1960).[3] He left his office to enter the US Navy as a Lieutenant. The merchant ship "LaSalle," on which he commanded a gunnery crew, was torpedoed off Capetown, South Africa, with the loss of all hands.

Joseph "Joe" W. Ellwanger

Pastor Joe Ellwanger was born in Selma, Alabama, in 1934 and came to Milwaukee in 1967 as a uniquely prepared religious leader having served as the only White pastor in strategic planning meetings with Dr. Martin Luther King Jr. He was a key figure in the civil rights movement in America.

Joe served as pastor of the African American Saint Paul Lutheran Church in Birmingham, Alabama, from 1958–1967. During that period, he was involved in the march for civil voting rights from Selma to the State Capitol in Montgomery. He was the only White pastor in Birmingham who took an active leadership role in supporting equal rights for Blacks. He also spoke at the funeral for one of the four girls killed in the church where Dr. King offered the eulogy.

Joe was one of sixteen pastors who met with Governor George Wallace, and later with President Lyndon B. Johnson, to support the Voting Rights Act of 1965. He wrote about his passions in his book, *Strength For The Struggle, Let My People Go.*

Ellwanger continued to be active in Milwaukee as pastor of the Cross Lutheran Church. His many activities included working with MICAH (Milwaukee Inner City Congregations Allied for Hope), the Black Panther Party, founded Project Return (a ministry for people returning from prison), and organized WISDOM (a statewide coalition of social justice groups campaigning to reform the criminal justice system).

In 2008, he received the Fred L. Shuttlesworth Human Rights Award, the highest honor bestowed on an individual by the Birmingham Civil Rights Institute. In 2016 he received an award from the Interfaith Older Adult Program to continue his work to end mass incarceration in Wisconsin. As pastor emeritus, Joe continues helping returning citizens to find employment.

———

Learning about the men and women who have contributed to the work in Milwaukee informed how to move forward in our work. But at the base of it, we were called to *"agree with one another I appeal to you, brothers, in the name of our Lord Jesus Christ, that all of you agree with one another so that there may be no divisions among you and that you may be perfectly united in mind and thought"* (1 Cor. 1:10).

1. The active ways we serve are:
    Helping Ministry Leaders help themselves
    Building Unity within the Christian Community
    Bringing Building Facilities up to occupancy codes
    Ministry Support services

Resource Information
Prayer Networking
Urban Ministry Leadership Training
Ministers to Milwaukee
Partnerships
Servant Leadership Development

2. We praise God for these early BASICS leaders:

Board of Directors:
Arthur Riemer, Chair: Hobert & Svaboda
Lawrence Clancy, Vice Chair: Cooke & Franke, SC
Wesley "Buzz" Taves, Secretary: IT People Unlimited
Marty Felde, Treasurer: Esparanza Unida Incorporated
Fred Jones, Director: FMJ Enterprises
Barbara Horton, Director: Darryll Hines Academy of Excellence
Cordelia Taylor, Director: Family House

Advisory Board of Reference:
Dennis Kuester, Chair: M & I Bank
Terry Anderson: Omnitech
Ned Bechthhold: Payne & Dolan
Rev. Stuart Briscoe: Elmbrook Church, Minister at Large
Elvin Danielson: Retired
Joe DeRosa: DeRosa Corporation
William Eisner, Sr.: Willian Eisner Associates
Rev. Dr. Marc Erickson: Eastbrook Church, Senior Pastor
William Godfrey: Retired
Gwen Greeler: Velvac, Inc.
Tim Hoeksema: Midwest Express
Basil Jackson: MD, PhD, ThD, JD
John Koss, Sr.: Koss Corporation
Martin Kraninger: Retired
Milt Kuyers: Faustel Inc.
Richard Leep: Leep Development
Julius Morgan: Community Enterprises of Greater Milwaukee
Joan Prince, PhD: University of Wisconsin-Milwaukee
Armour Swanson: Retired

Staff
Arnold Quakkelaar, President and CEO
Ed Edwards, Vice President and COO*
Dick Ahlgren, Project and Volunteer Management*
Jeff Bennett, Project Manager
Terry Bolda, Director, Public Relations & development
Jack Congleton, Data Mapping
Roger Dynes, Training Programs
Jay & Sue Maddux
Mark Mallwitz, Director of Prayer, Outreach, and Partnerships
Dan Puza, Web Team Leader of Database and Websites
Norma Quakkelaar, Reception and Administration
Jim Ramsey, Marketing, Projects, and Program Management
Rick Skotske, Projects Manager
Lois Stefanowski, Director of Prayer and Ministry Outreach

Jane Turner, Manager of the Information Center
Rev. Frank Villa, South Project Manager

3. There are significant characteristics of socialism that remain in Milwaukee today, such as the park system, the city grid system (N-S-E-W Street structure), and the emphasis on reducing pollution, congestion, and overcrowding. They valued recreation by developing the Lincoln Memorial Drive, which is now the world-famous Lakefront Festival Complex.

BASICS WAS BORN

1996

For God is not unjust so as to overlook your work and the love that you have shown for his name in serving the saints, as you still do. Hebrews 6:10

What: Explain the dynamics of how God leads to start an urban ministry.
So what: Encourage ministry leaders to persist in fulfilling God's calls.
Now what: How to recognize signs and wonders of God's work to change lives.

In February of 1997, the IRS issued our Letter of Determination that BASICS in Milwaukee, Inc. was accepted as a 501(c)(3) nonprofit organization. Brothers And Sisters In Christ Serving in Milwaukee was official.

Our first office was in my home, but it quickly moved to an office in downtown Waukesha. The office was donated by a fellow elder at Elmbrook Church, Phil Lee. We shared the office with Phil and the Fellowship of Christian Athletes.

In 1998, we moved into the facility of the Milwaukee Outreach Center on South 27th Street just north of National

Avenue. This happened because of the gracious support of Jack Brown. Jack had the special gift of encouraging anyone ministering to disenfranchised people. He became a dear friend.

It was strategically important for BASICS to be recognized as an integral part of organizations bringing solutions and assistance to the social problems of the city, so we were fortunate to secure an office in the Milwaukee Enterprise Center at North 4th Street and West Hadley. It was an ideal location on the fifth floor in the southwest corner. We could look out our window and see our target area of Milwaukee.

Our current BASICS office is located much closer to the center of Milwaukee: an ideal location at 2224 West Kilbourn Avenue, Milwaukee 53233.

CHURCH FACILITIES
RESTORATION AND RECONCILIATION
1997–99

An extended phase of my Milwaukee research was to find church pastors whose facilities were being inspected because community leaders wanted to close storefront churches. These buildings were often located in old business districts where there was a desire to restore the tax base, reduce crime, and create a new pride in the neighborhoods. The pastors of these churches were sent letters to inform them of the new city codes established by the city for churches. The rules were restrictive and caused a deep concern because there were virtually no funds to pay for the restoration and changes required.

The result of this dilemma was addressed by a pastor and a prophet who organized a movement to keep hands off God's property. Pastor Sam Jones and Prophet George Nathaniel III circulated petitions to stop the attempt to destroy churches in the inner city. They both had been trained as community organizers to control civil unrest and unite neighborhoods to stop violence. The whole situation lacked a solution and drove people to hate their public leaders.

BASICS searched for ways to build bridges from the suburban churches to the urban churches, and it seemed God was leading us to bring resources from the suburbs to adopt these churches by building relationships, restoring facilities, and reconciling our differences through prayer, care, and share principles Jesus teaches.

The petitions generated over 33,000 signatures, which at that time was the largest number of signatures ever submitted to city hall. The proposed codes were put on hold and the crisis was averted. The work of BASICS continued, and many wonderful cross-cultural relations were built during the next five years.

The primary goal of BASICS was to serve outreach ministries and neighborhood churches through the effective collaboration of caring, compassionate, and loving brothers and sisters in Christ to unite communities.

With my background in construction and management, a project management program was designed and defined by BASICS to use trained volunteers willing to come into the city to restore these buildings. By restoring church and ministry facilities, we have developed excellent working relationships with over one thousand volunteers. It was an impressive network of servants fulfilling God's call to love their neighbors east of Mayfair Road and the Menomonee River.[1]

A caution: Outreach ministries have a desperate need for facilities. A donated building is initially seen as a blessing, but it can quickly lead to major diversion of valuable resources to restore and maintain a deteriorating building. The cost of restoration is often exorbitant and is complicated by the added costs to meet all city building code requirements. A carefully prepared cost analysis is important to have before making decisions to accept such an offer. From the perspective of "with God, all things are possible," faith and prayer are essential! One example of this can be seen with Rev. Bobby Sinclair.

Building Bridges of Hope

This is the story of Mount Herman Missionary Baptist Church in the central city of Milwaukee. It's a story of how God blessed the vision of Pastor Bobby Sinclair who has two full-time jobs: one as a pastor and the other as a supervisor of electrical inspectors with the city of Milwaukee.

During 1995 Pastor Sinclair and I spent many mornings in prayer for his church, which at the time numbered approximately fifty people. In that year their facilities limited the number of attendees. They had an urgent need to find a larger building so they could continue to grow.

Pastor Sinclair's vision led him to acquire an abandoned 11,300 sq. ft. True Value Hardware store on Atkinson and North 18th Street and renovate it into a worship center for the neighborhood. After much prayer and work to find funding for the project, the Southern Baptist Convention came up with 75 percent of the funds needed. The other 25 percent came from members who in faith took out second mortgages on their homes. That enabled the church to move ahead on the project.

Another challenge arose. They had to sell the original church building and move out in eight days, but they had no place to go since the new building wouldn't be ready that quickly. But nothing is impossible for God!

Pastor Sinclair contacted six neighboring church pastors to participate in the renovation project. The response was a miraculous demonstration of brothers and sisters in Christ serving together to build God's Church. Over forty volunteers cleaned out the entire inside of the building. They painted the walls, cleaned every nook and cranny, completely stripped the floor and built a pulpit and platform complete with a choir loft. The work was completed in eight days, and the first worship service was conducted with great celebration and thanksgiving—worshipping God for his miracle of love and unity through the multi-church fellowship.

The new True Value Worship Center enabled over two hundred people to attend. Four people from the neighborhood made commitments to the Lord to change their lives and trust in God that day. BASICS's part in the project was to donate seven dollars for each hour of volunteer labor which totaled five-hundred hours. A $3,500 check was given to the church by BASICS as a thank offering to help pay for materials required. Praise our great God for his faithfulness!

–Rev. Bobby Sinclair

Funeral Home to Community Youth Center

One July a dark, drafty, wet, seventy-year-old garage of a funeral home was transformed into a bright, clean, modern activity center for the Lao Christian Church at 2316 West National Avenue. It took only a little over a month. Approximately thirty men and women from both the Lao congregation and the suburbs worked together with awesome results.

Attached to the rear of the church building, the garage had only been usable for a storage area since the church purchased the former funeral home three years earlier. They now needed more space for their growing youth ministry envisioned by Pastor Bouathong "BT" Vangsouladta who founded the church as an Elmbrook daughter church twenty-two years earlier.

The BASICS volunteer project manager, Owen Purvis, along with many volunteers and contractors, donated not only their time and talents, but also materials and funds to make the process run smoothly with a great spirit of cooperation and unity.

Pastor BT shared how:

The old garage has been converted into a beautiful room in the building. No one ever dreamed to see this. It's like when we came here to the United States and thinking we were worthless and waiting to die. But someone cared enough to share the Gospel of Jesus with us, and we accepted Christ as our Savior and Lord. We are new in him!

During the working days, we saw the men from BASICS working together with dignity. They never once argued or became angry toward each other. We saw the love in them. Our men said, "Pastor, if our men work together like this it would be unique." The men from BASICS are so pleased to come and work here in the near South Side of Milwaukee to serve the Lord instead of going far away. Here the mission is at our doorstep in a multicultural setting. God's love is *real*, and they are the witnesses!

–BT, Pastor Lao Christian Church

TOURS AND GROWTH
1998–2001, 2007

Our marketing strategy in the beginning was unique because we were advised by John Schmidtke, one of our ministers to Milwaukee, not to tell what we were going to do, but instead let others tell our story by word of mouth, sharing testimonies of what we did. This was a brilliant idea that worked very well. We decided to show what was going on by giving tours of our work. This also gave suburbanites an opportunity to move out of their comfort zone and go east of Mayfair Road where they were afraid to go. The tours were initiated by suburban churches for their people interested in urban ministry.

Northbrook Church in Richfield, Wisconsin, was one of the first to sign up for annual tours. Tours were held on Saturday mornings at the church with a light breakfast at 8 a.m., a brief orientation to Milwaukee and the rules of the culture, a description of the religious history of Milwaukee on the bus while traveling to the work sites, visits to the ministries and meeting the ministry leader(s) for a description of what they were doing, followed by prayers. Lunch was served often at the Milwaukee Rescue Mission where we would eat with those who were homeless and then tour their facilities to see their work in action. The tour usually ended around 4 p.m., with most of us exhausted and overwhelmed by what was seen. The experience created lasting impressions and resulted in the tourists becoming involved as volunteers and/or donors of their time, talents, treasures, touch and/or tears.

This strategy, implemented over a five-year period, built the BASICS brand and reputation for God's glory. It became evident that most of the "tourists" had no idea of the rich faith history of Milwaukee. We were taking affluent residents out of their comfort zones fifteen miles from home and into another world of many cultures they didn't understand, and in many cases, were afraid of. On one of the tours, an African missionary commented that missionary work in Milwaukee was more difficult and challenging than what he experienced in Africa.

As BASICS grew and as many volunteers became staff members, it became necessary to not identify them as pastors even though they often were called to do functions that pastors did. In the inner city, we were working with many people who had no church or pastor connections and often didn't want any relationship because of past hurts and/or not feeling worthy or good enough to go to church. We were often asked to conduct weddings and funerals, and we always encouraged people to become church members and accept the pastor as their spiritual guide. When they resisted that direction, we accommodated them as Ministers to Milwaukee. This led to BASICS being recognized as a missions agency for urban Milwaukee ministry. Our strategies may have begun with tours and grown into a missions agency, but the foundation for everything was prayer.

---

1. The following are some of the more than fifty facilities we assisted in restoring:

    Mount Hermon Missionary Baptist Church, Pastor Bobby Sinclair
    Family House, Mother Cordelia Taylor
    Lao Christian Church, Pastor Bouathong "BT" Vangsouladta
    Win-A-Soul Church, Apostle David King
    St. Luke's Emmanuel Missionary Baptist Church, Rev. Dr. R.E. McCrory
    Christian Family Gathering, Rev. Rick & Maria Jenkins
    Scott Christian Youth Center, Mother Naomi Scott
    Mount Horeb Baptist Church, Rev. Roy Hopgood
    Harvest Center Ministries, Darnell Robinson
    Amazing Ministries, Rev. Clarence Hill

Matters of the Heart Ministry, Rev Theresa Thomas-Boyd
The Milwaukee Outreach Center, Jack Brown
Transitional Row, Eddie Johnson
Iglesia Pentecostal Church, Rev. Jaime Martinez
Intercession Ministries, Ms. Sharon Mays-Ferguson
Pleasant Hills Missionary Baptist Church, Rev. Lester Barnes

FOUNDATIONS OF PRAYER AND MIRACLES

1997

Ask, and it will be given to you; seek, and you will find; knock, and it will be opened to you.For everyone who asks receives, and the one who seeks finds, and to the one who knocks it will be opened.
Matthew 7:7–8

What: Explain the value of working together with other ministries to experience the importance of sharing God's resources to build his Church, his way.
So what: Show how working in harmony within the family of faith is God's way.
Now what: To build unity in Christ's Church as a model and example to the community.

PRAYER WALKS IN CITY HALL
1996–98

BASICS was built on a foundation of praying for God's direction in everything we hoped to do, and so it made sense to begin our ministry to the city of Milwaukee with prayer at city hall. We decided to start with a prayer walk beginning on the top floor at 6 a.m. so we could be finished before workers came at 8 a.m. We called the mayor's secretary and told her what we wanted to do, and she felt that would be a great idea since the mayor was a preacher's son. She was sure he wouldn't refuse us. For the first year of BASICS, we met on the first Mondays of each month to pray at the door to each office from the top floor to the mayor's office on the first floor.

During one of our prayer walks, one of the guards confronted us saying we were not allowed to pray there anymore because of security risks. We tried to explain that city hall would be at risk if we didn't pray for the city! That didn't change his mind, so we went over to the city hall annex building across the street. After several months, he found us there also and told us to cease and desist.

By this time, we had established our BASICS office in the Milwaukee Enterprise Center on North 4th Street where they had a large conference room where we prayed until we moved our office to the City on a Hill building at 2224 West Kilbourn Avenue. We prayed in the large main lobby of that building until it was renovated in an affordable housing facility. To this day, every Wednesday morning at 8:45 a.m., the BASICS prayer group meets in the chapel for prayer. We've had as many as thirty people attend, but lately only a handful are there.

For the past decade, BASICS has been publishing a monthly prayer calendar to lead us all to pray for specific ministers to Milwaukee and their related ministries in the city.

MARCH FOR JESUS
1998–99

Throughout the nation, there was a growing desire to build bridges between urban and suburban residents to show they care for each other. There was also a fear of one-on-one confrontations that could lead to violence.

A march with people coming into the city seemed to be a good way to show compassion and build friendships. Much thought and preparation went into planning these events and involved many opportunities for volunteers to get involved as follows:

- Getting permits from the municipality for parades
- Obtaining city variances for noise (loud music)
- Getting a radio station to broadcast the event
- Getting cars/trucks to carry the speakers for simultaneous sound throughout the parade
- Food and water for participants and residents
- Free Bibles for anyone who wanted them
- Tracts for those who didn't want Bibles
- Church groups with flags, banners, and signs
- Police protection to provide crowd control
- Preliminary flyers to announce the event
- Distributing flyers
- Donating to cover the costs of the event
- Prayer before, during, and after the event

Hundreds of suburbanites came to participate, many with their families. Most residents watched from their porches. It was a fun two-to-three-hour experience for everyone and served to show a spirit of community. It also displayed much more work would be required to make a difference in the lives of disenfranchised citizens who were invisible.

During the mid 1990s, another movement of prayer began nationally within the Mission America efforts to evangelize the nation by encouraging Christians to reach out to their neighbors through their homes as lighthouses of prayer. Believers in Milwaukee participated in this effort to obey what Jesus instructed his followers to do. Here is a story of one of them as told by Mark Mallwitz.

Maria's Lighthouse of Prayer

One of our dear sisters in Christ, Marcia Vanderleest, considered her house to be a lighthouse of prayer. Marcia spent a significant amount of her time in prayer while also keeping her house open for prayer to anyone who wanted to join her in going to the throne of God.

Marcia actually had a lighthouse made and put on her front lawn so people could see and know that her house was a lighthouse of prayer, love, and hope. For many years, Marcia would pray and invite others to pray and take seriously the charge of being a lighthouse for Jesus.

One Halloween, Marcia invited children and their families to come to her house to be listened to, loved on, receive some food and candy, and of course—to be prayed for. Many children and their families came all afternoon.

In a neighborhood void of many godly outreaches, people were seeing the love of Jesus from one woman and a small group of friends. As the event was finishing, a dear brother in Christ, John Wegner, who is now in heaven, said to all of us, "Let's pray for one more person to come and be blessed."

Looking down the street, there was no one coming in any direction, but we prayed together asking the Lord to bring one more. Almost immediately after we finished our prayers, a woman came staggering down the middle of the road with her little boy. They were in harm's way and needed help.

Marcia and the team went into the street to encourage the woman and her son to come to her lighthouse, receive some food, coffee, love, and prayer. After a while, the woman began to speak and act more clearly. Marcia loved on them both with several bags of food, toys, and books before sending them on their way.

This story did not make the evening news or receive any awards, but for this mother and her child, God used Marcia's lighthouse of prayer to potentially save them from disaster. God used this encounter to bless this woman and her son with hope and joy that brought big grins to both of their faces.

That day God taught us the power of asking for one more opportunity to shine the light of Jesus Christ for his glory. This experience did not change Milwaukee, but it sure changed this mother, her son, and each of us. Someday we may see what the Lord did with this lighthouse prayer.

–Mark Mallwitz, Minister to Milwaukee

CALL TO PRAYER AND WORSHIP
2001–03

We all remember where we were on September 11, 2001, when the Twin Towers were destroyed and the Pentagon was hit by commercial airplanes. I was at work in my home office on that Monday morning at 8 a.m. when my wife Norma came downstairs very distressed saying, "Arn, you must see what's happening on TV!" We watched in shock to see the first tower burning, the second tower struck by a second plane, hearing of another plane hijacked and still in the air, fearing we were witnessing the start of a third world war. When the Pentagon was hit, it seemed to confirm the worst. It resulted in a call for America to pray, and that's what we did.

I clearly recall going back to my office praying to God: "Please help us! What do you want me to do, especially as a leader of your people?" Immediately an image came to my mind of the recently completed Miller Park Stadium in Milwaukee.

That picture stayed in my mind for several months. It just wouldn't leave. During one of my Monday morning meetings with my dear friend and colleague, Mark Mallwitz, I shared my experience with him. He said he had a similar vision. Was God trying to tell us to use the stadium to call the faith community of southeast Wisconsin to pray? We decided to ask God to show us three special signs to confirm this was something he wanted us to do.

The first concern we had was whether or not we could even use Miller Park for such an event, which we decided to name A Call to Prayer and Worship. We called Miller Park to find out who we should talk to, and we were told to submit a proposal, business plan, expected size of the audience, and date. When we explained BASICS was a Christian nonprofit ministry, she informed us that the Miller Park Board had not yet received such a request and had not yet set a policy for such an event, but she agreed to set up a time to meet.

We arranged a date to meet, and we decided not to go with a group of business executives in suits but instead with a group of former gangbangers in street clothes. At our meeting with the senior vice president of stadium operations, we explained that our intent was to hold the event with no fees or entertainment but only to have prayer and worship. We had no funds and no idea how many would attend. At the end of our meeting, we asked if we could go into the stadium to pray about it, and we were allowed to do just that.

We couldn't pray at home plate as we had hoped because the field was under repair, but we got as close as we could on the first-base side in the bleachers behind the dugout. Steve joined us in our hand-holding circle of prayer. We knew God was with us as we prayed.

When we got back to the office, we were given approval to proceed. We set a date that fit the schedule. We got the three-hour event at a price of one-sixth the normal price, but were told they would have to charge for the parking because that was a separate contract. We stepped out in faith and signed the contract knowing that if this was in God's plan, he would provide the resources his way.

The next concern we had was to find sponsors. I called one of our advisory board members and told him what we were doing. He agreed to pay the full stadium fee with three conditions: that we invite twenty-five pastors and/or ministry leaders to give a three-minute prayer or devotional; that the speakers would only mention the name of Jesus and not their own name, title, or organization; and no beer would be sold or allowed into the event. We knew this was God's way, and we agreed fully!

The third concern was how to pay for the remaining $22,500. We still had to pay for parking, sound system, stage, lighting, security, and other expenses. On the Monday morning of the event week, a woman who had heard about the event called our office saying God compelled her to call us to say that if this was to be a worship event, there should be a thanks offering. At the last minute, we organized a group of ushers to pass popcorn buckets for a worship offering. Exactly $22,501 was raised. All praise to God for his faithfulness!

A little over 10,000 souls attended the first year, and they experienced a touch of heaven. One of our Lutheran brothers exclaimed that he was so inspired at one point in the worship, he prayed and even raised his hands to his waist! Miraculously, God inspired BASICS to facilitate this event for three years with amazing miracles occurring each year.

The final event was blessed by a ministry in Racine who provided an inspiring demonstration at the conclusion of the worship. He released a single white dove that represented our connection with heaven as the orchestra, choir, and people sang all four verses of "Amazing Grace." After the dove circled the stadium, it exited through the dome followed by the release of a flock of white doves that symbolized the Christian's eternal life with God in heaven. All glory and praise was given to our Lord and Savior, Jesus Christ! Mark Mallwitz was my God-sent partner in this exciting event and here is his story of God's work in Miller Park.

Mark Mallwitz on Miller Park

Has God ever called you to something so much greater that your mind could comprehend or imagine? Has he stretched your faith so much that you did not think it could go any further, but yet he proved to be faithful? That is how the Lord stretched me. He blew me away and transformed me forever as he allowed BASICS and myself to host the first three Christian events at Miller Park called A Call to Prayer and Worship. There is no way that something of this magnitude could ever have taken place without God's calling, providing, directing, and being in charge. It was a God-event!

From the vision itself, to securing the stadium, to organizing the event, and providing the $60,000 each year in supernatural was, God was in control! And even now, almost fifteen years later, it is with fear, awe, and wonder that this story is being written to the glory of God! In 2002 the Lord was giving myself and Arn the same vision independently of each other of hosting a sacred assembly at Miller Par. And when God brought us together to discuss our deepest desires, we realized that our visions aligned. There was no doubt that God was calling us.

That year we started working. Arn began securing the stadium and I handled the details of such a large event. We met frequently, sharing our common passion. We prayed for God's guidance and confirmation. The first action item was prayer during the year before the event. Each month a remnant of faithful prayer intercessors would meet at Miller Park and prayer walk around the stadium, asking Almighty God to show us what he wanted us to do or not do. There is no doubt God heard those prayers and directed all our plans according to his good, pleasing, and perfect will. God led us to several key themes:

The gathering would be open to all people of faith and focus totally on the Lord Jesus Christ by worshipping, singing, confessing, repenting, and praying for our city, state, and nation.

We would invite twenty-five pastors and ministry leaders to speak for three minutes without mentioning their name, title, or organization—only the name of Jesus!

There would be no charge to attend, including parking, God would provide the funds!

God provided the publicity, the program, the participants, and the stadium. We had no idea how it would happen, but each year God miraculously paid all the costs, confirming his blessings.

We prayed for God to lead us to find kingdom-minded men and women who could lead us in all aspects of cross-racial and cross-denominational worship. God answered these prayers with a huge choir and orchestra that led us in worship all three years. It was thrilling to be a part of such diversity, love, and unity worshipping our God for three hours. It was a touch of heaven. God miraculously opened doors for BASICS ministers to speak at multiple locations during that three-year period to promote the event in churches, Bible studies, radio stations, newspaper articles, television program, all indicating God's blessings on the call to prayer and worship.

And what did God do with this gathering to change Milwaukee? I don't think we will know until we get to glory, but for three hours in these sacred assemblies, there was certainly an anointing of the Holy Spirit. Paul wrote:

If my people, who are called by my name, will humble themselves and pray and seek my face and turn from their wicked ways, then I will hear from heaven and will forgive their sin and will heal their land. Now my eyes will be open and my ears attentive to the prayer offered in this place. 2 Chron. 7:14−15

This God-honoring and powerful demonstration of love for God and our neighbors brought us together for three nights in the most segregated city in America. For thine is the kingdom, and the power, and the glory forever. Amen!

MILWAUKEE PUBLIC SCHOOLS COVERED IN PRAYER 2003–19

Prayer has always been the foundation of God's work through Brothers And Sisters In Christ Serving in Milwaukee. We found many followers of Christ had ideas and visions of ministries to start in Milwaukee's urban communities, but they didn't know how to do it. They often expected BASICS to do it or find someone who would. A rapidly growing concern in the entire Milwaukee area was the children and youth in Milwaukee Public Schools (MPS). We wholeheartedly agreed and began the process with prayer through our Wednesday morning prayer team!

A valuable insight was given to me by my pastor and mentor Stuart Briscoe who said, "If God gives you a vision of ministry, just do it! If you fail, that's OK. You learned what doesn't work. Anything worth doing is worth doing poorly at first." BASICS has adopted this spirit when training ministry leaders, but we add a support team of experienced ministers to Milwaukee to help people fulfill God's plan as God leads and provides his way.

God answered our prayers by sending Valerie Petrowiak, a woman of prayer who had a great passion to encourage people in the church pews. She adopted a school in Milwaukee to pray for the principal, teachers, students, and staff of their school as often as possible. At the time there were over two hundred public schools in the MPS system, and our goal was to have at least one person committed to each school. The Holy Spirit quickly led enough people to cover every school, and prayer leaders were selected to contact the principles to ask for the needs of their school to pray for. The response was amazingly positive, which sent a signal that the Christian community was alive and well in caring for all our children.

The communication lines opened up widely to help us understand the tremendous needs, concerns, and opportunities for serving. Shortly after the prayer network was established, the Milwaukee Rescue Mission called BASICS asking for help in distributing 10,000 pairs of children's underwear that was donated by a Wisconsin underwear manufacturer. It was a huge blessing for the givers and receivers that year since many of these children rarely were given clean underwear.

This led to prayer walks around the schools; during weekends we asked God to stop the violence in the schools. This resulted in many school principals inviting the prayer teams into the schools during school hours. Volunteers were later able to do more:

- Provide hats, gloves/mittens, and scarves, which were handmade by older women of churches
- Bring jackets/coats, boots, shoes needed during the winter months, which were donated by church families whose children had outgrown them
- Give cookies, bookmarks with scripture verses of encouragement, cards for prayer requests, etc
- Give Bibles for those who wanted them. BASICS set a goal of providing 40,000 Bibles to anyone as part of our FAMILY initiative (Fathers And Mothers Involved Loving Youth). Over 30,000 have been distributed.
- Provide academic and tutoring help as teachers requested to help students who were falling behind.

Just completing homework assignments eliminated many incompletes on report cards

- Offer prayer and encouragement during lunchtime to those students who desired
- Give Teacher and Staff Luncheons to show appreciation for their work
- Redecorate teacher's lounges during summer breaks

Major academic improvements occurred in a number of schools where these services were provided at no cost to the MPS. Many lives were miraculously changed. Praise our Lord!

CARING FOR THE COMMUNITY
1997–2003

The Leadership Foundations of America (LFA) was a significant blessing to me when forming the BASICS organization. As previously mentioned, Christian leaders in several major cities in America had been inspired by the Pittsburgh Leadership Foundation under the leadership of president Reid Carpenter and founder Sam Shoemaker. Having a passion for a city is at the heart of the LFA. They modeled their organization after Jesus Christ's passion for Jerusalem when he cried over the city of Jerusalem. Many men and women all over the world are experiencing life-changing calls to bring God's healing and truth to their cities.

During a Leadership Foundation Conference in Los Angeles in 1997, I visited the Dream Center, a large hospital that had been abandoned after having suffered damage from an earthquake. It was being restored by a nonprofit ministry in Phoenix to function as a community center for disenfranchised citizens living in extreme poverty. The Dream Center idea planted in my mind resurfaced when a similar situation developed in downtown Milwaukee.

At the end of the twentieth century, my good friend Patrick Vanderburgh, president of the Milwaukee Rescue Mission (MRM), mentioned the rising demand for their services. They were looking to expand their facility, so I mentioned to Pat that he may want to take a look at the nearby Sinai Samaritan Hospital that was up for sale, originally listed for sale at $25 million but reduced significantly with still no offers. The MRM board toured the huge 320,000 square-foot property but decided not to pursue acquiring it because of the restoration costs and risks.

However it occurred to me and to several other Christian leaders that, with God's help, this hospital could be like the Dream Center for Milwaukee's disenfranchised citizens. This vision was shared with my two friends Pastor (now Bishop) Walter Harvey and Prophet George Nathaniel III. The three of us agreed to pray that God would somehow make this facility available to the Christian community for one dollar, or whatever God's plan was to be. We prayer walked around the complex several times asking God for a miracle. He had one in store for the summer of 2000.

The Convoy of Hope, a faith-based nonprofit organization, selected Milwaukee to hold one of their events. This came about because of a conversation with two Milwaukee Assembly of God district leaders at a Convoy of Hope conference in 1999. They shared their driving passion to feed the impoverished poor people through children's feeding initiatives and community outreach. The location chosen for the Milwaukee event was a vacant parking lot of the Aurora Hospital. They arrived with a semi-truck loaded with food to be given freely to everyone in the area who came to the event. The result was overwhelming with an enormously positive response from the neighbors surrounding the abandoned hospital.

In early August of that year, I was leaving a community meeting on Martin Luther King Jr. Drive and ran into a realtor involved in trying to sell the hospital. I asked if the Aurora Hospital owners had ever considered donating the property to the faith community. The answer was "No, but I'll mention it to the Aurora senior management." Weeks later Diane de la Santos was appointed by Aurora to study the possibility and feasibility of transferring ownership of the property and if it could be accomplished by the end of that year. Through a series of miraculous steps, the ownership transfer became reality. But God wasn't done with us yet!

A legal entity was required to accept the ownership. It was decided that the organization that hosted the Convoy of Hope event held in the vacant lot of the hospital displayed the spirit Aurora wanted to convey to the neighborhood. Diane was the leader God chose to bring everything together. The City on a Hill was born as owner of the hospital and an affiliate of the Assembly of God Church Presbytery (a group of pastors who serve as the board) of Wisconsin Northern Michigan District (WNMD).

A temporary study team, led by Walter Harvey, was appointed to establish the new entity, business plan, and obtain an IRS determination as a 501(c)(3) nonprofit organization. In 2003 Reverend John Davis was appointed Board Chairman with Diane De La Santos as Executive Director of the City on a Hill. BASICS became one of the first tenants in the facility. Another miracle was to happen. God's plan was not yet completed. The faith of his saints was yet to be rewarded.

The BASICS monthly city-wide prayer meetings were quickly moved to the building-D lobby, which was a beautiful, elegant place to thank and praise God for his marvelous answers to our prayers. The Assembly of God Presbytery of WNMD with its many churches throughout Wisconsin and Northern Michigan demonstrated a tremendous spirit of generosity and faithfulness in their support of God's work in the extensive and impressive restoration of the facilities and the new ministries incorporated into the City on a Hill. Praise God for his miraculous blessings that continue to this day!

THE FOUNDATION OF GOD'S PEOPLE SERVING

1997

As he approached Jerusalem and saw the city, he wept over it and said, "If you, even you, had only known on this day what would bring you peace—but now it is hidden from your eyes. The days will come when your enemies will build an embankment against you and encircle you and hem you in on every side."
Luke 19:41–43

What: To demonstrate God's blessings when believers work together by showing God's love.
So what: Describe a few of the many ways God has been and is working in Milwaukee.
Now what: Inspire believers to do God's work, God's way.

MINISTRY STARTUPS AND RECOVERY
1997–2017

When Jesus saw Jerusalem at the triumphal entry, he cried because he knew what was to come. We can only imagine what was behind his tears. Our souls are also touched when we look at the mess our world is today and try to understand how God wants us to respond as his disciples. We know we are to be Jesus to others, but where do we start? What Jesus said was where I started:

Scripture says believers are heirs as God's children: *"The Spirit himself testifies with our spirit that we are God's children. Now if we are children, then we are heirs—heirs of God and co-heirs with Christ, if indeed we share in his sufferings in order that we may also share in his glory"* (Rom. 8:16–17).

My challenge and guide to restoration in the city was to serve in God's *heir force* to:

- Be *aware* of where God is working and join him there (mission)
- Be in *prayer* for God's wisdom and discernment (intercession)
- Show I *care* by loving my neighbor (compassion)
- Be ready to *prepare* friends to obey God's commands (discipleship)
- Be *there* wherever God calls me to serve (mobilization)
- Be an *heir* in God's kingdom (worship)
- And do this all *God's way*!

Applying these principles has been my challenge during twenty-two years of helping Christians in Milwaukee who are called to start a ministry. There is a pattern of three stages I've noticed when many believers embark on starting their own ministry:

- Doing my work—my way (ego-driven for self-gratification)
- Doing God's work—my way (outcome-driven and measured by numbers)
- Doing God's work—God's way (worship-driven to glorify God)

The gifts I continually pray for are wisdom, knowledge, understanding, and discernment. They are critical in doing God's work in cross-cultural settings. God has created us with the ability to choose right or wrong, good or bad. It is critical that we as ministers of the Gospel show and tell the truth of Jesus Christ to help people decide in whom they are going to believe. It's a matter of life and death!

God has created every person with a purpose, and he loves everyone. There are millions of people who have never heard the compelling message that requires a response regarding life and death. People who have faith in Jesus Christ have hope in eternal life and love God above all and love their neighbors as themselves: "*And now these three remain: faith, hope and love. But the greatest of these is love*" (1 Cor. 13:13). Showing and telling neighbors the love of God can lead them to become believers in Jesus Christ through the Holy Spirit which leads to hope in eternal life and faith in God.

Applying these truths and equipping Christians to serve is why BASICS exists. Applying these truths can lead to revival in Milwaukee.

John Jones' Story

I first met Arn Quakkelaar while he was the chairman for the construction of Elmbrook Church. That day was cold, rainy, and overcast, but I came out to film the progress of the building for the Sunday morning updates.

Arn carried himself like a businessman: clean-cut in a three-piece suit. Arn already stood out from the first moment I saw him; he had this spark, this excitement in his voice, a kind of passion that showed his tenacity and commitment to the project. He was trekking through the rain and mud—*splosh, splash, splot* —I still remember the footage I got of his every step; the weather didn't deter him from giving his presentation. He knew exactly where everything was supposed to be whether it was somewhere in this giant hole in the ground or covered in a muddy heap somewhere else.

That's what struck me about Arn. He works outside the box and pushes others to do the same because that's what the Lord has called him to do. He's a man of God in a time where there may be few left. He reminds me of someone like Moses, called to change the world in the late years of his life and to follow the Lord into the unknown wilderness.

Meeting Arn was a God-sighting for me. By the time BASICS started, I'd known Arn for years. Whenever we worked with each other, we really clicked. He's just the type of guy I can relate to and be motivated by.

BASICS has given me structure, security, and encouragement where I needed it most. It remains a constant support to an ongoing ministry.

For a technological time as this, God is bringing this ministry to fruition. Arn and the leadership at BASICS helped make it possible through the Lord Christ's direction in my life's journey.

-John Jones, BASICS - Minister to Milwaukee

TRANSITIONAL ROW
AND HOPE STREET
1997–2019

When I was doing research on urban ministries, I read an article in the *Milwaukee Journal-Sentinel* about a ministry called Transitional Row on Michigan Street between 24th and 25th streets. They were working with men and women who were victims of drug and alcohol abuse. Eddie Johnson was the director in charge of eight houses adjacent to each other and committed to providing recovery services in what appeared to be a Christian outreach ministry. I called Eddie and went to visit him.

The Transitional Row experience turned out to be my deep exposure to the ravages and abuses of all types, even to the death of a young man who had overdosed and died at my feet while his friend was giving him mouth to mouth resuscitation. I got to know Eddie over the next year by visiting almost daily to learn first-hand how addicts lived and survived or passed into their eternal home. My presence there seemed to have a calming influence to some but confrontational to others. My attitude was to help and encourage a healthy, godly lifestyle.

Getting to know Eddie's inner thoughts and passions led to a deep understanding and empathy for addicts who were trapped into a disease I call "decision dysfunction." Decision dysfunction happens when body and mind pain causes an intense desire to escape the consequences of their decisions. I learned from my direct personal relationships with addicts that when they hit rock bottom with an intense desire to die, they needed some glimmer of hope that could only come from a relationship with Jesus Christ.

The message of God's love and forgiveness is the greatest truth that could ever be shown and told to these brothers and sisters created by God for a purpose. But who would be willing to tell them when they had ears to hear? That's what Jesus did when he was on earth, and that's what I feel called to do now! Jesus heals!

It was at that time God led a group of very special BASICS volunteers to form a team of uniquely skilled brothers to surround Transitional Row (T-Row) as an action team. The T-Row business model was for the ministry to be self-sustaining through the rent money of the residents. That money would pay for all the costs of rent, building maintenance, repairs, etc. A difficult and virtually impossible goal. Eddie spent 90 percent of his time trying to collect rent money before the residents could spend it on drugs and alcohol.

Group Bible studies and other life skill classes were offered but didn't keep them from the bad decisions that destroyed them. We knew they needed a relationship with Jesus Christ to totally occupy and heal their bodies, minds, and souls. Eddie seemed to know exactly what these people were struggling with, and they respected him.

Maggie Hatfield, a resident of T-Row, was serving with Eddie as a silent partner. She knew every one of the residents. She had the wisdom to know what was going on every day and hour of the week even though she was not able to read or write and lived in extreme poverty while taking care of her sick mother.

Then a disaster struck. Eddie disappeared! We had no clue

what happened to him, but we strongly suspected that he relapsed into drugs, which was exactly what happened.

Fortunately, the BASICS action team stepped up and operated T-Row until a solution could be found.[1]

Before Eddie disappeared, he had written a simple grant request to a major Milwaukee Foundation. They sent a representative to visit T-Row for their normal on-site review. They were so impressed with the tremendous need and impact being made, they decided to make a large contribution to T-Row. This may have been what stimulated Eddie to celebrate with a relapse (which often happens to addicts).

Knowing the situation and risk of misuse of funds, we informed the foundation and requested they send the check to both T-Row and BASICS to insure proper use of the funds under BASICS control. When Eddie finally returned, he admitted to the relapse and agreed to go to a recovery center. Ed Edwards and I brought him to a drug rehabilitation center in Illinois for a minimum of three months. Eddie never returned, and we lost track of him.

The BASICS action team then assumed operational control of T-Row and began praying and searching for an organization willing to adopt T-Row. God miraculously answered our prayers. we learned that a 501(c)(3) in Milwaukee called the Samaritan Inn, a Christian ministry who BASICS had been working with on one of our restoration projects, was looking to expand their outreach to disenfranchised people. After meeting with their board, Scott Martin, one of their board members, was assigned to take over the leadership of T-Row; the transition and transformation of Transitional Row became reality. Praise God for his faithfulness!

Shortly thereafter, T-Row was dissolved. Operations were taken over by the Samaritan Inn and moved to a building on the northeast corner of Capitol Drive and 26th Street under the new name, Hope Street. Praise God for using brothers and sisters in Christ to do his work, his way! Hope Street is still an exciting ministry that continues to grow in miraculous ways.

Mark Mallwitz's Testimony

Have you noticed how the Lord will do multiple things at the same time? That is what almighty God did in my life and in the lives of the men and women who lived in a group of houses called Transitional Row. These homes were primarily for people who were low income and were dealing with drugs, alcohol, addictions, and hopelessness.

This ministry opportunity was my first real experience with poverty and addiction, and wow, God really opened my eyes! *"Forget the former things; do not dwell on the past. See, I am doing a new thing! Now it springs up; do you not perceive it? I am making a way in the wilderness and streams in the wasteland"* (Is. 43:18–19). Little did I know God was doing a new thing in my heart as well as the hearts of the people who lived there. The ministry itself would be a way in the wilderness and streams in the desert.

Arn Quakkelaar, who would eventually become my Christian mentor, teacher, shepherd, friend, and brother in Christ Jesus, invited me to come and see this facility, meet some of the residents who lived there, and see if God would show me how I might help these dear people.

My initial impressions of Transitional Row and the people who lived there came from a place of ignorance, arrogance, and misinformation. The problems seemed too large. I thought the people would never be able to get out of the cycle they were in. What could I possibly offer?

The Lord used Arn to show me the greatest gift is love. Arn would simply listen to everyone as if he were listening to the most important person in the world. He loved each person as if they were his brother or sister. He hugged each person and told them that Jesus Christ loved them and so did he!

God allowed me to spend time with people who did not think, act, talk, or dress like me or anyone I knew. But God was allowing me to see that each of these people had a lot of the same desires, goals, and aspirations I did! They wanted a better life.

They loved their families. They were open to prayer and loved to share their stories with anyone willing to listen.

And as I listened, my fears, arrogance, and misinformation began to fade into the background. Each time I went to Transitional Row more love grew through relationships. Relationship with God first, then one another. The more time you show God's love to people, the more they see how they can trust you. Then the deeper and more meaningful the relationship can be. Then ministry can really take place!

As God allowed us to go forward in faith with Transitional Row, we saw that not only were the people in the program in need of a heart change, the organization itself was about to collapse unless God intervened and got things back on track.

And that is what the Lord allowed Arn, myself, and several other humble servants to do just like Isaiah, *"And I said: Here am I. Send me!"* (Is. 6:8).

Through asking God to direct our steps and using Arn's leadership skills, the problems and shortcomings of the past began to be brought into the light of Jesus Christ. Over a period of several years, the ministry that had appeared dead was brought back to life in an even greater way than it had ever been before!

Today, Transitional Row is called Hope Street. Hope Street is home to about forty men, women, and children and is stronger than ever as it helps people find the hope of Jesus Christ!

The ministry has been a beacon of light for the forgotten people of Milwaukee for over twenty years, and has received national, state, and local recognition. Glory to God!

God taught me many lessons through Transitional Row during this formative start of my service for him in Milwaukee: No one is too far, too hard, or too lost for Jesus Christ; we can indeed bring the little things to God, offer them to him, and watch him grow them for his kingdom and for his glory; prayer was the foundation of everything we did, and without prayer, we did not have a prayer; the greatest gift is love, and God demonstrated his love to me through Arn, the other servants who came to Transitional Row, and through the people we were serving the residents of Transitional Row.

Again, when I began serving at Transitional Row, I had no idea that this first exposure to serving the Lord Jesus Christ would become the calling that the Lord would have on my life.

And twenty years later, God is still allowing me to deny myself, take up my cross daily, and follow him. It is a privilege to show the love of Jesus Christ and tell the good news of Jesus Christ just like he had allowed all of us to do at Transitional Row.

God not only changed the organization of Transitional Row, the residents who lived there, and the people who served obediently, he also did a new thing in my heart! I began to see things through his perspective, and I will never be the same!

–Mark Mallwitz, Minister to Milwaukee

FROM GANG WARS
TO AN OASIS OF HOPE
1991–2018

During the early 1990s, street gangs grew rapidly and became more violent and dangerous throughout the country causing inter-gang warfare, drive-by shootings, turf wars, and homicides. In Milwaukee, one out of every six homicides could be linked to gang activity stimulated by the availability of guns. Gangs in Milwaukee were the primary distributors of drugs into the metropolitan area with fast-growing increase in robberies.

The gangs in the Borchart Field neighborhood at that time were: One Way, German Outlaws, Castle Folks 16 & 17, Deep Garfield Posse, 26 Vicelords, Brothers of the Struggle, Clark Street Gangsters, Monroe Gangsters, and 2-Hustlers. The crime was mostly drugs, but they also committed thefts of all kinds.

There was a constant flow of cars from the suburbs coming to neighborhood alley fast-drug gang houses similar to fast-food restaurants. Such an alley gang house was at Ring and North 11th Street, the only remaining alley made with paved bricks in the city.

This alley was built right up to the foundation of a cottage house located at the edge of the bricks where a window of the house was conveniently located to lower a bucket for cash to be raised from car windows to the dealer and drugs dropped to the customer. The transaction could be completed in under a minute—truly a fast drug sale.

This drug house was also the location where the drugs were mixed with rat poison to increase the potency of the product. The gang used young teenage girls in the nude to mix the drugs in the second-floor rooms to ensure that the girls wouldn't hide the drugs in their clothing. One of the girls was caught concealing drugs in her body cavity and was immediately murdered. When police found the body, an order was issued by the city to close and demolish the building.

When I toured that den of iniquity before it was torn down, I felt the evil spirit my first step into the house, smelled the odor of death, saw the blood on the floor, satanic symbols and graffiti on the walls, and the bags of rat poison in the basement. It was truly a horrible experience. It was frightening and led us to immediately pray for God to cast out the demonic power in that place.

The building was removed, and a pine tree was planted in its place as a symbol of life with hope, God's way.

It was shortly before this episode that I met one of the most caring, gracious, giving, and forgiving people I've ever met, "Mother" Cordelia Taylor. She, her husband James, and their eight children were in the process of acquiring eight properties along the alley and North 11th Street to establish an organization called the Family House. It was to be an oasis of hope for abandoned, poor, and disenfranchised elderly citizens with no place to go for safety and protection from crime and illness. These were the homeless, helpless, and hopeless neighbors being ignored. They were often found by a police officer or a social worker and brought to the only place that would take them in day or night seven days a week.

Mother Cordelia Taylor was (and is) a small but powerful woman of God and committed to prayer, faith, and love. She gives hope to the hopeless in her neighborhood dominated by gang activity and gang wars. Gunshots were heard frequently and increasingly until one day a violent gang war broke out involving the drug house and one of the opposing gangs one block east on North 10th Street.

After daily calls to the police with no response, this courageous lady decided she would stop the war by going to the media.

On the way to the television station on Capitol Drive, she decided she should tell the police what she was doing. So she stopped at the District 5 station on 4th and Locust and told the desk clerk that she was headed to Channel 4 WTMJ-TV to explain about the war going on in her neighborhood that no one was responding to except for her. When she got back home from the TV station, her entire neighborhood was surrounded by police. The Family House hood was cleaned out. Her property was eventually transformed into a Family House oasis for hope constructed by volunteers and donor contractors from all parts of the Milwaukee area. This became an outstanding model of people working together to do God's work, resulting in many miracles! But there's still much more to this story.

Mother Cordelia Taylor could certainly be called a living example of the Good Samaritan as she took care of hundreds of broken victims of violence, abuse, and sickness. When she was a twelve-year-old child living in the South, something devastating happened. Her father was a hard-working and frugal sharecropper who saved every penny with the goal of being able to buy the seed for his farm in the spring without having to get a loan from the local bank. When he refused to take out a loan for the seed, the local bankers brutally killed him. Cordelia's grandfather aggressively sought justice, but it never happened.

She could easily have lived a life of hate and anger, but Cordelia followed God's way and forgave in a spirit of love and compassion.

Mother Taylor set her life's plan to work to rebuild her community to overcome the ravages of poverty and crime into a loving community of people who cared for each other and could live with hope and without fear. She is truly a Good Samaritan.

James and Cordelia Taylor raised their family of eight children in their home at 3269 North 11th Street which became one of the most violent areas of the inner city. Eventually they were able to escape and buy a beautiful new family dream home in a northern suburb, only to sell it and move back into their family home on 11th Street—exactly the opposite of what most people were doing.

Cordelia was working as a registered nurse in a care center but was disturbed by the deterioration in the quality of care offered by the facility. The facility's first priority was to produce a profit. Their second priority was the quality of medical care. She complained about this every night.

One night after coming home from work, she was complaining about this again to James as he was reading the newspaper. Finally, he put down his paper and said, "If you don't like what they are doing, why don't you do it yourself your way!" So she did! She quit her job, went back to school, and became certified as a care center administrator.

This planted the seed for Family House, which put Mother Taylor's faith into action. By combining her incredible energy and wisdom with prayer and the gift of compassion, she demonstrated her trust in God by showing and telling the love of God to the people in her community. She respected and loved her neighbors because of her deep understanding that God created everyone for a purpose and should be respected as a child of God. That spirit changed hearts and lives. It gave hope to her neighbors who were hopeless, homeless, and helpless. But she also admits there were times of doubt and even fear that she had made a mistake. She would go to her bathroom to cry and pray so James would not see her. She didn't give up, knowing that God is always faithful to those who love him and believe in his power.

After opening her first home for eight people, she and several members of her family bought a few vacant houses next door and began restoring them to invite more needy friends to join the Family House long-term care facility. Over the years, the entire block became a well-maintained and impressively integrated model of community transformation. It even included a medical center in the former grocery store across the street that had been burned out during the 1960 riots.

Parents, their children, and youth were a deep concern for Cordelia and her family because they knew that if a child is trained up in the way they should go, when they are old, they will not depart from it (Prov. 22:6). Family House programming encouraged fathers to build loving relationships with their children. Mothers were given food and taught how to prepare good meals. Children were encouraged to visit with the residents who loved to see them. Students were shown how to get better grades in school by reading and doing their homework. Teens were taught to respect their teachers and obey their parents. During this period, the neighborhood was peaceful with virtually no violence, a remarkable change in what had been a violent crime-ridden hood.

When Family House was fully operational, between three hundred to five hundred community people were being served per week—a remarkable example of God's work through his people of faith, hope, and love. Family House grew with facilities for up to fifty-eight residents and employing twenty-seven neighbors including Cordelia and the Taylor children. With an enterprise of this size and complexity, it became increasingly evident that a plan was needed for succession of leadership. Cordelia selected her granddaughter Joi Jackson to be groomed to take over her role after graduation from college. Unfortunately for Milwaukee, Joi moved east, got married, and didn't return.

The search continued with an urgency often found when a ministry was founded by a gifted visionary reaches the inevitable age of exhaustion. Several realities set in:

- The demands and scope of leadership duties becomes overwhelming and difficult, if not impossible, to maintain.
- Physical and mental limitations set in, requiring an increased need to delegate work to more capable staff.
- The effort to raise funds to expand successful growth

becomes more and more difficult, especially with changes in technology and governmental regulations.

- Costs of operations continually increase, requiring significant skills to avoid costs and find efficient, new ways of providing the services needed.
- The time required to train and groom new leadership is a full-time job, which expensive consultants are rarely able to do and funds are not available.
- Building new relationships with ministry partners and funders takes an immense amount of time to build trust, respect, and commitments required.
- In the case of Family House, many residents were getting old and required health services beyond what the staff and facilities could provide.
- Financial demands far exceed the available funds, so debt was increasing to an unacceptable level.

Mother Taylor faced these challenges and continually prayed with her family, staff, and supporters to find an elegant solution to continue to rebuild her community and serve those who were disenfranchised. One brilliant idea came to her mind after she realized that the number of residents was rapidly declining, and there was a need to find a new funding source. Family House could partner with another organization with a similar mission and vision. Family House could expand its role of caring for aging citizens to include the growing number of men and women returning to the 53206 (a Milwaukee zip code known for poverty) community from prisons. Such an organization was at that time searching for a facility that could house returning citizens and teach them a new way of living following the spirit of Family House. That ministry was GENESIS in Milwaukee, Inc.

In 2015 this collaborative concept was presented to the boards of both organizations, and a study team made up of members from both ministries was organized to develop a plan of action to explore the benefits to both ministries. During 2019 when the transition period was in process, the facility became a target of hood scavengers. The Good Samaritan became a victim in the neighborhood she loved and served for so many years.

The Family House was attacked and destroyed by a small group of the people she worked so hard to help. A beautiful oasis of hope became a target by a few individuals who were led to bite the hands that feed them. Why would they feel it was right to do such evil?

They broke down the doors and smashed windows to get into the facility and cut the wires of the security system at the control box to silence the alarm system. They then unlocked the exit doors from the inside so others could get in to steal and vandalize. They spray-painted the interior walls with graffiti symbols and demonic words and indiscriminately destroy and ravage everything. They cut off water lines and electric wiring to get the copper, leaving the water to flood the basement. They stole or smashed everything of value. They left the beautiful, well-furnished interior in shambles.

The Family House-GENESIS study team tried hard to keep this vandalism from happening. We held a neighborhood party to inform the neighbors of the plan to continue Family House by providing food, videos, fun, and games. In preparation for this event, we met with community and government leaders to explain the plan and purpose. We conducted surveys of neighbors who said *yes!* and local pastors who said *yes!* However, several local political leaders said, "No! It will never happen."

Due to the local political resistance, assessing the cost of restoration and debt recovery, the project was dropped. Many prayers are being offered that God would provide signs that he wanted the group to renew its efforts to fulfill Mother Taylor's vision.

The reality of the destruction to the facilities forced us to re-analyze the real factors at hand. Finding solutions to the disasters of poverty is what Mother Taylor and many others working in the neighborhoods are desperately trying to find. As those who believe God is the creator of all things, is all-knowing, all-present, and all-powerful, we understand that he is in control of all things and holds us accountable to do what he commands. God gave us the responsibility and ability to make decisions in whatever circumstances we are placed into.

As an engineer I do my very best to learn every detail of a problem, every possible solution to the problem, every cost and benefit of each solution, and then evaluate the outcomes to society and the beneficiaries. Looking, for example, at the stages in the deterioration of houses in the inner city, I've observed firsthand the stages and characteristics of change and the consequences/outcomes:

- Owner occupied and mortgage loan paid off: home is well-maintained.
- Owner occupied with mortgage loan being paid: home is clean and neat.
- Occupant is renting with good payment record: home is well-kept.
- Occupant is renting with bad payment record: house is deteriorating.
- Occupant has been served eviction notice: house is being ransacked.
- Occupants move out and take with them items of value: house is destroyed.
- Occupants become homeless or repeat the life cycle: house is vacant and open to gangs.
- House is gutted. Anything of value is taken by scavengers: house is infested with vermin.
- House is taken over by the city: house is boarded up.
- House is set on fire or bought by a developer: house must be protected.
- House is demolished if not bought: vacant lot.

The big question is: Who will solve the problems of housing and poverty in the inner city?[2]

Mother Taylor spent almost thirty years trying to address all the issues facing her neighborhood, and many people came to help her. But it takes a united community working in harmony to focus on making good decisions to solve economic and spiritual malaise.

Mother Taylor and her family could not do it alone. I believe it will take an infrastructure of partnerships with citizens who love their creator Jesus Christ, their neighbors, and themselves. There is no other way to bring God's kingdom "on earth as it is in heaven." I praise God for what he has done in giving us a touch of heaven at Family House in 53206.

The rest of this story is yet to be told. God's work is not finished yet. We are watching and praying.

WIN-A-SOUL MINISTRY
1999–2001

With an urgent call to reach lost souls for Christ and to help families overcome a variety of crises, Pastor David King purchased an abandoned tavern in the heart of a dangerous part of Milwaukee's inner city and started Win-A-Soul Ministries. With drug abuse, killings, shootings, and prostitution rampant on the streets, Win-A-Soul Ministries had plenty of work to keep busy.

However, an assortment of legal and financial difficulties grabbed hold of the ministry from the beginning. The building Pastor King purchased on a land contract had numerous previous code violations. While the first floor was approved for use as a sanctuary, the upstairs apartment was deemed unfit for living by the city inspector. The previous owner also owed about three years of back taxes and the roof was in dire need of replacement. A friend who knew about BASICS told him to call our office and talk to Arn.

After assessing the situation, we contacted an attorney friend, Rev. Frank Villa, who found that the owner of the tavern could be cited for nondisclosure. He decided to reduce the price substantially to only five hundred dollars, provided that someone would resolve all outstanding debts, back taxes, and utility bills to clear the title and transfer ownership. BASICS was able to negotiate and clear all the debts as well as work with city inspectors to correct all code violations. Pastor King then joined with other ministries and churches to not only spread the healing power of the Gospel, but to

83

help families and individuals improve their ways of life by empowering them to help themselves.

Pastor King formed a nonprofit organization called SWEEP (Soldiers, Walking, Evangelizing, Empowering People) that resulted in establishing a community justice center at Win-A-Soul Ministries with four other cooperating churches in the area. His goal was to help the whole person to enable them to become healthy citizens following God's way.

Summer nights on the streets of some neighborhoods in the city are like Sodom and Gomorrah, especially from midnight to 4 a.m. on Friday and Saturday nights. These are the times when decent people stay inside but street people come alive.

But not Apostle/Pastor David King.

I saw Pastor King at an inner-city listening session in 1998 where citizens and community leaders met to discuss their deep concerns and complaints about the criminal activity in their neighborhoods, which were called hoods because of the hoodlums taking over control. Solutions to the problems were difficult and rare. Police were unable to get cooperation from the residents who would not inform police on what they knew for fear it would result in severe consequences, even death, for them or their families.

Pastor King was energized by the immensity of this situation and asked the police if they would be willing to help him and God deal with the problems with a new strategy. They reluctantly agreed to try his plan for midnight raids and to stay away from the area around his church on Friday nights while he took over from midnight to 4 a.m.

His church met at a tavern the city had closed because of numerous problems and the dilapidated condition of the building. Pastor King was able to acquire the building and requested that one of BASICS' projects be to renovate the building into a church and community center. He wanted counseling offices and health facilities upstairs to replace the apartment, and a worship center to replace the bar. The church became known as the Win-A-Soul Ministry Center, and its members were concerned members from the community who were passionate about changing their hood into a neighborhood. They had virtually no funds to pay for anything, but the partnership with suburban partners through BASICS helped them make a difference.

Pastor King's plan was that church members met on Friday night from 10 p.m. to midnight to pray for their neighborhood to change, for them return to safety, and for the outreach team be protected during the midnight raid to follow. At midnight, select men would go onto the streets surrounding the church to stand and pray in front of the known gang drug houses while Pastor King, dressed in his street clothes, entered the house with only God's protection. The community knew Pastor King was a man of God. He was highly respected.

Pastor King would then go into the house alone to offer Jesus Christ to everyone in the house as a better way of living. He spoke under the authority of God's power to tell them to leave immediately. The drug dealers, pimps, prostitutes, johns, customers, and anyone else there were invited to meet at his safe house for counsel, medical attention, or rescue, without the fear of being arrested by the police. Many responded, were given counsel to warn them of their bad decisions, and some eventually became members of his church.

It was not uncommon on a hot night for the local prostitutes to walk the streets entirely nude. Pastor King would confront them and tell them to "Go get dressed!" They would obey his commands.

One of the neighbor ladies refused to attend his church when invited because her father was murdered on the steps of the tavern. After much encouragement, she finally came to visit a church service. When she saw and experienced the love of the people that went to Win-A-Soul Church, she changed her attitude, became a believer in Jesus Christ, and joined the church.

The power of God was clearly demonstrated through answered prayers. The Win-A-Soul Community Center thrived and brought peace and unity to the neighborhood for several years. Pastor King was selected as the director of Young Life–Milwaukee as part of a major Heartlove Community Center built by a group of Christian business leaders, staffed by believers, and eventually included a Christian school. Many family services were provided that brought harmony and love to the neighbors of the hood on North Martin Luther King Jr. Drive in what had been one of the most violent areas of the city.

GANG OUTREACH
1998

During the mid to late 1990s, the near South Side of Milwaukee was plagued with growing gang violence and killings between the Latin Kings and the Spanish Cobras. Marty Calderon and Luis Pizarro grew up in the area and became believers in Jesus Christ. They were each uniquely called to serve God as street evangelists to reach out to the gangs in those neighborhoods. They got to know each other even though they ran with members of different gangs. They were both opposed to the gang wars and worked with both gangs to stop the violence. The gangs respected them both as men of God and listened to their words of wisdom.

On a late Wednesday summer afternoon, the day after the funeral of a Latin Kings gang member who had been shot and killed by a Cobra, the Holy Spirit led me to call Marty to find out if we could meet with the Kings gang that night. My concern was that there was a high probability that a retribution killing of a Cobra could occur that night and, with God's help, we should try to stop it. Marty called the leader of the gang to ask if we could meet him at the gang house. He agreed to meet with us on the porch of the gang house around 7 p.m. Marty and I then went to a restaurant to have a quick bite to eat and pray for God to protect us and be able to convince the gang not to kill but forgive, a concept they probably foreign to them. I also called Norma to let her know I would not be home for supper and to pray for our meeting.

When we arrived at the gang house, the leader of the gang was sitting on the porch waiting for us with another gang member. We had a few opening comments, and I was introduced to the two. One gang member had a bad accent and couldn't pronounce my name correctly. He simplified my name to Mr. Arms. Marty told them we wanted to tell them about what Jesus did to those who killed him.

He forgave them! Marty then asked if the entire gang could join us? They said yes and suggested we go to the backyard. Within minutes the entire gang of around ten teenage boys and a few of their girlfriends joined us to hear what Marty had to say about forgiveness.

Marty gave a simple, straight-forward explanation about Jesus in the Garden of Gethsemane where the soldiers came to arrest Jesus. He told them about Peter, who cut off the ear of the High Priest's servant, Malchus. Jesus told Peter, *"Put your sword away!"* Jesus picked up the ear and put it back on fully healed. The gang all listened intently.

It was beginning to get dark so we asked them if we could stand in a circle and do what we typically do as believers when we gather together to pray—hold hands. Only the boys participated while the girls watched and listened.

After Marty prayed for them to forgive the Cobras, I gave each of them a hug and told them "Love you man! And God loves you too!" I noticed several of the boys had tears in their eyes. I suspect the boys were stunned that an old, white-bearded man loved them when most of them didn't even have relationships with their own dads.

Marty and I certainly felt the presence of the Holy Spirit that night. The name Mr. Arms took on a deeper meaning that night with arms of love. I found out years later that Mr. Arms was thought to be bringing arms to Milwaukee from Chicago. God has a great sense of humor, and the miracle of it all was yet to come.

At the end of our visit, we invited them to attend a church service with us on Sunday. They declined our invitation because they were afraid to leave their neighborhood, but they invited us to come back next Wednesday night. And we did.

Later that week, Marty was talking with Luis (the street evangelist working with the Cobras) who told Marty he had an unusual conversation with one of the Cobras who had observed our meeting while walking through the alley behind the Latin Kings' gang house with a gun in his pocket. He explained to Luis, "This was a strange meeting. They ended the meeting holding hands in a circle. Gangs just don't do that! For some strange reason I felt compelled not to shoot anyone."

The King-Cobra gang war entered a period of ceasefire.

The following Wednesday night we asked if they were ever afraid. Every one of them answered *yes*! Suddenly, all of them ran away in all directions leaving Marty and I standing alone. When the all clear signal was given, they all gradually returned. As they returned, it gave us an excellent demonstration of what happens when we are afraid and what we can do to overcome that fear.

More warning signs were given that night leading them to ask: Why aren't you guys afraid? Marty told them about the power of prayer and trust in Jesus. He told them that Jesus takes care of us in all circumstances and Jesus will take care of them too if they put their trust in him.

At the end of our meeting, the gang leader asked if he could pray to Jesus as we stood in our circle holding hands. He prayed a simple, beautiful prayer: "Please, Jesus! Help me not to be afraid anymore, please!"

After our hugs that night, I asked the gang leader, "Why are you so eager to learn about Jesus?" He told me this story:

When I was about eight years old living in the gang house with my mom and brothers, we were poor, and we didn't have any food to eat for breakfast one Saturday morning. My mom told us kids to sit at the kitchen table, and we were going to pray for food. While she was praying, the doorbell rang and there stood two men each holding two bags of groceries. Mom asked them, "Why are you doing this?" They said: "Jesus told us to." Ever since that day I've wondered, Who is Jesus? Now I know, and I believe in him!

A few weeks later, the gang leader was riding in a car with one of his friends when they were pulled over by the police who found drugs hidden in the trunk. They were both arrested, found guilty of drug possession, and eventually put in federal prison in New York. When Marty got a message from him, he was praising Jesus for answering his prayer by putting him in prison where he was safe and away from fear.

Our new gang leader friend and brother passed away from pneumonia in 2017. But he passed away into the arms of Jesus as a child of the King!

Marty Calderon's Testimony

The law eventually caught up with the various Latin Kings and Spanish Cobras during the weeks after our meetings with them. They were sent to prison where I continued to meet with them. Each of these gang leaders took a Bible and accepted Jesus into their lives. Other members of the gang asked if they could also get Bibles that didn't look like Bibles, so Arn found some paperback editions.

My calling is to reach the lost souls and the brokenhearted. Street gangs fall into that category. As one of seven evangelists in Street Talk Ministries, I lead a monthly meeting made up of police captains, a gang squad detective, probation officers, ministers, and aldermen. After determining the target areas, fellow evangelists and I pray and walk through the neighborhoods. We walk with the young men and women we encounter. I'm letting the Lord use me to save souls.

The rewards of this ministry are great. I get to watch these guys leave gangs, which literally saves their lives. The mother of the teen killed by the Spanish Cobra gang member has forgiven her son's killer, accepted Christ, and joined my Bible study. The rival gang leaders who came together for the meeting have become friends and are thinking of starting their own businesses together. The rival gangs even came together last summer for a barbeque.

Only God knows how many lives have been physically saved

since Arn and I last met with the Latin Kings gang leaders in October 2002. But as of June 30, 2003, there has not been one drive-by shooting or gang killing in that neighborhood. For an inner-city Milwaukee neighborhood, that's a long time.

–Marty Calderon, Street Pastor with Street Talk and God's Touch.

LIVING IN THE SHADOWS
OF MILWAUKEE
2008–18

During the winter of 2008, there was a growing community awareness of the plight of homeless and helpless people, invisible and ignored citizens. The mayor of Milwaukee, Tom Barrett, called a listening session for community leaders to address the homeless issues and discuss possible solutions the city should consider. Listening sessions are intended for the people affected but it's generally difficult for them to come. That was true of this meeting also.

However, a couple attended this meeting who were obviously homeless. They had heard about the meeting on the street and came even though not formally invited. The agenda for the meeting was quite structured and had little time allocated for open questions from the floor.

As the meeting was about to end, the homeless woman stood up and introduced herself as Laura Marsh. She said she had been living on the street for several years and asked if she could explain what it was really like. She was reluctantly allowed to speak, and she began to tell about her diary explaining the details of her life. Her hope was to ask the mayor if he could help her write and publish her story in a book. She was told to talk to the mayor after the meeting was adjourned.

Many people were gathered after the meeting to talk with the mayor. Laura was able to shake his hand, but that was all. I felt led by the Spirit to tell Laura I was interested in talking to her and invited her to come to my office the next morning at 9 a.m. She came promptly the next morning with her street friend John, her protector (street women are often abused unless they have a man to protect them).

I was impressed with Laura's promptness and intelligence. She let me read a little of her diary which had great insights into her life trying to survive in a hostile and dangerous part of the city. She gave me a copy of her diary that a friend had typed for her, so I took it home to read. That summer I edited her stories and organized them into a book format and had it printed by a church print shop with the title *Living in the Shadows of Milwaukee.* That was the beginning of a much larger story.

Laura's book was published and sold on Amazon while she was still homeless in the summer of 2008. During that October, she and John gave Norma, me, and a videographer a tour of the shadows neighborhood. From 4 a.m. to 10 a.m. we saw firsthand the places and conditions described in her book. We met and became friends with many of their friends, a life-changing experience, but this was not the end of her amazing story.

The doctors had to remove a large part of John's skull to relieve the swelling of his brain and put him into a coma. Laura spent much of her time in the hospital chapel to pray, where she experienced a God moment. She felt the Holy Spirit telling her John would be OK. The nurses kept telling her, "He's not going to make it and you are going to have to expect to live without him." But she knew God was with him and her. She lived in the hospital for several weeks with no food. She slept in the visitor's lounge. Then one day she was told by a case worker she could no longer sleep there and had to leave.

The case worker called every place she could think of to find a place for her to go, but they were all filled up. Laura had no place to go and no family to call, but she knew a man who helped her write her book. Maybe he would know what to do. The case worker called me and asked if we could meet with her and Laura to discuss the situation, so we went to meet them. Norma and I agreed to take Laura into our home, and she lived with us for a year as an adopted member of our family at thirty-five years old.

Norma's Perspective

In July 2009 my husband Arn was at a meeting on homelessness in Milwaukee with Mayor Tom Barrett. Two people who were homeless came to the meeting; Laura, a thirty-five-year-old White woman, and John Hines, a thirty-seven-year-old Black man living together on and off the streets of Milwaukee for the last four years. John was encouraging Laura to write a book about being homeless. When Arn heard she wanted to get it printed, he asked her to tell him more about the book. They met, and Arn decided to help her publish the book.

Then on August 23, Arn received a call from Laura saying John was shot in the face by a robber, and he was being treated at Froedtert Hospital. The bullet went through his left cheek and out behind his left ear. His brain swelled and he had a stroke, giving him only a 3 percent chance of survival. Laura had no place to go and was staying in the family center of the hospital.

Labor Day weekend Arn got another call from Laura. The hospital would no longer allow her to stay in the family center. She had to leave with no place to go. The shelters were full. We also knew it would not be safe for Laura to be out on the streets without her protector. Since we had an extra bedroom, we said *yes!* and invited her to stay with us. We went to get her.

When we met with the hospital case worker, she asked me, "Do you know this woman?" I said, "Not yet!" The case worker said, "You are the most unusual couple I've ever met." I then met Laura for the first time, and during the next year, we adopted her into our family.

The Lord's confirmation of our decision came when I sat down at my piano the next day to play songs from the Hymnal for Worship and Celebration (the old songbook from Elmbrook Church) and opened it to pages 314 and 315.

The first song was titled, "Let Your Heart Be Broken." The lyrics told me to let my heart break "for a world in need—Feed the mouths that hunger, soothe the wounds that bleed, give the cup of water and the loaf of bread. Be the hands of Jesus, serving in his stead."

The second song's lyrics were equally as powerful: "Reach out and touch a soul that is hungry... a spirit in despair... a life torn and dirty... a man who is lonely—If you care!" These words touched my heart so deeply, I cried. It was like God was confirming exactly what Arn and I just decided to do. The next year would change our lives as well as Laura's and John's. Truly God was working in all our lives.

Labor Day evening we brought Laura home. The following morning, I made her breakfast and lunch. Arn brought her back to the hospital and offered to pick her up on his way home from the office that night. We continued to supply her with food for her to make her own lunches, provided bus passes, and got her a cell phone to call us when she needed a ride home from the bus depot.

Arn did not go out looking for someone living on the streets, but we saw how God sent this precious person to us. Laura has been coming to church with us and is now enrolled at MATC (Milwaukee Area Technical College) taking three classes through a Pell Grant she applied for and received. She is getting excellent grades and hopes to earn an associate degree in business.

On March 11, 2010, John's head was filled with excess fluid and required surgery to put in the appropriate drainage tubes. Surgery was on March 12 (Laura's birthday). Sunday he was again experiencing excruciating pain, and on Monday he was back in surgery. Arn and I saw him Monday nigh,t and he talked to Arn quite a bit about God. John recently told Laura he thinks God has something special for him to do. That's why he didn't die. Laura asked him, "What do you think God wants you to do?" He replied, "Oh I don't know yet!"

I really love Laura and John! They represent God's miraculous gifts to us and many others.

—Norma Quakkelaar

Laura nursed John throughout his year of recovery. She taught him how to walk, talk, eat, dress, read, and write. She wrote two more books while suffering many health problems, then entered Milwaukee Area Technical College and married John. They now live in their own rental home. Neither are able to obtain employment because of their disabilities. We assisted them in getting Supplemental Security Income (SSI) and served as their payee to monitor their spending. Laura and John work hard to be able to get into the workforce. Norma and I are continually in contact with them to witness the miracle of their lives. Praise God for his goodness to those who love him!

STRETCHERBEARERS
2004

One day a scantily dressed woman entered the BASICS office. She captured the full attention of everyone. She asked to see Mr. Arms to talk about starting a ministry to help street girls who desperately needed someone to care for them. It turned out that God was working in Annie Schrader's life, the madam of prostitution in Milwaukee. Annie had become a believer and was led by the Holy Spirit to start a street ministry called StretcherBearers.

God had a way of bringing people like Annie to BASICS to do his work in the streets. Helping her was a little risky and risqué. But didn't Jesus work with prostitutes? So why shouldn't we? Many of these women were sick and desperately needed what Annie was offering, but the authorities didn't understand or believe in what Annie was doing. They continually tried to find her and put her in jail. God spared her from jail time, a sign that God was with her, and she felt his presence.

Annie was a gifted writer and strategic thinker, which enabled her to write grant proposals that generated an impressive funding stream. We worked together to apply for her IRS 501(c)(3) nonprofit designation and it was granted. She was on her way as president of the StretcherBearers Ministry under BASICS.

The role of leadership in a caring enterprise for girls with significant physical, emotional, psychological, and spiritual problems was overwhelming and fully absorbed her twenty-four seven. She seldom got a good night's sleep and often came into my office exhausted.

One day she came in terribly distressed because one of her girls died in her arms that morning. Annie also had an urgent need to recover. Annie wanted a helpmeet. She prayed that someday God would send her a good Christian man to marry.

A few months later she excitedly came into the office and announced that she found her man. He was a biker who had overcome his drug addiction, was going to church with her regularly, and became a believer. She was ecstatic and praised God for answering her prayers. A few weeks later he decided to confirm his relationship with his Savior and was baptized.

The next day he was found dead with his bike in an alley behind the drug house. He relapsed from a drug overdose while celebrating his new life in Christ.

This turn of events from the tremendous high to the lowest low virtually destroyed Annie's spirit. She dropped out of ministry, checked herself into a treatment center, and eventually left the city. Annie still calls frequently to tell me she's OK and still walking with God—still faithfully serving her Lord on the streets and making a difference in street girl's lives, God's way.

GANG LEADERS AS COMMUNITY LEADERS 2001

In the late 1960s, White Flight and Black Migration were combined to change the culture of Milwaukee to what is now the most segregated city in America. Many suburbanites remember growing up playing hide and seek in the neighborhoods now called hoods where violence, shootings, and killings are far too common.

What happened?

Jobs left town that took with them the means to support families. Local and federal government agencies intervened by offering welfare income to mothers to help them raise their children, but on the condition that the fathers could not stay in the home. This broke up the family structure.

That led to prayer, Bibles, and the Ten Commandments being removed from the public schools. Robbery, crime, disrespect for authority, greed, lack of integrity, and eventually shootings and killings became common. The only jobs left in the poverty neighborhoods were illegal ones: selling pot, girls, hard drugs, stealing cars, etc. Even the language in movies and songs on the streets became earthy—the type of swearing our mothers of the past would wash out our mouths if they caught us speaking that way.

Because of powerful gang leaders, neighbors became afraid of each other and became prisoners in their own rented homes. Landlords couldn't keep up with the costs of house repairs. Store owners were losing their profits due to robberies. Government money to fix the problems went to pay the salaries of the privileged and rarely reached the disenfranchised people it was intended to help. Taxpayers became tax-takers and politicians had to focus on getting more taxes and votes—a depressing picture of life in the inner city.

Hood leaders now control and impact the communities far more that the mayor, alderpersons, or even the police. What if these gang leaders were challenged to work with the neighbors and other partners in the hood to take on projects to correct the problems themselves? Right now, relationships with gang leaders are contentious and hostile.

The gang leaders I've gotten to know are not all bad, and I think a little love and care go a long way and should be tried. BASICS and other ministries in the city have tried and been successful.

An often overlooked resource in the city is a network of older believers who still live a Christian lifestyle with values that are God-honoring.

One example is a man I mentioned earlier, Minister Frank Woods who was raised in zip code 53206. The former gangbanger and gang leader who was educated in the prisons became a believer in Jesus Christ in prison, and he is now the executive director of GENESIS in Milwaukee, Inc.

Consider how positive it would be to build a network of community partners, church pastors, volunteer mentors, corrections officers, business owners, employers, and nonprofit ministries all working together in harmony to heal lives that are broken.

The power of prayer, care, compassion, and loving neighbors all working on projects together with adequate funds under the control of people who can make a difference as owners of their neighborhoods.

Does this sound insane? I believe this is what God intends if we truly love our neighbors! There are neighborhoods in the inner city where this is happening, God's way!

Minister Frank Woods is building such an infrastructure today in 53206, following the example of Mother Cordelia Taylor who did this for thirty years at her Family House (also in 53206) where she demonstrated her love for her neighbors with fantastic success in healing the lives and souls of abandoned residents.

Frank and I met at a meeting with a small group of young African American men from Milwaukee who had a deep concern for their community and wanted to do more than just talk. They wanted to do something to change unsafe hoods into safe neighborhoods. They saw the inner city becoming a prison with captives who needed to be set free.

They formed a team called the Captive Project under the very capable leadership of Pastor Richard Brown. It became a 501(c)(3) nonprofit organization under BASICS.

Before Frank became a believer, he ran with a street gang, became its leader, and ended up in prison where his life took a totally new direction working for his Lord. Frank was a gifted rapper and powerful speaker who impacted many young gangbangers by giving God-focused concerts in many Milwaukee County parks during the summer months.

His passion and ability to communicate led his team to develop and produce videos that showed how to transform the community. Frank's life story is an inspiration for Milwaukee.

DRIVE-BYS TO STOP-BYS
2000

In 1999 many people were concerned about an imaginary problem called Y2K. People feared computers would quit working at midnight on January 1, 2000, leading to major business software systems and programs to stop. Businesses would come to a screeching halt. No one seemed to know for sure what would happen, but large amounts of money were spent to hire consultants to fix the suspected problem, and nobody knew how to do it.

A similar situation was happening near South Side where a significant increase in crime was happening in the gangs, but nobody seemed to know how to fix the very real problem and very little money was available to do it. A handful of community leaders became sick and tired of being sick and tired of the killings that took so many lives. Three large churches (two suburban and one urban) recognized the need for an outreach ministry for Spanish-speaking residents in that area and so they formed a partnership together. Pastor Jose Padin was chosen and Centrobrook church was established at National Avenue and South 11th Street. They didn't drive by but stopped by to make a difference.

BASICS was invited to assist in renovating an old warehouse to serve as a worship and community center. Many volunteers participated in the project and many families from the neighborhood became involved. It was during this time that I met Marty Calderon, the son of Pastor Al Calderon. Marty was a former resident in South Side who knew many of the gangbangers and was committed to stop the violence and work directly with the youth face-to-face. Marty joined with Luis Pizarro, a similar street evangelist who worked with opposing gang members. Their presence in the community where the violence was occurring had a major impact on these young people because they knew someone truly cared for them. Marty and Luis showed and told God's love.

The highest crime area around Lapham and Mitchel Streets experienced a major drop in violence as a result and received much attention from the city and community leaders from the mayor to aldermen and judges. There were many prayer walks in the area where the police would allow Marty and his friends to gather on the streets to talk with the gang youth and not be bothered. Marty and Luis were skilled at knowing how to avoid and respect the territorial drug boundaries between the Latin Kings and Spanish Cobras where violence would most likely occur. Understanding the mindset of these youth was critical in building mutual respect and trusting relationships, which led to reducing the violence.

The results of this work by Marty and Luis has been remarkable in stimulating change in Milwaukee's South Side. God is certainly at work. Many programs, events, and movements have begun which bring faith, hope, and love to our communities.

The outcome of this activity could be viewed as two highways with different functions and goals. One is helping with practical needs such as food, clothing, shelter, health and safety—leading to survival. The other highway focusing on spiritual issues involving prayer and telling the truth about life and obeying God's laws— leading to eternal life. These two paths are very different and many times in conflict with each other. It raises the issue of the separation or integration of the church and state governments.

During the eighteenth and nineteenth centuries, religious organizations had a major role in providing for the needs of people through their generosity; hospitals and churches were built to serve the needs of the poor. But during the twentieth and into the twenty-first century, the government has taken over much of this role and the religious role has diminished. BASICS has openly decided to unite the functions of prayer, care (compassion), share (evangelism), prepare (discipleship) into all we do as our worship and thankfulness to God for what he has done for us. You'll read much more of this later in this book to help you see how you may be called to serve and be blessed being a blessing to others and to glorify God.

---

1. This action team was made up of: Art Riemer (prayer); Ed Edwards (business operations); Paul Merrican (accounting); Mark Mallwitz (human

resources); Pastor Roy Bowens (pastoring and teaching); Jack Brown (social services); Pastor Jodie Joiner (local pastor to the residents); Maggie Hatfield (receptionist and administrator); myself.

2. Some of the influencers who are responsible for deciding what will happen with these houses are: property owners, landlords, banks who own the mortgages, renters, government officials, politicians, and neighbors (residents and gangs).

Citizens who are often volunteers willing to help solve the problems include: church people, foundations, and businesses, and corporations.

BUILDING RELATIONSHIPS OF RESPECT
AND UNDERSTANDING

2002

The Spirit of the Lord is upon me, because he has anointed me to proclaim good news to the poor. He has sent me to proclaim liberty to the captives and recovering of sight to the blind, to set at liberty those who are oppressed, to proclaim the year of the Lord's favor.
Luke 4:18–19

What: Provide a guide to help believers know how to do God's work in urban communities.
So what: Give examples of how Brothers And Sisters In Christ Serving (BASICS) showed God's love to their neighbors.
Now what: Give glory to God who is bringing his kingdom and power through us.

A major change in my attitude working in the inner city related to my view of poverty. My mistaken opinion of God's view of poverty was based on Scripture where it states: *"If a man will not work, he shall not eat"* (2 Thess. 3:10). After reading and studying what is said just prior to this often quoted passage, I found Paul commanding the Thessalonians *"to keep away from every brother who is idle and does not live according to the teaching received from us."* Paul goes on to say, *"We were not idle when we were with you,* nor did we eat anyone's food without paying for it." Paul wanted his ministry to not be a burden to the Thessalonians, but a model or rule to follow for getting help as a servant. Putting it all in this context, the emphasis is on the servant but rather than those in poverty. Paul goes on to warn about being idle: "not busy but being busy bodies who must settle down and earn the bread they eat (2 Thess. 3:14–15). That changed my understanding of God's way and his view of poverty.

Our brothers and sisters in poverty are often in their situations because of social circumstances and/or the consequences of bad decisions made by themselves or others. God tells us to love our neighbors and move on to help them survive teaching them God's way, regardless of the causes.

The following stories demonstrate different ways God used brothers and sisters in Christ to respond by serving in unique ways that may help you decide how God is leading you to serve him.

PRISON AFTERCARE
NETWORK (PAN)
2002–2019

In 2005 a joint effort was started by BASICS, Salvation Army, and Prison Fellowship of Wisconsin to form a network of ministries serving in prison ministries throughout Wisconsin. Instead of ministries not being aware of what each organization was doing, what prisons they were working in, when they were visiting, how they were operating, who was involved, etc., it seemed to make a lot of sense to build a communication vehicle to encourage the Christian faith community to work together.

After several meetings, it was decided to form the Prison Aftercare Network of Wisconsin as an agency to coordinate, communicate, connect, and encourage prison ministries to work together by meeting together monthly for prayer and information related to reentry of prisoners back into the communities they came from. After one year of operations, PAN of Wisconsin won a national award for its innovative accomplishment of bringing together over one hundred prison ministries to assist citizens in their returns home.

BASICS had done a three-year study of the restorative justice concept introduced nationally in the 1990s. Our purpose was to map out all the known activities related to incarceration at that time in the social justice system of southeast Wisconsin. The study in 2002–2005 resulted in a linear responsibility chart that identified what happened to offenders from arrest to when they return to their homes.

The goal of this effort was to identify how the Christian community could change the lives of prisoners through showing the love of God and telling the truth of Jesus. This model became the seed for establishing a Ministry called GENESIS in Milwaukee, Inc. under BASICS.

Mike Moses' Testimony

I was born again in 1976 and three years later, God made it clear that I was to be in ministry. I had been watching a documentary about the killing fields of Cambodia. I was moved by the story of the nearly two million people murdered by the Khmer Rouge. I asked God what one Christian like me could do about all that was going on in the world? He told me, "Start where you are, start with what you have, and start with what you know." I was already a practicing pharmacist, but the first thing I did was seek volunteer opportunities at the church where I had been attending since childhood. I helped in the youth group and in administrative roles. I started graduate studies at Trinity Evangelical Divinity School, and I eventually graduated with a master's level certification in Biblical studies.

At the same time, I began serving on short-term, foreign mission trips to the Dominican Republic and then to Mexico, finally totaling fourteen journeys. I wanted to serve as a missionary instead of as a pastor. But I was convinced that this was something I would do full time when I retired from my profession. Three decades of clinical and administrative work within hospitals passed. I decided it was time to begin missionary work. My wife was not interested in my first thought of working in Africa, so I was guided to talk to and shadow Arn in urban missions.

In 2006 BASICS became my ministry home. Discipling high school boys became a major focus for my work, and I began to see how God had been preparing me for this. While that continued, I learned of the scourge of modern-day slavery and the human trafficking taking place globally and locally.

I began a period of public speaking at high schools, churches, and professional conferences. Most everyone asked me if slavery was happening here and now. The answer is yes. Thousands of people were exposed to this truth, and today it is much more widely understood to be a current issue.

In 2007 Arn made me the BASICS liaison to the Prison Aftercare Network (PAN) council, and I found myself being pulled to an area I never had seen myself doing—prison ministry. My pastoral visits with inmates consisted mostly of evangelism and discipleship to brothers in Christ who were incarcerated. I also began preaching in the institutions. This was a huge eye-opener to me! I had a pretty typical attitude toward criminals—if you do the crime, then you do the time. I didn't think highly of those incarcerated. However, one of the first men I ever visited had such an incredible testimony of transformation. He taught me that real change does happen. Highly despised former murderers and sex offenders can become brothers in Christ.

Several years before I answered God's call to ministry, I prayed the prayer of Jabez: *And Jabez called on the God of Israel saying, "Oh, that you would bless me indeed, and enlarge my territory, that your hand would be with me, and that You would keep me from evil, that I may not cause pain!" So God granted him what he requested.* (1 Chron. 4:10)

Recently, as I was traveling to one of the prisons, it struck me how God has answered that prayer. Instead of having influence for the Lord only at home, at Bible study, and at church, I now have a territory that covers most of the state of Wisconsin. In addition to the high school Bible studies conducted in Milwaukee, I preach in and make pastoral visits to state correctional institutions from Racine in the southeast to Green Bay in the northeast, to Stanley in the northwest and to Prairie du Chien in the southwest, with many points in between. I counted twenty-seven facilities to date and growing. As I ministered to the at-risk high school boys, I came to intimately know them and some of their situations. One was a young man orphaned at age eight and raised by his septuagenarian grand aunt in a part of town another student called "the troubles." He became like a step-grandson. We had him to our house for meals and out for movies, plays, and restaurants.

My wife and I learned from him and another student with whom we had such a relationship that though we had always been taught to pull ourselves up by our bootstraps, many of these families had no boots. Generations of poverty, lack of a live-in father, terrible education, and little available training for skill building has left many young men in an untenable situation and with little hope for a bright future. I pray that exposing them to God's Word and spending time with them edifies them and glorifies the Lord Jesus.

–Mike Moses, Minister to Milwaukee

COMMUNITY WAREHOUSE
1998–2019

When God's way and my way don't agree, I've found that God always has a more elegant solution and I must pray, watch, and be patient. Prayer has always been the best antidote to eliminate the frustration and disappointment that ensues when I'm wrong. Let me explain. BASICS spent a significant amount of time, talents, and treasure during the late 1990s restoring and renovating ministry facilities to facilitate his work. We often thought we had all the answers, but we were committed to God's plan with patience.

It became increasingly evident that an opportunity for a new ministry would be to take surplus "stuff" from the basements of many suburban homes and enable these brothers and sisters to donate that to poor families in the inner city, and take a tax write-off in the process. To do this would require a facility and program to collect, transport, clean up, and distribute the stuff, and this would also require setting up a project to organize the resources, people, funding, and probably a 501(c)(3) nonprofit ministry to run it—just the kind of work BASICS was good at doing. But it would take a lot of effort and divert our attention away from our primary mission to facilitate ministries. God had a much better solution, and he was about to show us his way.

After some investigation, we found two leadership foundations, one in Pittsburgh and another in Chicago, already operating storehouses with great success but were not yet self-sustaining. Several BASICS board members decided we should visit the storehouse in Chicago to learn how it was done. The outcome was that three of our board members decided to leave and start a new venture and call it the Community Warehouse.

Bob Hill, George Bogdonovich, and Ed Edwards (then COO of BASICS) used their God-given talents and skills to establish the storehouse in Milwaukee's South Side but with a limited scope of materials. They would only offer new materials needed for reconstruction projects related to ministry facilities and residences. Manufacturers and distributors supplied materials from surplus inventory that could be donated or sold at reduced prices. This stimulated the repair of many dilapidated houses in Milwaukee's inner city.

It was during this period that Habitat for Humanity was established in Milwaukee which is now run by Brian Sonderman, a strong man of faith and wisdom. He has been instrumental in building a network of construction related partners helping to improve city neighborhoods. God was at work but was not done yet!

There still remained the stuff in suburban basements that needed new homes. God worked in the hearts of many brothers and sisters who had developed relationships with their neighbors in the inner city through their volunteer experiences and tours with BASICS and other ministries. A movement started with families adopting families across the Menomonee River Valley to share their stuff.[1] This led Mike and Susie Hayden to start a giving ministry called Helping Hands to work with employees of businesses and corporations to donate their stuff within the marketplace. Mike built a network of volunteers to pick up, deliver, and meet people in poverty and distress by demonstrating God's love in practical ways. He often gave his testimony to those he felt would be blessed in knowing his story.

When delivering gifts to people in need, Mike told them how to choose the greatest gift of all—God's love and forgiveness, his eternal life!

MIKE HAYDEN'S MESSAGE

I want to share a promise with you.

If you were to die today, would you want to know that you could spend eternity in heaven or in hell?

In the Bible, God says he so loved the world that he gave his one and only son Jesus that if you believe in him, you will not perish in hell but spend everlasting life in heaven.

To believe is more than an intellectual agreement that Jesus Christ is God.

It means to put your trust and confidence in Jesus Christ that he alone can save you. Please put Jesus Christ in charge of your present plans and eternal destiny.

Believing is trusting his words as reliable and relying on him for the power to change. If you have never trusted Jesus Christ, let this promise of everlasting life be yours.

It's as simple as praying: "I believe that Jesus Christ died on the cross for me and shed his blood for my sins. By putting my faith in Jesus Christ, I will always know that whenever I die, I will spend eternity in heaven with you not because I am a good person, but because of what Jesus Christ did for me. Thank you for this promise. Amen."

-Mike Hayden, BASICS - Minister to Milwaukee

THE GOSPEL THROUGH
RAP MUSIC
2007

One of the principles of the BASICS Ministry is facilitating activities that a single church would not have the resources to do in order to spread the gospel and to initiate actions never done before. The Captive Project was that outside-the-box kind of ministry.

God sometimes uses the word-of-mouth strategy to accomplish his work and to bring those he has chosen to come together to do his will. That's what happened with Richard Brown, a tall, handsome Black man from the inner city who was referred to me by Tom Keppeler, urban ministry pastor at Elmbrook Church. Richard is an enthusiastic and articulate man with a creative mind looking for new solutions to difficult challenges. Being raised in a Christian family and church in Milwaukee, he uniquely fit my desire for a person to lead a movement to reach inner city youth with the good news of Jesus Christ. I prayed my plan aligned with God's plan.

I was particularly impressed with his connections to the guys and gals he was discipling on Saturday mornings at 6:30 a.m., the most unlikely time for young men to be awake and want to study the Scriptures. The teaching sessions were directed at preparing them to write rap music with strong messages from Scripture and sound theology. God brought a solution to the challenge of communicating to inner city youth. Praise the Lord!

Shortly after meeting with Richard, I met Frank Woods and his mentor, Rob Honey, who were the two first rappers of the Captive

Project. We discussed my vision of someday organizing a movie ministry that would show the desperate conditions facing youth in the city and then show what a life in Christ could be. They were excited and responsive to the vision and were immediately onboard.

Over the years, the Captive Project has been inspired by and led to work and perform with Lecrae Devaughn Moore, known as "Lecrae," a well-known American Christian hip-hop recording artist, songwriter, record producer, and actor who helped modernize Christian music.[2]

One of their first rap songs was titled, "We Comin 4 Ya!" I've included the lyrics in Appendix 5.]

Richard Brown's Story

One day in May of 2007 made a huge impact on me and my wife Aurelia. A young girl named Jasmine Owens, who nobody really knew or remembers, will always be remembered by the Captive Project team. She was out jumping rope in her front yard when two guys decided that their disagreement was significant enough to shoot at each other. One of those gunshots killed Jasmine. That event sparked us to be much more aggressive about doing something to change our neighborhood

We have been doing ministry in Milwaukee's inner city for a number of years before this, but for some reason this particular event really hit us hard. We decided to ask the Lord for guidance on how we could stop this violence. Originally our thought was to pursue a ministry that would get us into these high crime areas to preach the Gospel and help these people get into a relationship with Christ. The name we chose was Christ and Richard Productions following the model of Lord & Taylor. Taylor went into business but kept failing, so he decided to make it the Lord's business and promised to give a tenth (tithe) of all his profits to the Lord. The business became very successful.

While putting together a proposal for our new ministry, I

went to Pastor Mike Murphy at Elmbrook Church to talk about my ideas and possible funding. Mike asked if I knew about BASICS in Milwaukee. I said "No, if someone else is doing this already, I want to know about them." So I set up a meeting with Arn Quakkelaar for an hour, which turned out to be four hours. We hit it off right away. He had been praying for a ministry leader who could help bring the Gospel to the inner city through a culturally accepted urban arts approach. Rap music became the vision!

The Captive Project was birthed from that discussion. Luke 4:16–29 became our theme verse during the first year, and our slogan was, "We comin 4 ya!" We arranged more than twenty outreach events in disenfranchised areas using the urban arts to preach the Gospel and enter into discipleship relationships with people. It has been an incredible ministry with our focus being evangelism, discipleship, and cultural reconciliation.

We have a great relationship with BASICS. The Captive Project helped show the body of Christ in Milwaukee and beyond that we could all come together for the cause of Christ. That was BASICS' theme, and that is what we did with them.

In 2008 at the Elmbrook Church Harvest Fest, The Captive Project had a booth and was able to perform Christian rap on their stage, the first rap to be heard from that stage. What was incredible about that week was that we felt the Spirit of the Lord was commissioning the Captive Ministry that week. The theme of that Harvest Fest was Luke 4:16–29: *"The Spirit of the Lord is on me, because he has anointed me to preach good news to the poor. He has sent me to proclaim freedom for the prisoners and recovery of sight for the blind, to release the oppressed, to proclaim the year of the Lord's favor."* We were also prayed over, encouraged, and anointed to do God's work.

That same year, someone from Green Bay felt called to do a Christian outreach event at Zeidler Park in Milwaukee to try reaching as many inner-city people as possible. We called the two-day event, Gospel Fest. Since Milwaukee is known as the City of Festivals, I asked the Lord to show up for us in a special way during the event. We planned to have our guys go up and perform followed by the well-known national rap artists. When our guys got on stage, it started to rain hard and the crowd scattered to find shelter. Our guys continued to perform but they were rapping in front of an empty park. I was inside a tent asking God, "What happened? I don't understand!" When the Captive team finished performing, it stopped raining and the national artist then got on stage and everyone came back to listen to the concert.

The second day, we followed the same plan. Our guys got on stage to perform, and it started to rain again! When that happened, I was praying again, "Lord what happened? Why?" The Holy Spirit spoke to me and said, "Didn't you want me to show up in a special way?" I looked up and there was a double rainbow over the stage while the guys were performing! The time was 6:30 p.m. When they got off stage, it stopped raining, and the national act performed for the returning audience.

During our follow-up meeting, the guys all agreed they felt the Lord had "baptized" the ministry and the rainbow was the seal. Fast forward a year later; we were at HOPE (Helping Others Prepare for Eternity) Fest dedicated to the Lord and located at the Wisconsin State Fair Grounds. I asked the Lord again for a special sign of his presence. HOPE Fest is a seventy-two hours prayer concert based on 2 Chronicles 7:14: *"If my people who are called by my name will humble themselves and pray and seek my face and turn from their wicked ways then I will hear from heaven and heal their land."*

The seventy-two hours were split into twenty-four hours for repentance, twenty-four hours for God's presence, and twenty-four hours for God's response. When the third day came, we were anticipating God would do something from heaven again, so we were looking at cloud formations and the birds flying overhead to see if they were doves, but they were only seagulls and pigeons. The weather forecast for the third day was rain. As I was giving my testimony to one of our guests, it started to rain hard. Along with the rain and the dark clouds, there was a strong wind that lifted me up out of my chair in the tent and toward the front opening to see a double rainbow!" I asked my son, "What time is it?" It was 6:30 p.m., the same time as the double rainbow appeared at Gospel Fest.

We were overwhelmed that God showed up to remind us of his faithfulness. This was our special blessing and testimony to God's work.

The following year, God showed up the same way at 6:30 p.m. with a double rainbow, but it was even more profound. The local news covered the appearance of the rainbow and everyone we had shared our testimony with called to tell us about God's rainbow in the sky—our constant reminder that he will never again destroy his world with a flood.

The Captive Project ministry is a ministry whose primary focus is to do what God has called us to do. The unity in the body of Christ through prayer is always the way to go. Bringing the body of Christ together by meeting to pray for God to show up is the goal of the Captive Project and BASICS. As we move forward, our next Hope Fest will introduce a full-size replica of the Tabernacle of God to bring the good news of Jesus Christ to the people of Milwaukee and beyond. Praise God for setting the captives free!

–Minister Richard Brown, Pastor, Converge

Converted Drug Dealer and Gangbanger Discipling other Drug Dealers and Gangbangers

The Captive Project, an initiative of BASICS in Milwaukee, has been conducting urban outreaches in the parks of Milwaukee using the Christian arts since 2007 and has ministered to tens of thousands of people.

Since the Lord has been using our ministers to serve in high crime areas, we knew we would encounter many prostitutes, drug dealers, and homeless people. Our objective was to rescue victims with the Gospel of Jesus Christ. But the Lord has also called us to go after the perpetrators. By prayer and trust in God, we have been able to specifically target the drug dealers and gangbangers in the city with the love of Christ.

Frank Woods, one of the Captive ministers, has had contact with some of these dealers who are looking for answers on how to change their lifestyles. Frank is credible with these drug dealers and gangbangers because he was one of them in his early years. He came from a fatherless household and joined gangs that became his father figures. Through his gang activities, he spent time in prison. It was there that Frank became a believer in Jesus Christ. In addition to loving Jesus, he also loves rap music.

Through a series of events, he learned about the Captive Project and BASICS and was invited to join.

Now after becoming a disciple for Jesus Christ, he's talking with other drug dealers and gangbangers who have a hard time believing God will accept them because of the things they have done. They think, "Jesus is for the people that aren't as bad as I am. So why try?" Many believe they are in so deep with the gangs that they can't return. During a Bible study, one of the dealers asked, "Can God forgive me even if I killed someone?" Another said, "I have a lot of blood on my hands." One after the other all centered on *the* central question: "With all that I have done, can God forgive me?" They don't understand the limitlessness of God's forgiveness. Frank is slowly getting through to some of them that the sins of murderers or adulterers are completely and permanently forgiven the moment he or she accepts Christ as their Savior.

–Richard Brown

MILWAUKEE COUNTY PARK OUTREACHES 2006–2019

One of our first opportunities to do a park outreach event came out of a surprising project involving some of the men and women of our volunteer team. They were asked to paint a house across the street from an inner-city county park. The owner of the house was poor and didn't have the funds to pay someone to do it, so BASICS was asked by the minister to Milwaukee who lived in the house if we could do it if the owner bought the paint. We stepped out in faith that doing this favor would bring God glory.

Marcia Vander Leest, a young, single woman and minister to Milwaukee was called to teach the children in her neighborhood about Jesus during the summer vacation and was inviting the children to come into her home. The response was so great that there was not enough room in the house, and she began searching for an alternative place to meet. Maybe the park across the street? Concurrent with her dilemma and prayers for a solution was the BASICS response *yes!* to her request to paint the house she was renting.

As the volunteers worked on painting the house, the children in the neighborhood would ride their bikes to Marcia's summer school and watch the painters put up the scaffolding and ladders and the women planting flowers in the backyard garden. The children were fascinated to watch the work and asked lots of questions. A young boy came on his bike but the chain broke loose, which started a "chain of events." A volunteer came down off his ladder and reconnected the chain to the delight of the boy. Other children asked the volunteer, "Can you fix my bike too?" This led to many children bringing their bikes from home to get them fixed. Some who had no bikes asked, "Can you get me a bike?"

The house got painted, and the owner was overwhelmed by the generosity and spirit of the team. But the diversion of bike ministry to kids incentivized the team to brainstorm how to bless this neighborhood with bikes. How about a bike giveaway outreach in the park? The ideas escalated resulting in a unique plan that would bring the entire neighborhood together.

The word was sent out from BASICS that anyone with unused bikes could bring them to Mark Mallwitz's home in Menomonee Falls for a bike giveaway in Milwaukee. And anyone who could fix bikes and willing to volunteer could come on Saturdays to repair them. The response was far beyond anything we imagined. A local bike shop heard about the project and donated parts, special bike repair tools, and even used and new bikes. God's people provided over one hundred bikes to be given at the outreach event along with over twenty-five volunteers who fixed the bikes weeks before the event. An amazing response!

There are many stories of how God set in motion activities that overwhelmed organizers of the Bike Giveaway, including a Vietnam veteran who repaired bikes for kids as a labor of love and to overcome a health problem suffered after the war. He donated twenty bikes. But perhaps the most interesting miracle concerned bike helmets.

One week before the event someone mentioned that the kids should have helmets. It was a great suggestion, but there was no money left to buy them. Then Mark and his wife Lisa had a surprise visit from a couple who heard about the event and gave them a bike $500 for whatever was needed, not knowing anything about the helmet idea. Mark learned of an organization on the West Coast that sells bike helmets worth $30 for kids to nonprofit ministries at $4 each. Mark hurriedly called to place an order and managed to get it through only ten minutes before the shipping department closed. After nervously waiting and praying, the shipment arrived at his house Friday afternoon. The total cost $400 plus shipping at $100 for a total cost of $500 what was donated by his friends! Praise the Lord!

The Bike Giveaway started at 10 a.m. with games, food, a Bible story of David and Goliath by Ray Jablonski (with a ten-foot pole to show how tall Goliath was), a powerful message by Pastor Lamar Beverly-Davis, free Bibles for anyone who would promise to read them, *and* a free bike to anyone up to sixteen years old. It was fantastic to see the parents come to be a part of the celebration and fun.

All one hundred bikes were given appropriately to the size and sex of each child. Many received their first bike. The excitement and spirit of unity was fantabulous! In addition to the bikes (and since the weather was beginning to turn colder) over 400 blankets, comforters, and sleeping bags were given along with Bibles and handmade bookmarks with scripture verses on them. Several churches brought tables, chairs and paper products. The experience was an amazing example of God's people showing and telling God's Love.

At around 4 p.m. all the bikes were distributed, but three children were left without a bike—a five-year-old old boy, an eight-year-old girl, and a twelve-year-old boy. They were devastated, and we didn't know what to do but pray. As we were praying, a man drove into the park on the grass with a trailer to where we were praying. He had forgotten about the event until that morning and was afraid he missed it. He decided to take a chance and still come. He delivered three bikes precisely suited to each child. A miracle occurred before our eyes. God is so good!

This event was so successful and opened our eyes, hands, and hearts to do a major series of park outreach events throughout the county park system, and those events are continuing to this day. Praise the Lord!

MOBILE MEDIA MINISTRY
2011–19

God works in remarkable ways that can only be arranged through his divine appointments.

When we moved to Wisconsin in the early 1970s, Norma and I attended the Brookfield Christian Reformed Church with our five boys. We always sat in the front row so the boys could see the activity on the platform rather the backs of pews and heads. We also wanted to meet new people coming to church by introducing ourselves to them after the services and inviting them to our home for lunch. Most often these were young people who were entertained by our active boys.

On one such occasion, we met two single guys who had been hitch hiking in front of the church on West Burleigh Road. It was cold and started raining, so they came into church to get warm.

We became forever friends.

On another Sunday, we met two young ladies, and we invited them to join us for lunch. One of the girls' names was "Lori," later to become Mrs. John "JJ" Jones. We got to know JJ when we started attending Elmbrook Church where he was the video producer organizing the rapidly growing video ministry of the largest church in the state of Wisconsin. JJ and Lori were a beautiful couple with amazing personalities and inspiring desires to serve God.

We became forever friends with them also and enjoyed watching them build a beautiful family.

JJ had worked as a cameraman for a local network TV station and had a phenomenal talent for shooting, reporting, and producing on-site news reports that communicated real-life stories of inner city Milwaukee. Being a very astute and creative communication genius working in the city, he noticed a for sale sign on a retired mobile medical care center van which had also been used by the Milwaukee Police Department as a mobile police command center to address the problems of crime in the inner city.

That's when God gave him the vision to use that van for a ministry to bring God's truth to his neighbors in the city.

JJ and Lori began praying that God would lead them to fulfill that call to serve, and over several years and numerous miracles, the Mobile Media Ministries became reality in the form of Big Blue. Miraculously JJ was able to buy the van at an unbelievably low price, but he had no commercial driver's license to drive it and no place to park it. For several years a farmer allowed him to park the van in his suburban field where it could have rotted and become unusable, but God provided protection with weeds, trees, and bees to grow around it to be hidden with a bee hive on the door to keep out scavengers.

The cost of renovating the van to accomplish his vision was overwhelming, but many friends of faith came alongside to provide everything needed, including changing video technology. Initially JJ planned to use slide projectors and screens, then video projectors, which led to high resolution LED video screens only available from China—leading to three trips to China to learn the new technologies.

Big Blue eventually was completed with three large video screens on the side, a sound system, remote cameras, and a classroom inside. JJ was now able to show and tell God's truth anywhere God would lead him even though his greatest supporter and encourager, Lori, passed into the arms of Jesus and never saw the final outcome.

JJ's mission is to bring hope into parks, church parking lots, the streets in Milwaukee, and beyond. Recently a truck repair company on the South Side has offered to keep Big Blue moving wherever God leads.

Praise the Lord for all his blessings!

John Jones' Message

For years, my vision for serving God in the city was to go out on the streets to show movies and videos that I could speak into with a huge media van. I wanted to share Christ to those who had no knowledge of God and no hope for the future. I had a van already that I was going to outfit for just this kind of outreach by installing large screens into the sides. But I had no clue how this was going to happen.

Mark Mallwitz reintroduced me to Arn when he brought me to BASICS in Milwaukee for the first time. It was the perfect connection—a God thing. Here was this man I knew from before who inspired me and shared a passion for reaching the city just like I did, and he was the founder of this place where I could collect donated funds and goods for my ministry, a place where I could connect with other ministers and passionate people for the sake of the Kingdom of God. Here I had structure and friends to help me keep on track and keep me moving forward.

For a long time I'd have monthly meetings with Arn and Mark to talk about my van and ministry. We discussed the spiritual side of things, prayed with each other, and refocused on the goals ahead. Without the structure and encouragement there, I don't think I would be where I am today with my ministry or my walk with God.

Through their mature leadership and moral support, I had a sense of security in my journey. I became a better steward of what the Lord had given to me, and I was accumulating more support from others around me. I made relationships with churches, pastors, and organizations who could fill in the gaps of what I couldn't do myself. It got my van off the vacant lot it sat in for over a decade and onto the streets. Mark and Arn were with me on that very first day, the day of our maiden voyage.

Even when I was about to take a crucial trip to China to purchase my first LED screen, Arn was there to encourage me. He invited me to his house to share my vision and plans with a group of friends. When I got there, there were already close to thirty people in attendance. I was working so hard on my van and so excited to give my story that I collapsed from dehydration while speaking. After that, everyone was telling me not to go to China, even though I needed to, so I could receive important product training from the manufacturers. No one in America knew how to maintain these screens.

"What if you collapse in China?" they were saying. But Arn looked at me and said, "JJ, go ahead." He never doubted. Arn was one of the first people to believe in my vision, and I went to China. It was a fantastic time and a trip I will never forget. The Lord has been leading me step-by-step, meeting-by-meeting, person-by-person, to bring this ministry to completion.

Arn has also shown me new ways to grow. My heart has only grown bigger from serving with BASICS and Arn for the last several years. Arn shared a story the Milwaukee police had told him. They said the saddest thing they see on duty is when there's a homicide or accident, and they mark off the area with tape, the family and friends of the victims show up on the street corner and cry. Arn was the first person to suggest the media van be used as a comforting balm in times like this. We could drive out to protect and pray with the families inside the van with a warm hand and drink instead of leaving them to cry on the cold

concrete all alone. After many years, I can now drive my media
van myself, so this is a new part of my ministry that can be
implemented to reach my city with the love of Christ and
something I think is important for Milwaukee, which ranks in the
top ten most dangerous cities in our nation.

–John "JJ" Jones, Minister to Milwaukee

FATHERS AND MOTHERS
INVOLVED LOVING YOUTH
2009–17

In 2009 God led BASICS to focus our attention on the family,
and we felt the name should have a special meaning and challenge,
so we established the acronym of FAMILY: Fathers And Mothers
Involved Loving Youth. We desired to help families stay or become
healthy and were worried about how so many young people fall
into addictions, crime, sexual promiscuity, pregnancy, abortion,
and human trafficking.

Silver Ring Thing

We started with an existing national movement addressing the
issue of teen pregnancy. In 2009 BASICS started working to help
teens, both boys and girls, learn the risks and consequences of
premarital sex. This training encourage teens to make a virginity
pledge based on God's design for building a family. Those who
pledge wear a silver ring which constantly reminds them of their
promise to God to be sexually abstinent until marriage.

The first program was held at the Milwaukee Area Technical
College in downtown Milwaukee. It was attended by a large
number of teens and their parents. The two-hour, high-energy
event included music, videos, dramas, special effects lighting,
comedians, and speakers. The messages are all focused on telling
the truth about love, dating, second chances, and life relationships
leading the teens to make a decision to remain pure until marriage.

To seal that pledge, they were offered a silver ring to show their pledge to purity.

This program has been offered several times in Milwaukee and is a tremendous help for parents to communicate God's way to their teens in a peer-to-peer context. It also provided awareness for an even more dangerous reality.

Human Trafficking Awareness

A dangerous condition for teens exists in Milwaukee that most citizens are not aware of, and it is critical to the safety of both boys and girls. Milwaukee is the mecca for sex trafficking, particularly in group homes where runaway teens often go.

The underground sex trade is thriving in Milwaukee. Milwaukee is tied with Las Vegas as the third-highest city for rescue of young people during FBI raids. In 2011, according to Dana World-Patterson, the chair of the Human Trafficking Task Force of Greater Milwaukee, Milwaukee was the highest city for rescue of young people during FBI raids.

The majority of victims were twelve- to seventeen years-old African American girls from the north side of Milwaukee. Traffickers are both men and women. Milwaukee's underground has been known for involvement with sex trafficking since 1942. During World War II, when they were in the city for training in Chicago during the week, soldiers would spend their weekends in Milwaukee where the girls were plentiful and available.

In 2010 BASICS received a grant to start a program to teach parents and their teens about the dangers of human trafficking. We assigned one of our ministers to Milwaukee to head this effort in the Milwaukee public schools. Approved by the school board, the program taught human-trafficking-awareness classes for junior and senior high school students, even though middle school students and those older than high school age were all at risk. These classes continued for several years until the funding ran out.

Intercession Ministries

A Christian social worker working with youth in the inner city became overwhelmed with the lack of facilities for young girls who were pregnant and wanted to keep their babies. The system was encouraging them to have an abortion; she felt this was unacceptable. Sharon Mays-Ferguson quit her job as a case worker in faith that God would provide for her to start a ministry for these girls to intercede on their behalf and teach them God's way to live in love. She named her ministry Intercession and prayed for God's guidance and a facility for the girls.

Sharon's prayers reached BASICS, and we sensed God's direction to restore and remodel an uninhabited, bullet-ridden gang house she acquired. The house was in bad condition but was structurally sound. One of our ministers to Milwaukee, Jim Ramsey, went with me to meet Sharon and assess the work required. He was impressed with her vision and the work she had already started doing. Jim explained the situation to his suburban church pastor, Reverend Fred Sindorf, and other men from the church to explore the possibility of adopting the ministry as a project for their small church. The decision was *yes!* and the work began.

The project became much bigger than we expected, but the church team was very generous and committed to follow God's leading. The Intercession home was completed and beautifully furnished. Sharon was a wonderful, loving house mother with girls that had never experienced such love. The ministry was set up to care for girls ages twelve to seventeen years old, but it quickly became evident that older girls needed the same care. Sharon began praying for the house next door (only four feet away) to be available so she could expand Intercession to include rooms for these older girls. However, the owner set the price high, and she didn't have the money.

One Friday afternoon, I got a call from Sharon saying the house next door was on fire and, being so close to her home, she was afraid it may burn her house as well. The firefighters amazingly were able to save Intercession, but the house next door was completely destroyed. Only minor scorching damage occurred to

Sharon's home and operations were able to continue after the repairs were done. Sharon eventually was able to acquire the vacant lot and two others next to it, giving Sharon room for expansion.

The Johnny Ferguson Family Blessings

In a meeting I had with Pastor Harold Moore of Mount Mercy Memorial Missionary Baptist Church, he mentioned an unusual family from his fellowship who had stepped out in faith to buy a house from the city, with the requirement of restoring it before they could occupy it. Johnny Ferguson and his wife were blessed with eight children ages one to sixteen, and they were eager to work together as a family to fix up their new home. Their goal was to move in by Thanksgiving Day of that year—an ambitious goal requiring lots of prayer and sweat.

The remodeling required demolishing the kitchen and bathroom, which was accomplished fairly fast but required much more electrical and plumbing work than expected. That work had to be done by licensed contractors. The work reached a standstill without the funds to keep going. They needed help. Pastor Moore knew BASICS had helped many ministries with facilities needing repair and asked if we could do the same for a family in need. In faith we said *yes!*

To continue the work, Johnny needed kitchen cabinets, a sink, stove, refrigerator, bathroom sink, toilet, bathtub, and two wall cabinets. It seemed impossible for them to get all the materials, pay for them, and get the work done by Thanksgiving. The day after Johnny told me of his dilemma I received a call from Brad Feltz, a member of Northbrook Church who had just finished remodeling his own home and had replaced a lot of what he took out of his house and was going to take to the dump. After realizing the good condition of the materials and appliances, he thought it might be of value to someone in the city.

I asked him what he had, and it was exactly the materials Johnny needed. When I told Brad the story of Johnny's family project, Brad offered to deliver all the materials to Johnny's home with his sixteen-year-old son. When Brad and his son meet Johnny and his family, they were so impressed with what the family was doing, they joined the project and all worked together to finish the project in time for the Ferguson family to have their first dinner in their new home on Thanksgiving Day. Wow! What an answer to prayer. But God was not done yet with the blessings.

A few weeks later, I received a call from John, one of The Barnabi Brothers, stating that his family wanted to bless a family in the inner city who was in need and working hard to improve themselves living God's way. There was no question in my mind that God wanted to bless the Ferguson family even more. John's family wanted to anonymously give Johnny's family Christmas gifts and asked for the names, gender, and age of each child, and also what they wanted with no limit on the costs. That Christmas was a blessing to everyone involved—an experience only God could have orchestrated with families adopting families in the family of faith, God's way.

BACK TO THE BASICS OF
FOOD, CLOTHING, AND SHELTER
2010

Seeing poverty in reality is a horrible experience. Few people realize how severe living with nothing can be. God gave me the opportunity to know people in Milwaukee who have nothing and must make tough decisions not only for themselves, but also for others such as their children. It's beyond horrible. Let me tell you about Lilly Lane (her name is changed to respect her privacy).

A group of dedicated Christian women living in the inner city were part of the Houses of Prayer Everywhere (HOPE) national movement that encouraged the women to walk and pray daily or weekly for every home in their neighborhood. As they walked past each house, their desire was to eventually meet and get to know each neighbor by name, and know how to pray for their specific needs. The following is the story of one of these women.

One day as Lilly was prayer walking in her neighborhood, she prayed for a specific home that seemed unusual because of the lack of activity with the window shades closed. It was almost to the point of appearing abandoned. She prayed for God to lead her into what to say as she walked up the steps and prayed that she would be able to build a relationship with whoever answered the door.

She knocked on the door because the doorbell didn't seem to be working. After what seemed to be ten minutes, she heard a slight noise and saw the curtain on the door open just a little. Eventually the door opened slowly, and a young woman cautiously said hello. She introduced herself as a neighbor who just wanted to find out how to pray for her. The neighbor girl was carrying a baby, and behind her were two little children about two and three years old with virtually no clothes on. The baby had a horrible breathing problem and was obviously ill.

After a few words of introduction, Lilly asked if she could just step in because it was cold outside.. Upon entering she noticed there was almost no furniture in the house, a very low temperature, and a musty odor. The neighbor was very cautious but seemed to quickly recognize her neighbor's good intentions and began explaining she had been abandoned by the father of her children. She had no money, no food, no phone, no refrigerator, and no one to help her. She was desperate and was overwhelmed that someone would come to help her, an angel from God.

The angel immediately arranged to get the baby to the hospital where doctors found the baby had pneumonia, diarrhea, and severe dehydration. Lilly, her husband, and the other women of HOPE got food and clothes for the children.. Over the next week, they arranged to provide the much needed help for this family to survive. The young mother was effectively adopted for a time until the family was stabilized. This condition is rampant in Milwaukee with invisible people barely surviving, and some not surviving. These opportunities to show God's love exist in many homes in the inner city.

Poverty can be exasperating to some who have lost all hope and resort to making decisions that literally destroy themselves. In desperation they will steal, sell drugs, or prostitute themselves to feed their children. They may even abort their unborn child to keep them from suffering a life of poverty. In these circumstances, what would we do without faith, hope, and love?

These stories repeat over and over. They clearly identify an opportunity to show and tell God's love to our neighbors by providing the basic necessities to people in poverty. Over the years, many ministries have arisen to provide networks of resources, primarily through people of faith and their churches, but often with rules that restrict the effectiveness of that help. The difficulties to people in poverty include:

- Not being a member of the church with a food or clothing pantry
- Having no transportation, therefore no way to get to the food and bring it home
- Restrictive schedules at food pantries that are only open for a few hours during the week
- Pantries that don't offer simple foods they can use (without stoves and refrigerators) and no paper products available
- The needs are often far beyond just food and clothing. They often need a good neighbor who understands them and can feed their souls as well.

Many of these circumstances have been recognized, and ministries have been established to overcome the barriers, but there is still much more to be done to heal souls that are suffering. People in poverty need to be taught how to make decisions that lead to survival and success. The lack of fathers with jobs living within the family would be a great start. Over the years BASICS has worked with ministries that help to provide food, clothing, household goods, and appliances to these invisible neighbors.[3]

BASICS has been providing a service of linking needs to resources through its Christian Communication Network for the purpose of helping connect to neighbors in need. In the Sermon on the Mount, Jesus teaches:

> *Be careful not to do your acts of righteousness before men, to be seen by them. If you do, you will have no reward from your Father in heaven. So, when you give to the needy do not announce it with trumpets, as the hypocrites do in the synagogues and on the streets, to be honored by men. I tell you the truth, they have received their reward in full. But when you give to the needy, do not let your left hand know what your right hand is doing, so that your giving may be in secret. Then your Father, who sees what is done in secret, will reward you.* Matt. 6:1-4

The prayer, care, share, prepare outreach model is used to show and tell God's love by our actions. This can be seen in the actions and testimony of Mike Hayden.

Serving the Invisible People in Poverty, By Mike Hayden

I was raised the oldest of five children and the son of a bank executive. in Wauwatosa, Wisconsin. As I look back at my childhood, I was an unhappy child who was incredibly insecure and angry. Some of those feelings I attribute to my father, a sports enthusiast, feeling like I was a failure. I excelled in sports to gain his attention. When I was performing well, he was proud of me.

I ended up being one of the best players, but my dad was often gone because his position at the bank required him to do a bit of entertaining. As a result, I didn't have an opportunity to spend much time with him. There were times I felt all alone. Growing up, I was a gifted athlete and that made my father proud. But it wasn't long before that would end, which triggered a tremendous amount of anger.

I come from a history of drugs, alcohol, gangs, and depression, and I discovered alcohol when I was a sophomore in high school, and there was a major problem developing. When I drank, my behavior became violent. I now realize that as the alcohol gave me a sense of freedom, the inner anger was released. It wasn't long before I was released from the basketball team for breaking the rules.

Basketball was my sport and well as my father's. I had colleges looking at me in my junior year and my future in sports seemed pretty promising. That all vanished, and I was drawn to guys like me who were down and outers.

My drinking became more frequent and put me in a downward spiral. I felt worthless, hopeless, and angry. I had various run-ins with the police and was arrested on more than one occasion. This didn't endear me to my father. I barely graduated from high school but was accepted into UW-LaCrosse on academic probation. I was an emotional mess and hadn't been in Lacrosse one week before I was once again arrested. I spent most of my time drinking, playing cards, and sleeping. I was placed on school probation for an incident in the dorm that almost burned down the dorm. At the end of that school year I was told not to return because of failing grades, and because I was considered a nuisance.

When I returned home, I was asked to leave, and that was music to my ears. I wanted nothing more than to be on my own. I was nineteen years old and called a friend of mine to find an apartment on the east side of Milwaukee we could afford. The premises were roach-infested and horrible, but I finally felt free from the control of my parents. I found more failures like me, and we formed a gang. We did what gangs do, but didn't use weapons—we used our fists. There was alcohol, drugs, girls (mostly run-aways), burglaries, break-ins, and fighting. We were a violent group, in fact, that was our trademark. We were known for violence. I then found I needed my "medicine" and would drink all day until I passed out. There were many mornings I would wake up with broken bones in a pool of blood, not knowing where I was or how I got there.

I believe it was only by the grace of God that prevented me from being incarcerated. One night I went to a church service and met a young man and he asked me, "Brother, are you saved?" I was drunk and looked him in the eyes and said, "You aren't my brother, and I don't know what you mean." He pulled out a Bible and showed me verses about salvation and asked me if I wanted to be saved. I shook my head in disgust and walked away.

But to be truthful, I was so out of it that I couldn't respond even if I wanted to. Something happened that caused me to think. Maybe I need to get right with God. Naw, look at the parents he gave me and the life I am living. He doesn't care about me; I am doomed!

I started to read the Bible along with some material on Christianity and began to think, "Maybe I don't have to continue living this way? Perhaps there is an answer? Is it God?" I went back to the church where I was raised, but I walked away as empty as when I went in. I was confused and came to the conclusion that God wasn't the answer and that I needed a good job and get married to the girl I was seeing. I did both and the void was still there. I was so disappointed. Both the job and marriage ended.

The Vietnam War was going on, and if I didn't get into the Army, I would get drafted and someone else would control my life. It scared me to death that some sergeant could tell me what to do, and I couldn't pop him out. I joined the Wisconsin Army National Guard, flew out to Fort Ord, California for basic training, and divorced my wife.

In the plane, I sat in disbelief. Mr. Tough Guy was shaking like a leaf. I was given a fanny pack with toiletries and inside was a pocket New Testament. In desperation I pulled it out and started to read the verses about salvation. For some strange reason this day they looked different from what I had read before. They made sense, but I couldn't understand how a loving God would take me just as I am. I had never experienced unconditional love in my whole life. I struggled and tried to get it out of my mind, but it wouldn't leave.

Finally I bowed my head and told God that I believed God sent his Son, Jesus Christ, to die for my sins; I believed Jesus paid the penalty for my sins by shedding his blood, and he wanted to be a father to me. I told God that I didn't know how he would want a piece of trash like me, but I was willing to accept this truth by faith. Then I lifted my head and something miraculous happened. I felt as though a thousand pounds had been lifted from my shoulders. I was experiencing a peace in my heart that I had never felt before.

I returned home after basic training and started my new life in Christ. I left my old friends, found a Bible-believing church, and I am still growing spiritually every day. It is because of my life experiences that I am drawn to inner-city youth, gangs, and ex-offenders. Many of them are in a downward spiral that I experienced, and it is a terrible place to be.

I was once there. I found the Word of God is powerful to those who believe. It is a vehicle for communicating God's ways. It is living, life-changing, and dynamic as God works in us. The demands of God's Word require decisions. We must not only listen to his Word, but also let it shape our lives and act on it in obedience. I accepted the Lord and he changed me and my ways of the past.

-Written by Mike Hayden before being taken into the arms of Jesus in a car-train accident in 2019

THE REST OF MIKE'S STORY
2019

Mike and his wife Susie dedicated themselves to serving the needs of the poor in Milwaukee during the last twenty-five years of Mike's life. They spawned the ministry called Helping One Another. It impacted many people with practical gifts but more importantly with spiritual gifts through the working of the Holy Spirit.

Some of the ways Mike and Susie loved and served people in the Greater Milwaukee area was to do what Jesus would do. Whenever they heard of a need, they would contact someone in their network or respond themselves to deliver what was needed. They established and developed an inner-city basketball program called Hoops for Kids and gave countless Milwaukee Bucks and Brewers tickets to inner-city youth. They served on several boards for urban ministries and would pick up and deliver thousands of household items from and for people all over the greater Milwaukee area. If they couldn't do it themselves, they engaged others in their network to help. They truly demonstrated the love of Jesus in their actions.

They called their ministries Positive Programs for the Family and Helping One Another. Their primary objectives were to show care and compassion for those in need, identify with the distress of others to help relieve their discomfort, and come alongside organizations that helped lift families out of poverty. Showing and telling God's love was at the heart of their ministries. One of Mike's favorite scripture verses to tell people as he served them was John 3:16–18:

> For God so loved the world that he gave his one and only Son, that whoever believes in him shall not perish but have eternal life. For God did not send his Son into the world to condemn the world, but to save the world through him. Whoever believes in the Son [Jesus] has eternal life. But whoever rejects the Son will not see life, for God's wrath remains on him.

---

1. A stark reality and alert to donors of stuff: "Good intentions should be combined with good stuff! Our neighbors don't need used tea bags. Occasionally donors in their enthusiasm to get rid of their stuff like stoves, ovens, refrigerators, cars, appliances, etc., give items that don't work. This can be an embarrassment and lead to negative results. When Jesus changed the water into wine for the wedding at Cana, it was better than the best wine of the day. We should give as to our Lord!"
2. The Captive Project team in 2009 was included Richard and Aurelia Brown, Frank Woods, Lawrence "LT" Winters, Robert Honey, Lavonda Agee, Eshekiah Winters, Cedric Jiles.
3. A few that have been associated with BASICS include:
    Food Ministries
    Feed My Sheep: Dave Van Abel, founder and Leona Rettinger
    Just One More: Chris Capper
    Feed the Children-Salvation Army, Debbie Thompson
    Clothing Ministries
    Threads of Love Quilting/Close-Knit Friends: Mary Cheney

Friend of Sinners Church: Dan and Sherry Quakkelaar
Household Ministries
Aslan's Warehouse: Ted Cheney and Don Richmond
Helping One Another: Mike and Susie Hayden, Ted & Mary Cheney, Dave and Karen Vogel, Marva Metzger
Caring Hands: Heartland
Woodlands Condo Association: Neva Hill
Morning Glory: Bryan Otzelberger

THE ACTS OF THE MINISTERS TO MILWAUKEE: POVERTY AND CRIME

2005

In my former book, Theophilus, I wrote about all that Jesus began to do and to teach until the day he was taken up to heaven, after giving instructions through the Holy Spirit to the apostles he had chosen. After his suffering, he showed himself to these men and gave many convincing proofs that he was alive. He appeared to them over a period of forty days and spoke about the kingdom of God. On one occasion, while he was eating with them, he gave them this command: "Do not leave Jerusalem, but wait for the gift my Father promised, which you have heard me speak about. For John baptized with water, but in a few days, you will be baptized with the Holy Spirit."
Acts 1:1–6

What: Show how God's people are doing God's work healing poverty and crime in Milwaukee.
So what: To provide inspiration and examples of what God's people have been doing.
Now what: Encouragement to do God's work as God leads.

The first chapter of Acts is Jesus' last compelling words to his disciples. He gave them specific instructions on what to do when he went back to heaven. If we are to be Jesus' disciples and ambassadors, these instructions could apply in principle to us also while on earth doing God's work:

- We are to do and to teach.
- Give instructions to those God chooses through the Holy Spirit.
- Show Christ; give convincing proof that God was and is alive.
- Speak about the Kingdom of God.
- Wait for the gift Jesus' Father promised and be baptized by the Holy Spirit.
- Receive power when the Holy Spirit comes on us.
- Be Jesus' witnesses in Milwaukee and to the ends of the earth.

These were the last words Jesus gave to his apostles. We should be willing and committed to do what Jesus instructed his disciples to do!

Throughout history, generations have faced plagues, famines, floods, earthquakes, and enormous disasters that resulted in decades of pain, suffering, pestilence, and death. Peace only came from God's intervention through his mercy and grace. God created us with the ability to make decisions—to believe that Jesus is God's Son, obey his commandments and worship him only. That sounds so simple and yet is ignored, avoided, resisted, and refused by so many choosing a path that leads to their eternal destruction.

Look at the reality of God's own chosen people, the children of Israel. They lived in Egypt in slavery, were rescued by God through his servant Moses, and then sent into the wilderness for forty years to be tested and strengthened before God fulfilled his covenant promise to give them the Promised Land. Doing God's work God's way was the thread of life and death—blessings and curses, good and evil.

Going even deeper into the dilemma we face as a nation is a fact few people in our country realize is that truth and integrity have died in American politics and media. Lying is now considered by the Supreme Court as protected speech. Under US law, false-hoods and even deliberate lies are fully protected by the courts under the First Amendment of the US Constitution. In today's world, it's up to the decision of each individual to determine the truth of statements made by politicians and the media. This drives the belief that there is no absolute truth, but we as believers take exception knowing that God's Word: the Bible is the absolute truth of our God.

Working in the community to address social disorder and law enforcement from a Christian perspective becomes a unique challenge for leaders following God's laws by speaking truth and being persons of integrity as God's ambassadors. We must always guard against being seen as hypocrites by doing or saying things not aligned with God's will.

BASICS has been and is a vehicle for God's ambassadors to fulfill God's call to serve him as the Holy Spirit guides us. Several areas of serving have surfaced where we have seen miraculous signs of God's favor and blessings. A few of these are described here to show how God has impacted Milwaukee bringing a touch of his kingdom and a peace that passes all understanding.

A Testimonial from The Lynde Bradley Foundation

BASICS was established by a group of suburban-dwelling Christians who were attuned to the problems of the inner city and knew in their hearts that they, being materially comfortable and physically capable, were obliged to do something to solve them. Though the sentiments that inspired them to act are not unusual, the fresh approach the founders of BASICS have taken in their efforts to make a difference should be upheld as a model for people of like mind throughout the nation.

From the beginning, the founders of BASICS have observed that there are faith-based programs already in place in inner-city neighborhoods that address the many challenges there. The leaders of these grassroots efforts are the very people who are most qualified to make decisions about how to meet those challenges because they live, work, celebrate, and mourn there day in, day out. It is this important discernment that sets BASICS apart from other groups of kind-hearted outsiders who start out with good intentions but end up either taking custody of and often misdirecting faith-based groups. Or they end up limiting themselves to merely furnishing extra sets of hands to do mostly ineffectual busywork, all in the name of charity.

BASICS acts as a problem-solving agent for faith-based organizations. It evaluates the individual needs of each group and aims to provide it with tailor-made solutions. It brings support to churches and faith-based groups by assisting them with management issues, helping them to locate resources within their community, and arranging the help of volunteers who have valuable skills to the table. BASICS encourages these small, grassroots organizations to plan for their growth strategically with an eye toward the future, and to form mutually supportive relationships with other neighborhood groups so that they may rely on each other to tackle common problems.

The real story here is not what BASICS does for the faith-based groups it assists, though in that capacity it has done a lot. Even more vital is the new and vigorous order of volunteerism it has inspired among suburban Christian congregants who used to be able to achieve relative self-satisfaction by writing a yearly check to the ever-elusive charity. BASICS has given materially comfortable members of our greater community what they have lacked all along—a vehicle to become fully engaged in civil society. Now, they are able to donate their time and talents as resources that will be as effectively utilized as those with monetary value. In return, they are rewarded with the tangible fruits of urban revitalization and the understanding that civic renewal is not a grand idea to be applied only to the inner city, but it is needed in every community.

—Alicia Campbell-Manning, The Lynde Bradley Foundation

A Testmonial from the Milwaukee Fire Department

The words of now-retired Milwaukee Fire Department Captain
Bob Anderson capture the essence of an ambassador of Jesus
working in life and death circumstances to show Jesus in his function as a firefighter—rescuing lives and souls. Here is his testimony
of showing God's love as a mirror of Christ.

Every day, Christian firefighters and police officers are exposed
to the aftermath of senseless violence and brutality that, after
time, dulls the sensitivity to sin's horror. If a man is shot in a drug
deal or a woman is beaten for infidelity, without condemnation
we risk our lives to help the victims. The hapless victims are not
forsaken and those taken by God are not forgotten. They are all
prayed for.

But quite often God allows us to make a difference in a
rescue or make a difference for those who grieve after the
ambulance speeds away. It is then that God calls us to come out
of our protective shells. If we hear God's voice, and if we trust
God to empower us, despite the danger we can respond to needs
just as he would. It is in such moments that compassion flows,
and we are illuminated as a beacon through the light of Jesus
who dwells within us. Jesus is the head, and we, the body, are
called to respond according to our spiritual gifts to become a
reflection of Jesus—created in Christ to do what he has prepared
for us. The following true story speaks of God using me as an
instrument in his hand.

It was around midnight when the EMS call for an infant
with troubled breathing sounded like it would be one of the
usual—a cold or the flu, or at worst an asthmatic condition. It
wasn't. As our fire engine arrived, a man waved frantically from
the sidewalk. We followed him as he rushed inside the house and
were directed to his one-year-old daughter lying on the bed on
her back with baby formula clogging her nose and mouth and a
small pool of it below her cheek. She wasn't breathing.

I immediately radioed for a paramedic unit as my company
began CPR on the lifeless child. Her extremities were cold, and

her eyes were glazed. Both bad signs. When the medic arrived, I rushed the infant to them and told them what I knew and then returned to the house to prepare the father. I found him in the bedroom trying to jam shoes on his five-year-old daughter and three-year-old son. The girl trembled with fear and the boy sucked hard on his thumb. The mother of the children, confined to a wheelchair, was putting on her shoes with hands that shook to violently to tie them.

The father kept shouting for an answer, "Why did this happen?" And the little boy whimpered from the shouting and the jamming. The father turned his anger on the boy, screaming for him to "Shut up!" I couldn't hold back and reminded him that the children were just as frightened as he was and that they needed love. He said I was right and hugged them.

I went outside to see how the paramedics were doing, but I didn't need to ask. I saw that the heart monitor was a flat line and they had stopped CPR. The paramedic base doctor asked the medic by radio if they were comfortable with a 10-99 and they concurred. That means it's over.

A serene grief common to firefighters poured over me. She lay on the cot, still, alone, yet with an expression of peace. She had been well cared for, squeaky clean, dressed in pink and white pajamas. Her velvet baby hair was gathered with small bands above her ears. She was a pretty baby, even in death. Her big, dark eyes that could not see looked straight at me. She was with the Lord now. Her eyes were on Jesus.

The medica would wait for the medical examiner, so I left them to tell my crew that the baby had died. But then I saw the father, nervously fidgeting with his face pressed against the back window of the paramedic van. The moment I dreaded was upon me. It's hard to tell a man that his little baby is dead. It's even harder when he has little else in the world.

Their lower flat was well-kept but very sparse with one queen-size bed for all of them, very little furniture, no kitchen table, and no toys. His wife was seriously disabled with what appeared to be multiple sclerosis. He looked like a working man, clean and well-groomed. He must have also been the one who did everything for his wife and children. He loved them.

I put my arm around him, acknowledged my deepest sorrow and told him that his baby had passed away. He looked at me in disbelief as if I had just run him through with a sword, pulled it from his gut, and then dropped the bloody steel to the ground. But the moment of disbelief quickly turned into a wailing rage. He ran into the house after first ripping the railing from the porch stairway. I followed him to stand guard over the children while he cried out, smashed a window with his fist, and threw what little he had against the wall. His wife joined him in grieving, but she could do nothing more than scream and pound the arms of her wheelchair.

I stayed in the bedroom with the children. The little girl cried and quivered and the boy stood silently in a corner with his thumb still wedged in his mouth. I held out my arms to the girl, and she ran to me. I picked her up and she snuggled into my fire coat; the boy began to cry and then hugged one of my legs with his free arm. I wept with them.

When the father returned to the bedroom, he stood spread-eagle with his hands on the door frame looking like a frustrated, powerless Samson whose face was smitten with rage. But then he saw his children. He saw me holding his daughter, and the anger drained from his face and turned to agony. He ran to his son, picked him up, and held him close while wildly crying for his little girl.

My guts were being ripped out, and I couldn't fix it. He looked at me and kept asking why it happened, and all I could tell him was that only the Lord knows, and that we just can't understand his ways. And I was speaking the truth because I certainly couldn't fathom why God would take this poor man's treasure from him. There I stood, a man committed to serving the Lord, feeling like an inadequate Christian since I couldn't give him any words. But words were not what God wanted and he turned my mind back to the change of the father's face from rage to brokenness. I didn't understand why the baby died but I saw the Lord's purpose for me. We don't always understand God's ways, but he is with us in the suffering. I could be a mirror of Christ for a moment while I held and loved his children.

–Captain Bob Anderson, Milwaukee Fire Department

TACTICS AGAINST POVERTY AND CRIME 2005

Over the last decades, numerous attempts have been made by leaders in the Milwaukee area to stop poverty and crime. These efforts were typically initiated and driven by churches in partnership with many public agencies and government organizations. The basic biblical principle was to assist the governing bodies within the community to reduce poverty and crime.

Working to build an effective social order to overcome the ravages of poverty and crime became a major effort by the law enforcement community. The Department of Corrections and the Milwaukee Police Department have the social responsibility to enforce the laws and insure community safety, so BASICS was in a unique position to work with them and other agencies to build links to the faith community network of pastors in the pulpits and people in the pews to unite their efforts through collaboration and cooperation.

The relationships of the faith community with government organizations had to be carefully understood and described to recognize that the governing bodies are committed to the rehabilitation needs of people under their supervision and that we were not favored in any way by working with them, especially with the Department of Corrections. The faith community not only helps with practical needs but, more importantly with the soul needs that ultimately can lead to peace and eternal life.

The acts of the faith community over the past decades have been impressive in trying to address the issues of poverty and crime. During the decades before and after the change into the twenty-first century, Community Justice Centers started a network of resources and facilities throughout the inner city. I believe the founders of these efforts were driven by a desire to accomplish God's work—to show love to our neighbors. Supporting and serving disenfranchised citizens includes cooperating with law enforcement, education, corrections, and wealth sources. God has opened many doors of opportunity to make a difference in the lives of the invisible and often abandoned people in communities of poverty and crime. These efforts were labeled as Compassionate Conservatism in the 1990s and are now often referred to as social justice.

During the 1990s, God moved in the hearts and minds of both local and national leaders to search for solutions to the serious social issues that resulted from the actions that occurred during the 1960s.

National and local community leaders largely from the faith community have risen up to develop community centers to provide the services that disappeared when fathers were not in the homes. Working with people in poverty and crime often involves one-on-one relationships with individuals who are at risk to help them improve their decision-making skills. A pattern evolved in working with impoverished people. Unless a person was experiencing a major life-threatening crisis, there was no incentive to make a decision to commit to change their lifestyle to follow Jesus Christ.

The role and functions of chaplains and coaches in our society seem to be more accepted and suited to impacting life changes. A chaplain, for example, is readily allowed to minister in hospitals, schools, jails, and prisons where they are frequently called to serve. Often, they are asked to perform funerals and weddings and even baptisms for individuals who have no church affiliation other than the BASICS minister.

In 2005, BASICS was searching for ways in which pastors and people of faith could work with the Milwaukee Police Department to reduce crime by following the principles God gives us in his word. Below are some examples of people of faith who have stepped out to reduce crime as street chaplains.

Milwaukee Police District 4 Community Outreach Initiative

Pastor Jay Fischer of Evangel Assembly of God Church has been working effectively with the Milwaukee Police Department as a chaplain to the community along with many volunteers from his church and his neighborhood. The model of outreach is used by the MPD in all seven districts of Milwaukee as an attempt to build closer relationships of trust and cooperation with all segments of the community. Here is the story told by Marcia Smith, a volunteer from Evangel Church:

> Pastor Jay has many stories and testimonies from his time serving as chaplain with the MPD and Salvation Army street chaplain team, responding to emergency calls where his counsel is urgently needed. He is passionate about his work with District 4 Police Department and is continually building relationships within the police department along with the faith-based organizations that assist the police department. Pastor Jay is the head of the local faith-based organization, and they recently honored the District 4 Police Department with an appreciation day (an annual event) with lots of food throughout the day to cover the various shifts.
>
> One of these events was the Millwood Outreach with the police department and faith-based organizations where a lot of burgers, brats, hotdogs, snow cones, french fries, and other foods were available at the Millwood neighborhood. Evangel has also hosted several funerals with ties to the police department. I know I'm only scratching the surface on the testimonies to be told. The Lord has opened many doors for Pastor Jay to get involved with our community, and he has touched many lives for the glory of God.[1]–Marcia Smith, Evangel Assembly of God

FEARLESS SOLDIERS OF MESSIAH
2006

Pastor Alvin Hull and his wife Suzanna, ministers to Milwaukee, were a special couple dedicated to serving the poor in the inner city. Both were prayer warriors and gifted in healing the sick. They joined our BASICS Wednesday morning prayer team to pray for the city and were led to start several ministries relating to helping individuals and families with special needs. Pastor Hull grew up in the inner city of Saint Louis, Missouri. Suzanna was from the inner city of Detroit, Michigan. Both had been impacted by the consequences of crime.

When Pastor Hull and Suzanna first met with Norma and me, they were convinced that God was calling them to Milwaukee as city pastors with many creative ideas of what God wanted them to do. His wife was excited and passionate about her role as a prayer partner to support whatever God was going to do. Below is a summary of some of the miracles God did through Pastor Hull's ministry as a Minister to Milwaukee in the BASICS team.

Pastor Hull started the Seek and Find ministry to find people in poverty and help them by showing God's love. It was amazing how God led them to pray for whatever was needed and how God would lead them to his provisions in miraculous ways. People would donate food, clothing, furniture, home furnishings, money for gas, help moving the materials, etc. A dry cleaner in the South Side offered to clean all the clothes that were donated at no cost. Another donor agreed to pay for the lease, the gas, and the insurance of a van to transport materials. Warehouse storage space was provided as needed by other donors.

A health clinic closed and donated twelve stations of exercise equipment, a paraplegic man paralyzed from a work accident was miraculously healed and began walking again, and a teenager (my granddaughter, Kezia) who broke her back in a swimming accident was miraculously healed through prayer.

Pastor Hull organized the Fearless Soldiers of Messiah, a group of eight minority, male street chaplains with a goal to stop crime in buses on dangerous bus routes and in restaurants where gangs would attack patrons. They wore black uniforms armed with Bibles to confront young teens being disruptive. The bus drivers and police deeply appreciated the impact they had in reducing crime. He was invited to preach and teach in jails and prisons as a chaplain and started a weekly inner-city radio broadcast that brought the Gospel to Milwaukee residents.

Pastor Alvin was instrumental in starting the street chaplains initiative in BASICS which led to the HOT (Homeless Outreach Team) program. He led a group of BASICS ministers into the Menomonee Valley to find the homeless tent city where mostly veterans were living year-around.

Pastor Alvin's wife Suzanna passed into the arms of Jesus after a long illness, but Pastor Hull continues to this day in full-time ministry as a chaplain.

Testimony from Pastor Alvin Hull

In 2014, the head Muslim chaplain at the Racine Correctional Institution asked me to preach to some of the men on a Monday afternoon. This is especially important because the majority of converts in prisons today are Muslims.

The Muslim chaplain was so impressed with the message and the reaction of the men that he asked me to continue to preach three times a month at Saturday night services for over three years. God has opened the door for me to serve as a regular volunteer chaplain at the second largest prison in the state of Wisconsin. The miracle of God is that the Muslim chaplain befriended us in an environment that normally isn't very conducive to hearing the word of God.

When Pastor Hull finishes his messages, he asks the inmates, "What's our motto?" In unison, nine hundred voices yell out, "Get Right! Get Real! Get Ready!"

Pastors and chaplains are similar in many respects. Both provide counseling and spiritual ministry to those in need. The primary differences lie in where, how, and to whom they offer compassion and care. A pastor is typically a denominationally ordained paid spiritual leader in a church.

A chaplain in BASICS is a minister of presence with

experience and skills in a certain area of work. They are available as a friend whenever and wherever they are to open their souls to share their needs on a personal and practical level. They are usually unpaid volunteers such as police officers, teachers, business leaders, etc. who are trusted and respected with the highest level of integrity. They are humble, caring, intense listeners, confidential, even when seeing and hearing the dirtiest and filthiest evil at its worst. They have a relationship with God and have the gift of discernment. They are willing to guide a friend when facing devastating difficulties.

—Alvin Hull, Pastor

MINISTERING TO LAW ENFORCEMENT OFFICERS 2000–2016

Testimony from Chaplain George Papachristou

In May of 2016 BASICS sponsored a cookout for all three shifts of the Milwaukee Police District 2 officers. Each officer was given food and a personalized thank you card made by local school children.

I cannot tell you what a great impact this had on the officers. They were sincerely touched by the generosity displayed to them. While they are used to having food dropped off for them from time to time, they have not had it done in the form of an actual BBQ. The officers working at night were especially impressed as they typically only get the leftovers from what may have been presented for the day shift, so for volunteers to be physically present for their shift meant the world to them. When I began chaplaincy, I was told that it is a ministry of presence, and that is exactly what was accomplished through God's grace.

We did receive some prayer requests, and many officers had occasion to speak to me in private regarding some of the concerns and worries. Prayerfully they were able to feel some relief having been able to just talk to someone. As a dear friend told me many years ago, we never know when we may be in a position to be Jesus to someone. In our flawed human way, through God's power, we are able to do that.

I have seen God open many doors with respect to law enforcement in the state of Wisconsin and in Milwaukee. The State Department of Justice partnered with the International Conference of Police Chaplains (ICPC) to train over three hundred law enforcement chaplains throughout the state. I was blessed to have been one of the ICPC Instructors who presented the twelve courses that allow a chaplain to attain the basic level of ICPC certification. This is now the standard of certification by the state of Wisconsin for Law Enforcement Chaplains.

During the past years I have had the honor to preside over weddings. I've also sadly officiated funerals for officers slain in the line of duty, two who took their own lives. In the aftermath of these tragic deaths, many officers have come forward with questions regarding their faith, which has led to Bible studies and support groups for law enforcement officers, including the establishment of Fellowship of Christian Peace Officers that meets monthly for support, fellowship, Christian education, and Bible study.

–Chaplain George Papachristou, Wisconsin State Police (Former BASICS Minister to Milwaukee)

---

1. The Chaplains of BASICS:

Pastor Alvin Hull: (see description from this chapter)

Pastor Edward Johnson: Serves as a prison chaplain at Racine Correctional Institution with Pastor Hull. He has been active in the Wednesday morning BASICS prayer team since 2012 and served as one of the Fearless soldiers of Messiah.

Bridget Sheehan: Joined BASICS in 2001. She provided professional chaplaincy services to incarcerated women for over twenty years; she ministered through Bible classes and recovery support. In 2000, she became the woman's chaplain at Milwaukee County Correction Facility, South. To many, she became a spiritual mom. Bridget is now living with her Lord.

Roger Dynes: Joined BASICS in 2002. He holds regular Bible studies on Thursday nights at Fox Lake Correctional Institution leading seven other volunteers; he co-leads weekly with the in-prison community Bible study.

Frank Woods: Chaplain serving in Racine Correctional Institute.

Pastor Steve Rogers: Senior pastor of Elim Tabernacle serving as chaplain of the Greenfield Police and Fire Departments.

Pastor Jonathan Misirian: Senior pastor of Southbrook Church serving as chaplain of the City of Franklin Police Department

Reverend Jerry Hageman: Served as a volunteer chaplain at the Milwaukee Secure Detention Facility and is currently a hospice chaplain serving in southeast Wisconsin.

Ted Persen: A police officer and chaplain with the Milwaukee Police and Fire Department.

Andy Stallworth: A police officer and chaplain with the Milwaukee Police and Fire Department

Mike Moses: Joined BASICS in 2006. Mike has educated many high schools, churches, and other ministries on human trafficking. He is a chaplain in the Wisconsin prison system.

Ron Koepke: Joined BASICS in 2007. He has volunteered in prison ministry for well-over twenty years. As a chaplain, Ron ministered throughout Wisconsin with his wife Alice. Ron is now living with his Lord.

Richard Schwoegler: Joined BASICS in 2014. He is actively working with the Milwaukee Police Department to start Christian-based groups in each police district of Milwaukee and start a chaplain's program for the MPD. He continues to serve independently as God leads him.

George Papachristou: Joined BASICS in 2014. Previously he was a chaplain for a high school football team, a mentor at Hope Street, a police officer for the city of Milwaukee, chaplain to the Big Bend Police and Fire Departments, and is certified as a law enforcement chaplain in Wisconsin

THE ACTS OF THE MINISTERS TO MILWAUKEE: ALONGSIDE GOVERNMENT AGENCIES

2011

But you will receive power when the Holy Spirit comes on you; and you will be my witnesses in Jerusalem, and in Judea and Samaria, and to the ends of the earth.
Acts 1:8

What: Show how God's people are doing God's work in Milwaukee within government spaces.
So what: To provide inspiration and examples of what God's people have been doing.
Now what: Encouragement to do God's work as God leads.

A significant change took place in the American educational system for elementary and secondary schools on May 23, 2001. It's called the No Child Left Behind Act (NCLBA). It required assessments of all students to accomplish standards-based education reform with standardized measurable goals. This legislation included new rules on religious freedom in our educational system which was to be implemented by the Milwaukee Public Schools (MPS) Board of Education. This occurred at a time when BASICS was concerned about not only the quality of education in inner-city schools but also the rise of disrespect and violence in so many of the elementary, middle, and senior high schools.

Fortunately, during this time one of the BASICS' board members, Dr. Barbara Horton, was also on the MPS board and was familiar with the NCLBA law and its requirements for a monthly report to the government on setting a policy for religious freedom and the status of implementing that policy. This situation aligned with my efforts to study the new law to determine how it would impact the BASICS strategy to have the faith community work within the schools.

Matt D. Staver, Chairman of the Liberty Counsel, came to our aid in helping us understand what role we could have in supporting the teachers, parents, and students. He also provided a guide for MPS on how to write their policy on religious freedom. This was a God-sent gift to us and guided us in the years ahead in working with the public schools. My understanding in having worked with MPS Superintendent William Andrekopoulos' staff in 2007 is that the proposed policy was reviewed by the MPS legal counsel, adopted, and became a guide for not only the MPS, but was used by the Wisconsin Secretary of Education, Dr. Linda Burmeister.

The rules for teachers in the NCLB Act stated that:

- Teachers cannot teach about religion but must remain neutral.
- Teachers cannot observe religious holidays.
- Teachers cannot promote religious beliefs.
- Teachers cannot practice religion in the classroom.
- Teachers cannot discuss personal beliefs in class.
- Teachers cannot encourage or discourage prayer or religious activities.
- Teachers are free to express their beliefs and take part in religious activities on or off campus outside of school hours when it is clear they are not acting in their official capacities as school employees.
- Teachers are free to meet with other teachers for prayer or Bible study before school or during lunch.
- Teachers may serve as faculty advisors for student

religious clubs, but they cannot endorse the activity as a school religious activity.

WORKING WITH PUBLIC EDUCATION
2003–19

Even though these rules applied to the teachers, we felt our volunteers should understand and follow the same rules as supporters of the teachers.

The first step in working with the education system was to pray for the students, teachers, administrators, and parents. God was already ahead of us and called several people led by Valerie Pietrowiak to form a prayer initiative called MPS Covered in Prayer. It was amazing how quickly people were led by the Holy Spirit to begin praying. Many of these volunteers were from the suburbs but were alumni of the MPS and had a deep love for their alma mater. The vision was to have at least one person praying for each school in Milwaukee and Valerie, with her team, built an email network of pray-ers to cover every school in the city. That goal was fulfilled within a year![1] Praise the Lord.

Through the information gathered from the email list, we eventually could find out the number of pray-ers for each school which enabled the team to assign pray-ers to the specific needs of each school, and eventually to specific projects, teachers, and principals. God blessed us with multiple ideas about how we could minister to the needs of students, teachers, principals, and even parents. Here is a short list of some of the activities that resulted from MPS Covered in Prayer:

- Prayer walks around the school initially and then inside as the principal would allow
- Prayer with principals, teachers, security administrators, and eventually with at-risk students
- Prayer led to care for students where the team would provide students with blankets, caps and scarves (many

made by the volunteers), mittens, boots, underwear, coats, and Bibles
- Student tutoring, life-coaching, and prayer as appropriate
- Lunchroom conversations and prayer as requested
- Teacher appreciation luncheons
- Teacher lounge makeovers done during the summer months as requested by the principal

The impact of all these volunteer activities was a blessing to everyone involved and had a deep impact on students and parents alike. This model of school support has been expanded to other cities in the Midwest and is continuing to this day.

The greatest number of pray-ers volunteered to pray for South Division High School, so that became our target school to start an expanded strategy for change following God's way. Dr. Maurice Turner was the principal of the school when we first explained the MPS Covered in Prayer vision and program. The school was suffering from devastating violence both in and out of the school. Almost every day as many as twelve police cars came on-site to address the consequences of gang activity.[2] It was a desperate situation that required every ounce of Turner's creative problem-solving energy and skills, including prayer. Maurice became a dear friend of BASICS as a brother in Christ.

Maurice Turner's Story

Have you ever seen God do something that was so much greater, so much larger, greater than your wildest dreams? That's what the Lord allowed BASICS to see the first time we went to South Division High School in 2012.[3]

Before BASICS was invited into South Division, there were routinely two or three squad cars in front of the school every day. Fights were breaking out daily between the ethnic groups, males and females, and even between parents and students. The school desperately needed divine intervention. BASICS had been praying for all of the MPS but not on-site until Marty Calderon invited me to meet the principal, Maurice Turner. He blew me away.

Mr. Turner was a former college basketball star at the University of Wisconsin-Milwaukee. A large man not only physically, but in his presence, spirit, and love. After a few introductory comments, principal Turner asked two questions I was not ready for: "Do you love Jesus Christ? Do you love the Bible?"

Feeling somewhat rattled, I said, "Yes! I do love Jesus Christ, and I do love the Bible!"

Principal Turner's response was, "You and your team are always welcome at South Division! I love Bibles. Can you get free Bibles for any students who want one?" Fortunately, one of the faithful servants on our BASICS team, Phil Helwig, was a member of the Gideon Ministry and was eager to help resulting in giving over five hundred Bibles to students, parents, and teachers.

Principal Turner proceeded to tell me that every morning before the students arrive, he and any of his staff are free to meet together in his office for prayer for the school, students, parents, and everyone who enters the school.

He also told me about the first day he was principal at the school. He greeted all the students at an all-student assembly, introduced himself, outlined the goals and objectives for the school year, and then proceeded to do something that was amazing. He announced that he was going to start the school year with prayer and that anyone who didn't want to participate could step out of the auditorium, or if they stayed, they should be silent or participate in the time of prayer. No one left the auditorium! No one disrupted the time of prayer while principal Turner asked our Almighty God to bless, anoint, and heal South Division High School!

After hearing all these things. I was dazed, excited, and like Peter on the Mount of Transfiguration when he didn't know what he was saying, I blurted out one more question: "Is there anything else you would like for me to know or do?" Immediately he said, "Would you like to be our prayer-friend in the cafeteria once a week?" The first lunch period was about to start, and he suggested I stay and check it out. I did, but I was not ready for what I was about to see.

As we entered the cafeteria, there were two men with rifles positioned in the lunchroom. There was chaos, pushing, shoving, shouting, yelling, and a tension that you could cut with a knife. After seeing this and not really knowing what I was doing, I told Principal Turner:,"Yes, I would be willing to come every Thursday and pray in the lunchroom and be a friend to whoever God would bring into my path." Each week for the past seven years, BASICS has had a presence in the lunchroom on Thursday praying for and with staff, teachers, students, parents, and guests—being friends with whoever God brings to us. God was bringing prayer and bibles back into a public school. Praise the Lord!

Over time, South Division allowed BASICS to have prayer walks several times a year as Principal Turner and others would direct us and tell us where the greatest needs were in the school for prayer, usually at the trophy case where most of the fights would occur. Gradually the need for two to three squad cars diminished to none! The lunchroom became quiet and rifles were no longer needed. Praise the Lord.

The school then allowed BASICS to host annual staff appreciation lunches where teams of volunteers serve lunch to the staff and teachers. Volunteers offer encouragement and thank them for their faithful service, then ask if they have any prayer requests. One of the teachers said she had been a teacher for over twenty years and had never felt so loved and appreciated like they did at these lunches.

The school then asked if BASICS would help encourage the students during parent-teacher conference times. Many of the parents were not able to attend the conferences ,and principal Turner felt it would be beneficial if a loving, caring adult would come and talk to a student for about ten minutes about how they were doing in school, what they could do to improve their grades, be available if there was anything the student wanted to share about their lives, and encourage them to do their best. This included helping with homework to eliminate incompletes on their report cards.

BASICS was blessed to do this with the guidance counselors who showed us how much potential many of the wonderful students had, and also showed us the needs of many of the students who come from broken homes or were homeless. After a year of prayer and volunteer involvement from the community, Principal Turner reported a significant improvement in test scores for the entire school.

Finally, BASICS was asked if we had any clothing such as hats, gloves, scarves, personal items, deodorants, food items like granola bars, juice boxes, or pop tarts that Mama Mac could have for students in need. Mama Mac was in the security department of the school and did an amazing job of caring for the students and helping them in whatever they needed. She even gave them breakfast snacks for the weekend if they didn't have food at home.

Here is a little history of Mama Mac's closet. Mama Mac's closet was started in 2008 to help students and families at South Division High School. She began by collecting winter coats from parents, staff, and the community for needy students. This led to giving clothing and hygiene products for both children and adults at shelters around the South Side. Mama Mac says, "I just want everyone to know how important it is to love each other. I couldn't do it without everyone's help."

BASICS has been blessed to share hats, gloves, and scarves made by widows in a loving ministry called Threads of Love at Elmbrook church. Other friends of BASICS have donated food items, personal hygiene products, shoes, and winter coats. The staff and teachers have made BASICS feel like part of their family and are simply known as friends of South Division. What a beautiful demonstration of the love of God through his people and the power of prayer. –

-Mark Mallwitz, BASICS - Minister to Milwaukee

Dr. Gregory Thornton's Desperate Call for Help

As superintendent of Milwaukee Public Schools, I write to solicit your help in saving lives. When I accepted my position, I knew the challenges we faced would be enormous. But I never thought that for our students the challenges would sometimes be life ending.

In the past several weeks, we lost four students on the streets of Milwaukee. Each young man was shot to death in a separate instance. They were boys who sat in our classrooms and laughed in the hallways and played ball in the parks. And now, all four of them are dead.

Poverty happens. Jobs go away. Hopelessness sets in. Children are on the street for long hours each day, seeing the interplay of drug dealers or gang bangers. The children become street tough. Some of them bring their anger and defiance to our schools. At times, their adult relatives follow them to school, and the fights can become more menacing.

The scourge is contagious. Milwaukee, we cannot turn our backs on these children and their families. And what about the hundreds of other Milwaukee children who are walking a thin line between danger and hope? They are the small subset of students in our schools who are frequently absent or truant, or who are quick to fight, disrespect a teacher, or disrupt a classroom. We cannot allow them to soon be on the same grim list of children lost to violence.

We need your help, Milwaukee! The lives of our young people are in the balance. Let's learn from recent events and assure that each child born in our city has hope of living a long life in which they know the support of the community around them.

–Gregory Thornton, Superintendent of Milwaukee Public Schools[4]

This plea served as a rallying call to expand the BASICS prayer efforts to include many other faith-based partners. God moved powerfully to expand the MPS Covered in Prayer project into a movement. Paul writes, *"May our Lord Jesus Christ himself and God our Father, who loved us and by his grace gave us eternal encouragement and good hope, encourage your hearts and strengthen you in every good deed and word"* (2 Thess. 2:16–17). God provided glimpses of encouragement and strength through several volunteers.

Deanne at Rufus King International Middle School (RKIMS)

After quitting my job as an administrative assistant at a Lutheran Middle School, I was introduced to BASICS and RKIMS. I was unsure of God's plans for me, but I knew I needed to be obedient to his call. When I was asked to do a prayer walk, it was clear that I was to pray for these students and teachers. I am honored that God would use me in such a way, and I am excited to see how God is going to use this ministry in the schools so I can partner with two amazing women: principal Tamara Ellis and vice principal Robin Swann.

Michele at Barak Obama School of Career and Technical Education (BOSCTE)

Today I attended my first MPS prayer walk at the BOSCTE, a school that serves K–12th grade. It was an honor to meet Principal Maurice Turner and to pray alongside such beautiful people who have a heart for the Lord and his people.

Maurice told us about the school and the challenges they face. He gave us a tour of the huge building that once held 3,700 students (as Custer High School) but now just 800. I was amazed to see beautiful woodworking, welding, and HVAC workshops along with a cosmetology lab and an auditorium built to hold over 2,000 people. We joined together to pray for the students in these workshops and also to visit the newly decorated teachers' lounge makeover done by volunteers from the BASICS's network and Elmbrook church.

There is so much potential amidst so much brokenness. The many opportunities for learning are not utilized due to lack of staff and student motivation. I was overwhelmed by the thought of what it would take to transform this school, the students, families, and the community. But as we prayed in the different areas of the school, I was reminded of how big our God is. His love and faithfulness are so great—I'm certain there will be a mighty work here.

Tamara Ellis, Principal, Rufus King

It's such a blessing to have women of God and prayer partners committed to praying for and with me, the staff, and the students. You are so valued and much needed.

Pray for our youth. Listen to their hurts. Teach them how to live God's way. BASICS was able to come alongside other government agencies as well.

COMMUNITY SAFETY COALITION
2000

In the year 2000, the Community Safety Coalition (CSC) was organized and established in Milwaukee as a non-sectarian partnership of law enforcement agencies, corrections, community-based organizations, faith communities, and others working together with the mission and vision to reduce crime, to promote safety, and to improve the quality of life in Milwaukee. The goals and objectives of the CSC was to be carried out through its diverse subcommittees, each of which were to define and develop their goals consistent with the CSC mission and vision.

The strategies articulated as ways to achieve their goals were to:[5]

- Minimize the impact of drugs
- Expand jobs and employment opportunities for inner-city residents
- Raise level of education among at-risk youth
- Focus on and remove illegal guns
- Analyze blocks or neighborhoods where violent crime persists
- Institute proactive approach to face crime directly
- Commit to "walk" and be visible on the streets by observing and talking to residents
- Declare a "ceasefire" and invest in blocks and neighborhoods
- Target irresponsible landlords who rent to drug dealers and/or keep nuisance properties
- Hold instructional and informational meetings for specific parolees/probationers and members of gangs
- Determine prayer sites in each police district
- Maintain after-school activities.
- Pursue truant students to keep them in school and off the streets during school hours
- Encourage daily school attendance

This impressive plan and many others like it have basically disappeared over the years even though the problems they were organized to resolve continue. Again, we ask: What have we learned? Why are we still having the same problems? What should the faith community do? Obviously, we must watch and pray! But God has a plan. We believe and trust in God for guidance in knowing God's way.

Mobile Command Centers

Working with Community Center initiatives gave BASICS an opportunity to learn the inside details of the living conditions within homes of poverty and crime. This turned out to be a precursor to understanding the characteristics that could lead to correcting the challenges of children and youth unable to escape the consequences of making bad decisions.

During the summer of 2007, the Milwaukee Police Department was facing significant increases in gang crime in twenty neighborhoods in the inner city. Consequently, they developed a strategy to use the large and retired Mobile Medical Center vans and revamp them as Mobile Command Centers to bring police and social services resources into the neighborhoods to help stop crime. This was done during the summer months in the county parks in an alternating schedule for two- to three-week periods in each of the twenty areas with the highest crime rates.

BASICS was asked to provide a coaching center in each van where local pastors and mentors would be available to talk to the youth and encourage them to be good citizens. Reading materials, board games, and Bibles were made available as they desired. If further assistance was needed, it could be arranged. This provided volunteers from the faith community a great opportunity to learn more about the problems facing youth in the inner city. This experience eventually led to the BASICS park outreach programs that are continuing to this day in inner-city parks.

Homeless Outreach Team (HOT)

The homeless population of Milwaukee kept growing in many cities in the nation, including Milwaukee, but it seemed little was done to address their problems. With my engineering problem-solving mentality, I felt it may be time to do an assessment of homeless citizens in Milwaukee. Having also had a homeless woman live with Norma and me for a year gave me access to the inner workings of street life in the shadows of Milwaukee.

As part of my investigation, I arranged a tour with Norma and a videographer of the downtown area where the homeless sleep on the streets. Laura Marsh (author of *Living in the Shadows of Milwaukee*) was our tour guide. We started at around four in the morning on a cold October morning while it was still dark, and we could see where the homeless were sleeping. Laura had alerted her homeless friends the day before that we were coming and told them why we wanted to meet them. She guided us to where her friends were sleeping and when they woke up, we interviewed them before they had to hide their sleeping bags and belongings.

Most of the people we met who were homeless were over-whelmed that we respected them enough to come and talk with them to try to help them overcome their dilemmas and understand their problems. Each story was significantly different, but we found several typical patterns that led them into homelessness:

- Eviction: They were in crisis because of something like a lost job, and were therefore evicted from their home.
- Disability: They were abandoned because they were physically or mentally handicapped, on prescription meds, or had HIV-AIDS.
- Chronic: They were abandoned because of addiction, and got money through panhandling.
- Criminal: They were in hiding and had warrants out for their arrest.
- Vagabonds: They were hermits by choice. Many of them were veterans who wanted to live free from any control.

The services enabling them to exist were provided by churches and social assistance organizations. Those I spoke with were able to attain meals in facilities and on the street, clothes to keep warm, bus tickets, legal services, medical services, and emergency housing when it was very cold.

In 2010, this information and our spirit of compassion led BASICS to organize these resources and volunteers into a group from the faith community who were called and already involved in serving the homeless. We called this group the Street Chaplaincy Program.

At this time, we also collaborated with Lieutenant Karen Dubis assigned to District 1 of the Milwaukee Police Department. Lieutenant Dubis had received training at a Problem Orientated

Policing Conference in Arlington, Texas. The conference had training from the Colorado Springs Police Department's successful Homeless Outreach Team. Lieutenant Dubis took some of that training and added to it and started a Homeless Outreach Team (HOT) within the Milwaukee Police Department (MPD). As part of this collaboration, the street chaplains volunteered their time to provide counseling for homeless individuals on the street. The MPD HOT received several awards for their service to the homeless community.[6]

In the fall of 2010, Lt. Dubis started the MPD Homeless Outreach Team (HOT).

> The HOT team takes a new approach to homeless issues by collaborating with shelter agencies, food providers, mental health care providers, BASICS, and a number of other agencies including providers of medical treatment, drug and alcohol treatment, clothing, and other services. HOT officers attended weekly meetings with local service providers, civil rights leaders, local homeless advocates, community members, and the homeless themselves. A new option was to meet with BASICS street chaplains as partners to provide on-call chaplains to respond to homeless individuals that the HOT team officers encountered. HOT team officers contact BASICS to request a chaplain's immediate response to on-the-street issues they encounter with the homeless. This strategic relationship between BASICS and the Milwaukee Police Department was a work in progress by Arn Quakkelaar for the past few years. The street ministry is an example of BASICS Rescue and Restore initiatives and BASICS's mission to bring hope to the hopeless in the Milwaukee area.
>
> –Kristina Betzold and Lt. Karen Dubis

ANGOLA PRISON
2015

In 2014 I became aware of the Malachi Dads program of

AWANA Lifeline through the Prison Aftercare Network of Wisconsin and was led to Chaplain Dennis D. Kuhens, volunteer State Director of Wisconsin Prison Fellowship who was successful in introducing the Malachi Dads program in the Prairie Du Chien Correctional Institute. Several of us on the GENESIS team visited his facility to see the great work he was doing in that prison. The friendship that developed involved his team visiting Milwaukee and resulted in an invitation to the GENESIS team to visit the Louisiana State Penitentiary (also called Angola Prison) to spend a weekend inside death row. This experience was an amazing answer to my prayers to be able to experience and understand what it was like to live in a prison. I truly felt this was part of God's plan for my life.

Angola Prison is a large land area surrounded by the Mississippi River in Louisiana and is called "The Alcatraz of the South." It covers 18,000 acres of land with its own zip code (70712) and radio station. Much of the land is used for farming, formerly called the Angola Plantation. It includes a village called the B-Line which is home to over 500 employees of the prisons. There are six prison housing areas, each have their own warden running the separate prisons.

Angola is often referred to as the farm because the land is used to provide food for the more than 11,000 inmates who work forty hours per week at four to twenty cents per hour. They raise food for everyone in Angola and the four other state prisons located in other parts of the state for the entire year. The prisoners raise cotton, soybeans, tomatoes, onions, cabbage, okra, beans, peppers, squash, strawberries, and eggs—all weighing over four million pounds per year. Livestock dominate the fields with beef cattle, cows, pigs, goats, chickens, and horses for inmate cowboys who perform for visiting families of the offenders.

Angola has more lifers than any other prison in the US and is the nation's largest maximum-security prison with over 6,100 offenders and 80 men on death row. Additionally, 85 percent are spending the rest of their lives in Angola and 90 percent of the inmates have no visits during their incarceration. Angola prisoners build the caskets for inmate burials conducted by inmate pastors.

In the years before 1960, Angola was known as a blood-drenched hell-hole where only the most violent criminals could hope to survive. This began changing during the 1970s when a restoration reform movement began to invade the minds of the state leadership. In 1995, Burl Cain was appointed Angola's prison warden, and he led the change in attitude. He believed religion and faith can change even the most violent and hardened criminals into productive citizens. This new approach significantly changed Angola into a model prison, recognized worldwide for having little violence. Gang activity was replaced by encouragement for inmates to join one of the many approved organizations or to organize their own. This enabled Christian faith-based ministries such as the Awana Lifeline Malachi Dads program to flourish as led by its Executive Director, Mike Broyles.

After our long trip in a van with five of us from Milwaukee, we arrived mid-afternoon on Friday, January 30, 2015. We were given a brief orientation at the B-Line Chapel and then brought to the reception center of our new home—a cell in the old death row. Our GENESIS team consisted of three of us who were "recovering citizens" (RCs) and two of us who had never lived behind bars. I vividly remember the RCs teaching me how to make my cot so the sheets wouldn't come loose at night. At supper that night we paired-up at tables of four with two lifers who were Malachi Dad's and two visitors to tell our stories. What an awesome experience!

The first lifer I was paired with, Freddie, told me he had been shot fourteen times. He had three kids, and his oldest son hung himself at the age of nine, all because his father was trying to satisfy the evil desires and demands of a woman who wanted the most powerful man to get guns and kill as many men as possible, and then when she was satisfied, they could have a family. He said that in an evil society, man's way is to "go down to gain respect." But God's way is to "go down to go up—God is in absolute control of my life now!"

Another lifer, Patrick, said he was innocent as part of a setup by the gang but didn't explain details other than that he had written about his story and that it had been published nationally. He is seeking a pardon. He's married to a faithful wife and has nine children (two sets of twins). His daughter was killed in an auto accident while on the way home from a rodeo event at Angola (he was not allowed to attend the funeral). Patrick is a musician on one of the worship teams, is a master chef and feeds 4,000 men a day, was the owner of a trucking business, and hopes to have his story published in a book. His oldest son was rejected by his mother at birth but is blessed with a pastor's heart, and they are very close. He's a Malachi Dad and hopes to serve God both in and out of Angola.

One of the chapel sessions was a worship service to celebrate the graduation of eighty-seven offenders who had completed the seminary training in Angola as Malachi Dads with twenty-two of them to become chaplains in the prison throughout Louisiana. We were part of anointing and commissioning them to go and preach the Gospel as our brothers in Christ. We all experienced the presence of God through the power of the Holy Spirit descending upon us in that precious moment.

Our three days in the death row cells, in chapel sessions, on tours, at meals, and seeing and sitting in the old electric chair was extremely subdued and sobering and impossible for me to explain. I couldn't speak or see through the tears of pain realizing in a unique way the consequences of sin and man's way of punishment, but realizing the tremendous gift of God who forgives me and gives eternal life. I couldn't stop thinking and wondering about how many of the men who died in that chair went to heaven instead of hell. How many never heard the Gospel or chose to put their faith in Jesus Christ and received hope in eternal life? Did they experience the love of God and the peace that passes all understanding?

The Malachi Dads and in-prison seminary have changed Angola miraculously. Can God do that in Milwaukee? *Yes!*

This experience dramatically renewed my passion to show and tell God's love to prisoners who were created by him for his purposes to live his way. Our GENESIS team returned to

Milwaukee with the vision and passion to start a seminary in the Wisconsin Prison System, and it is happening today through the efforts of a group of leaders led by Wisconsin Representative, Rob Hutton. Praise the Lord![7]

God is truly at work in Wisconsin! We must watch and pray and work as he leads us. This model provides a compelling reason for prison reform in America and Wisconsin.[8]

WISCONSIN INMATE
EDUCATION ASSOCIATION (WIEA)
2005

Observing God at work through his people over the past decades is a marvelous journey of miracles and relationships. The stories of all the individuals God is using to do his work is amazing, and all the intricate parts of the timeline may never be told. It's a great honor to see how God's plan brings his people together in divinely appointed ways that don't seem important at the time but when placed into a road map of events, show how magnificent our God really is.

Operation Transformation is a collaboration among the Wisconsin Inmate Education Association and Trinity University to establish a new Trinity Campus within the Waupun Correctional Institution (WCI), a maximum-security prison. The in-prison college curriculum is designed to transform inmates, families, and communities to reduce crime and improve communities by starting with inmates during their incarceration.

The WIEA campus provides a Bachelor of Arts in Biblical Studies for inmates and requires at least four years of study. Upon graduation, these graduates can serve as mentors or fieldworkers in prisons, jails, and neighborhoods upon reentry. These changed individuals would exist to bring peace, forgiveness, and reconciliation to inmates, their families, and communities throughout Wisconsin.[9]

Mentoring a Lifer

Over the past two decades, I've visited over half of the seventeen prisons in Wisconsin and have gained a much deeper understanding of the consequences of crime than I would have ever imagined. Having studied and charted all the steps in the incarceration process, it seemed very important for me to get to know personally the inmates who serve time in prison for extended periods of time.

My first opportunity came through an invitation from one of our BASICS chaplains to visit a prisoner who was interested in our work at GENESIS with returning citizens from prisons. This individual was led into a life of crime and was sentenced to life in prison. He was an avid reader and became familiar with the restorative justice process of looking at a crime from the perspective of the victim's families and the impact it had on their lives. This caused him to change his attitude from hostility to empathy, which altered his thinking and resulted in a desire to pursue reconciliation by defining ways to prepare a prisoner for reentry into society and escape the pattern of crime .

This was a divine God-appointed opportunity for me to learn how criminal thinking can be directed toward a rescue and restore process that can change a person's life into a new way of living. Even though my prison friend would probably never be able to live outside of the prison walls, he was used by God to develop a reentry program using principles God teaches us in his Word. His experience and knowledge inspired me to use much of his understanding to develop the GENESIS reentry, five-stage program. With the information I gathered from my prisoner-friend and the chaplain, we began the concepts of reentry which we use in GENESIS today.

Testimony of My Mentee

The world revolved around me, and my emotions ruled most

decisions in my life. A perpetual failure, I disappointed and hurt everyone in my life: failed my parents, abandoned my daughter, destroyed sibling relationships, dropped out of school, deserted or fired from every job, and I was a flop as a friend. Eventually my life spiraled out of control, and I turned to crime. My selfish choices and crimes escalated as I harmed others and killed an innocent person. An escape attempt, with more devastated victims, created a necessity to place me in solitary confinement for more than two and a half years. The first positive changes in my life took place during those early years of isolation because that is when I accepted Christ.

A missionary through Campus Crusade reached out to me while I was broken and alone in that cell. He spoke to me through those bars for weeks until one day we prayed together for Christ to come in and take control of my life. I was transferred to a new prison and released from isolation within a week. The chaplain at the new prison extended his hand and helped me build a positive social network with Christian inmates. The chaplain invested considerable time and energy helping me heal and understand how to become a Christian man. Two months later, God brought a businessman and minister from the community who also mentored and discipled me. Our friendship has remained consistent and close for over twenty-three years. A sibling bond was restored with my sister, and our close friendship could only be described as a blessing. Once God began building me into a new creation, I prayed for him to continue his work to change my character and value system.

Forgiveness from God does not absolve me from consequences associated with my past actions. Understanding and accepting responsibility for the harm I caused left me overwhelmed. My victim lost her life, the children lost a parent, and her family lost a loved one. Three men were traumatized during my escape attempt, my two-year-old daughter was abandoned by her father, and my parents were burdened with shame and sorrow, taxpayers have been saddled with bills for my treatment, welfare, and care. And the list goes on. I remember falling on my knees and asking the Lord: "What do you want me to do during these years of punishment?"

The words the Lord gave the exiles in Babylon in Jeremiah 29 provided me direction and encouragement for more than two decades: *"Build houses, plant gardens, seek the peace of the city into which I have carried you away; pray to me for their peace, and you too shall have peace"* The Lord began providing me with opportunities to be a peacemaker within the prisons, and he gave me the ability to be honest and love others. He also showed me how to love my daughter. Relationships with my parents and siblings blossomed over the years. I developed into a responsible person capable of maintaining steady employment (in prisons). God removed my fears and insecurities and empowered me to openly share with others. Plus I have been granted numerous chances to participate in treatment, educational, and personal enrichment activities.

–Testimony of my Mentee, Joseph Hecht (a lifer)

WORKING WITH THE
FEDERAL GOVERNMENT
2001–2015

As part of BASICS's ongoing search for ways to reach out to our neighbors in distress, we were constantly reminded of the high number of young men in prison having minimal to no relationship with their fathers. In 2000 an unofficial survey of one thousand homes in one area of Milwaukee identified only one home that had a father permanently living with his children and wife.

The families in that area had broken away from the traditional nuclear family structure, and teenagers were not maturing with the nurturing and guidance of their natural father. This reality was observed in many other urban areas throughout the nation and gained national attention. Federal funding became available through the Compassion Capital Fund Office of Community Services in 2005.

Faith-based, grassroots, charitable organizations were specifically encouraged to apply for these funds, and they were on a level playing field with government-funded social agencies to receive those funds. The money was to provide social services to low-income communities and provide alternatives to gang involvement, youth violence, child abuse, and generally to develop healthy youth. This goal certainly aligned with BASICS mission.

The 1990s seemed to be a time of awakening in the nation's desire to show compassion to urban communities, which coincided with President Bush's Compassionate Conservative movement. The Leadership Foundations of America were uniquely positioned to benefit from faith-based organizations being able to compete with non-government agencies to raise funds for their programs, and the Leadership Foundations aggressively encouraged us to pursue writing grants for this funding.

Many faith-based organizations, including BASICS, were opposed to the use of federal funds for religious outreach and evangelism. While wanting to strengthen the separation of church from state, we also wanted to work toward cooperating with the government to build integration and unity in the communities being served.

Was it in God's plan to provide us with a little bit of the world's wealth to do his work in Milwaukee? About the same time I received an invitation from Bud Ipema of the Leadership Foundations of America to join a collaborative effort by the LFA to form a multi-city group of Leadership Foundations, which BASICS was a member of, to work together with other cities to demonstrate the work already being done successfully to accomplish what the government was trying to do. In addition the LFA offered to provide technical assistance and funds to pay grant-writers to prepare the proposals.

At that time Arnold Brownstein had recently moved to Milwaukee from New York and was eager to work in ministry. He had joined BASICS with the faith that he would be able to raise a little financial support for himself and BASICS. He was a former government employee working in international diplomacy and was experienced in writing government proposals. Shortly after joining

BASICS, he was invited by the Department of Health and Human Services to be trained as a grant-reviewer to evaluate and grade Compassionate Conservative Fund grants. This gave him inside exposure to the government's review process. That, along with the LFA's offer of support, seemed to indicate God was showing us his plan to move ahead with a proposal.

At the same time, BASICS was getting strong messages from some of our donors that they would stop giving if we accepted government funding. My personal opinion was similar; I refused to pursue using any government funds because of the controls that would be placed on us that would limit us doing what God was calling us to do in bringing people to live according to God's ways. With signs coming from several directions, I felt BASICS should write a proposal with a very strong statement that we would not depart from our Christian-Judeo beliefs and mission.

Then in 2010, I was invited to a meeting at the White House Office of Faith-based and Community Initiatives in Washington, DC, to meet with government leaders to discuss the Compassionate Conservative Funding initiative. With funding from a donor, I was able to attend and the group met with Senators Joseph (Joe) I. Lieberman and Richard (Rick) J. Santorum, HHS-CCF Director Bobby Polito, and many other dignitaries who urged us to help them in their desire to include the faith community in demonstrating the power of transformation in the lives of youth. I sensed a divine direction to proceed and prayed God would confirm our decision.

In 2011 Arnold Brownstein wrote our grant proposal independent from LFA because the plan we developed didn't align with the LFA plan, and we prayerfully submitted it to the government not expecting it to be successful and not being part of the consortium with other cities. In September of that year, we received the denial of our proposal. That was our answer, and we praised God for giving us a clear answer to our prayers. We continued to do what God called us to do in park outreach events which absorbed all our resources and volunteers.

Then in January of 2012 I received a phone call from Washington, DC, Department of HHS's grant administrator requesting we apply for the 2012 cycle of CCF funding. I explained that we were deeply involved doing our ministry work in the city and didn't have the time or resources to write another proposal (which would take at least two people three months costing around $10,000 and only a 3 percent chance of getting an award), so I declined. The caller responded: "No, I'm not asking you to do anything more than saying *yes!* and I will resubmit the same proposal you submitted last year."

In September of 2012 we were informed that BASICS was awarded a two-year grant to provide one hundred mentors for one hundred mentees each year for prisoners reentering their communities from prison. This clearly was a miraculous answer from God.

GENESIS was successful in working with the churches to find mentors, and since we were already working in many prisons we found many suitable mentees. We fulfilled and exceeded all the requirements during the first year. And in 2013 we were awarded a second two-year grant adding fatherhood and motherhood training to our scope. This funding enabled the GENESIS team to prove and demonstrate our capacity to positively impact the lives of returning citizens. We gained national recognition for doing God's work in Milwaukee.

A tremendous blessing came to GENESIS as a result of administering the grants. We learned and established policies and procedures that fully aligned with all the rules of the federal government. Even though the funding has ended, our operations have benefited greatly from the experience. During 2016 and 2017, the GENESIS team studied best practices used throughout the nation and has developed a community infrastructure for different segments of the city to cooperate and work together without taxpayer funding and to become self-sustaining.

Another feature of the new GENESIS program is that the leadership of GENESIS team consists of both urban and suburban leaders. The board consists of business leaders while the staff consists of returning citizens who have lived through the five stages of transformation, all following God's way.

WORKING WITH REENTRY
2012–2019

In my corporate life I was a professional engineer of automated environmental systems, so I felt maybe God had prepared me to use these skills in the ministry of changing lives. I initiated a project to assess all aspects of the criminal justice system using the linear responsibility chart tool I developed for Johnson Controls and Rockwell—Allen-Bradley Automation. We would chart every step in a process to identify all the functions required to accomplish a goal in the quickest and most cost-effective ways.

We applied this methodology to the local corrections system and mapped out a journey through the system. Our study and research helped us to learn and understand a lot about the reality of crime and its consequences. But the whole system is far more complicated than we ever imagined. We gained a deep respect for the many professionals working in many different roles in the corrections system. The people we interviewed were district attorneys, judges, police officers, parole/probation officers, attorneys, community business leaders, residents, pastors, ministry leaders, politicians, and prisoners both in and out of prison.

The ultimate objective was to identify ways in which the faith community could help prisoners and their families adjust their lives to the difficulties inherent within the criminal justice system. A major outcome of the project was to learn how many people are involved and affected by the system. It became evident that an infrastructure of partners working together could be a tremendous opportunity for the entire community as part of a continuum of care combined with restorative justice to help returning citizens develop their new life living God's way. Over the following years from 2005 to 2012, the BASICS network began building relationships with many segments of the community to develop an understanding and infrastructure of resources for returning citizens.[10] I'd like you to know Frank Woods, one of the people leading this work as the new executive director of GENESIS In Milwaukee, Inc.

Frank Woods at GENESIS

In 2006 I was released from the Department of Corrections and transformed by the power of God through the redemptive work of Jesus Christ. In 2007 God in his sovereignty led me back to a friend who made a decision for Christ five years prior, which led us both to The Captive Project, a ministry serving under BASICS in Milwaukee. Led by this fearless leader, Arn Quakkelaar, we quickly saw a man devoted to the city. When I first met Arn during a luncheon. Meeting an older white haired, White gentleman made my stomach begin to churn, but he wasn't opposed to sitting at the table with ex-thugs from the inner city, which lessened my anxiety. He shared his plans for counter-cultural ministries to change the city.

After serving six years focused primarily on community outreach and discipleship, the opportunity arose with Arn's new baby of a ministry to focus on the prison population. Originally, my role would be to create bridges for churches and businesses to come alongside those released, but little did we know God had bigger plans. After hearing Arn's testimony of God's call on his life and his obedient answer, we began to secretly refer to Arn as Abraham, because he had forsaken the riches of the business world to serve amongst the poor. In 2009 by faith he was used by God to be a part of bringing a model for discipleship to ex-offenders returning home, restoring them back to society as returning citizens. To the natural eye, this gesture was miniscule, but to the trained, each part screamed how much these people were an asset to the community.

Soon thereafter, Arn was invited to Washington, DC, to sit at the table with government officials, as well as those in the national field of reentry, to discover new effective ways to bring resources toward ending recidivism and mass incarceration. Many throughout the city would agree that with his engineering background, the five stages he designed to reclaim life after prison has been duplicated by many whose operations mirror his research. Arn will never admit his role as a man used by God to show his grace and mercy to the invisible people of our community.

I am most thankful for how God blesses us through our different stories, and although we look different, have different backgrounds, and speak differently, God made us all. When we acknowledge this, we can then begin to experience life and see through each other's eyes. We can share in the things that make us so different, thus removing them. This is a lesson that came from the many lessons learned from Arn directly, but mostly indirectly.

In 2014 I entered the worst year of my life. My nineteen-year-old daughter departed from this world. What seemed to be a routine surgery turned into a long drawn out Labor Day weekend. I found out she had slipped into multiple cardiac arrest. My entire family and I were shocked and devastated by this. It nearly destroyed my faith.

I wondered why her and why not me. I remember being at St. Joseph's Hospital wrestling with self, anger, fear, vengeance, and brokenness. I was close to losing all hope. In my confusion outside the emergency room and outside the hospital, I could see my friend, "Abraham," Arn Quakkelaar. He stood focused toward my position across the parking lot as if he was in prayer. Every thought that wasn't of God left me, and I began to think about the healing that can only come from God.

We were in desperate need to hear from God, and that day showed me why we shouldn't ever forsake the assembling of ourselves. This was faith personified in Arn. It was contagious. Later, he and Norma shared a story from their life about their struggle after losing a child many years earlier. That conversation helped transform our healing. Since then we have often shared our story in the same manner.

In 2018 Arn went on emeritus status with GENESIS and BASICS to enjoy the fourth quarter of life and focus on his lovely wife. This move again was a lesson to pastors and ministry leaders alike concerning ministry. In August of the same year, Arn passed me the baton to continue this fruitful legacy of bringing resources to people like me, those returning to

Milwaukee from prisons to join in the efforts to make Christ's name known through serving him in their homes. The weight of that move has brought some gray hair to my head, but it has also showed me the true essence of ministry and leadership despite opposition, we must press on! I have been on the sidelines watching Arn for over fifteen years, and now it's time to use the tools he inadvertently gave through his faithfulness to God first, then all things after.

–Frank Woods, Executive Director of GENESIS in Milwaukee, Inc.

THE GENESIS PROJECT
2010

The GENESIS project grew out of care for individuals in our society who have been historically neglected after they leave prison. This growing population includes those who are homeless, those coming out of prison and other institutions, those who have aged-out of foster care, and others who truly need a new beginning. Only a few other ministries in Milwaukee are like GENESIS.

Early in 2010 BASICS began an investigation on the possible acquisition of a facility that could accommodate the vision and purposes of the GENESIS project. The goal was to provide a safe residence for citizens returning from prisons, those who are homeless, and others displaced in our society. The programs would provide volunteer work, social services, employment and skills training, life skills, and discipleship education to the residents. This comprehensive approach serves to ensure the vocational and financial success of the residents upon return to society. Outside businesses and services partners would be invited to provide services along with the GENESIS staff.

Pastor Sonya Graves' Testimony

As I thought about my experience at GENESIS, I considered

about all the men and women whose lives I touched. God allowed me to display his love, compassion, truth, and teaching into their lives. Working at GENESIS was a learning experience for me. Showing the love of Christ by visiting men and women in prison and then helping them as they came out was amazing.

There are many stories I could tell, but one that stands out is the session I had with a sixty-two-year-old woman who was released from serving her time in prison and was on probation. She was sent to GENESIS from one of the agents from probation and parole. The woman was told that if she wanted to change her life, she needed to go to GENESIS and speak with me. The woman came and met with me, and we talked for an hour on our first visit. She poured out her life to me about things that took place in her life when she was between the ages of six and thirteen. She was molested by a family member ,and when she told her mother, it was dismissed and rejected. She was told that it did not happen, and it was her fault. This woman carried this all her life, and it changed her life for the worst. We had intense, personal conversations. One day she said, "I finally can say it was not my fault, and I forgive the person who hurt me and my mother."

She wept bitterly in my office. She had a breakthrough, and I give God all the glory for what he did for her. Her life is moving forward with God at her side as a result of coming to Christ at GENESIS.

-Sonya Graves, BASICS - Minister to Milwaukee

For almost ten years God seemed to be leading BASIC to work with people both in and out of prison. The vision of the expanded GENESIS program became more and more clear, like getting the two government grants. All this seemed to say God wants to bless us with a facility that would accommodate the full GENESIS vision and mission.

Should we stay with one small building for the welcome center administration offices, or should we look for a larger facility that could accommodate classrooms, job training workshops, and on-site jobs for returning citizens to work with supervision? The State

Department of Corrections was also looking for solutions to over-population in the prisons and the many being planned for release into urban communities.

The GENESIS program addressed many of the issues discussed, and I was invited to present the GENESIS concepts to the Wisconsin Department of Corrections Community Justice Cooperating Council (CJCC) meetings in Milwaukee and Madison. The interest it generated caused me to organize a group of business leaders to develop detailed financial plans for implementation. During this period, God made our GENESIS team aware of four unique facilities to consider acquiring. The criteria we used to evaluate a facility was based on the ministry we planned to facilitate:

- A welcoming "home" atmosphere
- A private setting with space for quiet rest and time with God
- Space for Bible study alone and with a group
- A place for private counseling
- Kitchen for food preparation
- A place for meals together with other returning citizens
- A facility requiring upkeep and maintenance for chores
- A building with projects to teach skills for employment
- Classrooms and worship center
- Administrative office space
- Bedrooms and restrooms to house up to one hundred residents
- A space to do laundry
- A game room and exercise room.
- We thought a space to garden would be nice, but was also optional
- Garages for auto repair and inside parking for equipment
- Finally, parking

A convent setting seemed to fit our criteria well, and God amazingly opened the doors to consider four options. The team spent the next three years attempting to discern God's plan for the GENESIS program.

There were four options. It was difficult to understand what God's plan was when so much effort was put into the project we thought God was leading us to pursue. We continued to pray and watch for God's direction.[11]

We continued to pray that God would bless the GENESIS ministry. A new expanded vision was to look at acquiring houses in neighborhoods that would become a network of lighthouses in the community, and that each family house would become a lighthouse to give direction and build healthy neighborhoods where God's kingdom comes and his will is done. The plan gave direct control to the people in the neighborhoods where transformation is desired. To accomplish the lighthouse network, a house was acquired, and the new vision is currently being implemented.

Private Individuals/Family and Public Foundations

Jesus is the perfect master-leader. He is bringing his kingdom to our world. He is the model to follow as we are called to be his emissaries/ambassadors/disciples to bring his good news into the world in which we live. In searching the Scriptures to find clues on how we are to view getting the resources we need to do his work, he tells us in Matthew 10 that when he sent out his twelve disciples, he gave them specific instructions under his authority:

- Where to go: *"To the lost sheep of Israel."*
- What to say: *"The Kingdom of God is near."*
- What to do: *"Heal, raise the dead, clean the lepers, and drive out demons."*
- How to do it: *"Give freely because you have freely received."*
- Don't take any money: *"The worker is worthy of his keep."*

- Where to stay: "*Search for a worthy person and stay at his house.*"
- How to bless:"*If the house is deserving, give it your peace. If not, take it back.*"
- When to leave: "*If not welcomed or listened to, leave and shake the dust off your feet.*"

I've often wondered, "What did Jesus do on earth during his ministry that I can apply to the work he's called me to do?"

- He worked as a carpenter with his earthly father Joseph until he was thirty years old.
- He became homeless at the age of thirty to enter his ministry.
- He prayed every morning on the mountainside.
- He chose his twelve disciples and taught them.
- He lived with his followers and continually taught them.
- He taught and healed the people on the highways and byways and in the synagogues.
- He criticized the Jewish leaders who refused to learn his way and were hypocrites.

Jesus did all this without a business plan. All the provisions he needed were often provided by his followers. In Matthew 10:9, Jesus states, "*a worker is worthy of his keep,*" which is certainly true, but that requires people who value the work being done and are willing to pay for it. Jesus was able to pay his taxes by having his disciples catch a fish and find adequate funds in the mouth of the first fish they caught. Does this imply that God will provide in some miraculous way? I can attest to the fact that miracles do happen when we trust in God to provide in unexpected ways.

Over the years, God has amazingly supplied the provisions we've need to keep the ministry of BASICS moving ahead. We have occasionally run short of funds, but when we asked our network to pray, God always provided what was needed. This is why we have viewed fundraising as being much more than getting money. The resources we have needed have come through the giving of time, talents, treasure, touch, tears, and sometimes a check. This approach has significantly built our faith, hope, and love. And the greatest of these is love.

The people of faith have been loving and responsive and have come from many different perspectives. Over half of our donations have come from individuals who are actively praying, volunteering, working on projects, and serving in outreach. The rest comes from churches, family trusts, businesses, corporations, and foundations. God's people have been faithful; God is faithful! Praise the Lord!

---

1. MPS schools where on-site prayers, projects and Bibles have been offered are:
   South Division High School
   North Division High School
   Vincent High School
   Franklin Pierce Elementary School
   Bradley Tech High School
   Auer Avenue
   Alba School
   Vincent High School
   Rufus King Middle School
   Lincoln Center of the Arts Middle School
   Barack Obama School of Career and Technical Education
   Longfellow School
   Clark Street School
   Bay View High School
   Hope Schools
2. Some of the major issues facing youth and urgently seeking solutions today are:
   Pornography: on TV, games, and movies
   Apathy: lack of self-respect and loss of hope
   Truancy: lack of parental care and direction
   Illness: lack of good food, lead poisoning, asthma
   Domestic abuse: violence, rape, drugs
   Illiteracy: not able to read at grade level
   Teen pregnancy: abortion decisions
   Poverty: fatherlessness
   Unsafe schools: bullying
3. Some of the demographics are:
   Wisconsin's largest bilingual high school with 1,138 students
   Male: 53.5%; female: 46.5%
   Nationalities:

> Native American / Alaskan: 1.2%,
> Asian / Pacific Islanders: 13.4%,
> Black: 32.1%,
> Hispanic: 46.9%,
> White: 5.9%
> Multiracial: 0.5%
> 86.1% of students eligible for free or reduced-fee lunches.

4. Gregory Thorton, "The Silence is Deafening," Sep., 2012, www://www.j-sonline.com/news/opinion/the-community-sillence-is-deafening-4m49ktq-140383903.html.

5. The partner groups included in the Safety Coalition were:
> Milwaukee Police Department
> Probation and Parole
> Community-based Organizations
> Faith-based Organizations
> City Departments
> Health Services
> Education
> Business and Business Owners
> Prosecutors
> Citizens of the Community
> Facilitators

Some of the religious leaders involved in this effort along with BASICS Ministers were: Pastors Harold Moore, Carl Griffin, Donnie Sims, David King and Sister Rose Stietz.

6. Some of the persons involved in collaborating with the MPD Homeless Outreach Team were:
> Convener: Arn Quakkelaar, BASICS
> Lt. Karen Dubis, MPD District #1
> Kristina Betzold, BASICS administrator
> Pastor Alvin Hull, Fearless Soldiers of Messiah
> Darrell Bell, Fishers of Men Ministry
> Marty Calderon, Street Talk Ministries
> Bob Burmeister, Under the Bridge Ministry
> Pastor Richard Brown, BASICS Captive Team
> Frank Woods, BASICS Captive Team
> Officer Anthony Leino, MPD
> Officer Russell Barker, MPD
> Officer James Knapinski, MPD
> Reverend Edward Johnson, Fearless Soldiers
> Rev. Ron Cutino, Fearless Soldiers
> Rev. George Castro, Fearless Soldiers
> Pastor Ray Jablonski, HeartFire Ministries
> Raymond Jablonski Jr., HeartFire Ministries
> John Wegner, HeartFire Ministries
> Pastor Ansen Davis, Word Is God Ministries
> Pastor Denise Davis, Word Is God Ministries
> Pastor Demetrius Bryant, Word Is God Ministries
> Sonya Graves, Word Is God Ministries
> Pastor Martin Childs, Pilgrim Rest Baptist Church

Pastor George Claudio, Vineyard Church
Oliver Johnson, Prison Aftercare Network of Wisconsin
Richard and Gloria Gierach
Laura Marsh, Homeless Resident
Bob Burmeister, Under the Bridge Ministry

7. Highlights of changes at Angola:

Violence at Angola has dropped 80 percent since the seminary first opened.

Staff turnover dropped because the prison is a safer place to work.

All the gangs have disappeared. Gang leaders have become pastors.

As prisoners changed, the Angola "rule book" has changed. Men have proven themselves trustworthy.

Prison operating costs were reduced by $12,000,000 per year.

A dramatic reduction in the number and scope of prison riots.

Four hundred fewer security and administrative employees.

8. Note: Grove C. Norwood, founder and CEO of the Heart of Texas Foundation is using the Angola Seminary model to operate the Southwestern Seminary at Darrington Penitentiary in Rosharon, Texas. Grove is also assisting the establishment of a similar seminary in Wisconsin called the Wisconsin Inmate Education Association (WIEA).

Email Grove Norwood (Grove@HeartOfTexasFoundation.org) to arrange a trip for your state's key players.

9. Note: For more information, email info@WisInmateEdu.org

10. BASICS received national attention for this work. On October 21, 2015, the Justice Center of the Council of State Governments issued a national press release entitled "Second Chance Act Grantee Work Reflects Pope's Belief in Rehabilitation."

11. *The Gray Conference Center, Northeast Milwaukee*

Pros:

Formerly a convent meeting all our functional criteria and more

Building use aligned with the Genesis mission, vision and passion

Dedicated to Christian beliefs with Catholic beginnings

Received a $30,000 seed money donation to pursue acquisition

Owner and Diocese eagerly supported the transition

Cons:

Building was very large, old and costly to renovate to meet code requirements

Lacked municipal support because of political objections

The city wanted to use the facility for expanding the safety training academy.

Our offer to purchase was rejected. Project was abandoned!

The Saint Joseph Convent, Campbellsport

Pros:

A convent in outstanding move-in condition

Met all our criteria and more

A donor offered to buy the entire facility and give it to GENESIS

The community and its president were very supportive

Cons:

Distance from Milwaukee was a concern

Didn't meet Department of Corrections (DOC) restrictions

The owner took the property off the market after a verbal offer was made.

The project was abandoned.

Saint Coletta's Convent, Jefferson

Pros:

A convent had potential and strong local support.

Cons:

Distance from Milwaukee—didn't meet DOC restrictions

In poor condition—the cost to repair was too high

No offer was made. Project was abandoned.

More than twelve other sites were considered but none met our criteria and we began feeling God was not leading us to pursue other facilities. It was then that Ms. Cordelia Taylor mentioned her deep desire to transfer the operations of Family House to Genesis.

Family House, Milwaukee zip code 53206

Pros:

An ideal location for the population we were being led to serve

The facility uniquely met and exceeded all our criteria.

The approved land use aligned with the Genesis mission.

The owner was eager to transfer the ownership and work with us in reaching out to meet the needs of the neighborhood.

Cons:

The Family House debt was found to be very significant.

The vacated buildings became targets of vandalism even with additional security.

The project was abandoned until alternatives could be found waiting for God's guidance.

KINGDOM DEVELOPMENT

2015

Our Father, who art in heaven. Hallowed be Thy name. Thy
kingdom come, thy will be done, on earth as it is in heaven.
Matthew 6:9

What: To encourage the reader to develop a love for the people of
Milwaukee.
So what: To develop a spirit of evangelism to reach out to our
neighbors in love.
Now what: To commit to God by doing God's work twenty-four
seven wherever he leads.

What would the city look like if the Kingdom of God came to
Milwaukee? What picture comes to your mind when you pray for
his kingdom to come? Can you imagine a perfect city *"on earth as it
is in heaven"*? With what I've seen in Milwaukee, it's hard for me
to imagine what that might look like. Obviously, it would take a
miracle of God to make our city holy!

Nehemiah pictured that miraculous holy city for Jerusalem
when God's people were in captivity, and the city had been
destroyed. He prayed, and God heard his prayers and saw his tears.
Then miracles happened. Jerusalem was restored, but it took a lot

of work by many people, even with people who were opposed and resisted.

I haven't found a verse in the Bible that would even hint at Milwaukee being a holy city, but wouldn't it be great if Milwaukee could become known as a city for God? Many believers are praying for revival in Milwaukee, and we have seen many Christians in our city work diligently for that to happen. Many of the stories in this book would indicate that God is certainly at work in our city through the lives of his people. If we have faith the size of a mustard seed, it could happen. What would it take for us to begin the process?

Do you recall the heir force concept I mentioned earlier in this book? This was a vision God gave me that may be helpful to review as we consider our role in doing God's work in Milwaukee, his way!

My challenge and guide to restoration in the city was to serve in God's *heir force* to:

- Be *aware* of where God is working and join him there (mission).
- Be in *prayer* for God's wisdom and discernment (intercession).
- Show I *care* by loving my neighbor (compassion).
- Be ready to *prepare* friends to obey God's commands (discipleship).
- Be *there* wherever God calls me to serve (mobilization).
- Be an *heir* in God's kingdom (worship).

Could this be a way of applying God's truths to kingdom development in Milwaukee?

LISTENING SESSIONS
2016–18

Since 2016, the BASICS prayer team has fervently prayed about the painful problems people have on the streets. Many community leaders have held listening sessions to get closer looks at the hurt in the homes of our citizens, particularly those living in poverty and affected by crime. The mayor's office, the Department of Justice, the Police Department, and many churches and social agencies are digging deeper into what's broken and how to find answers with new approaches and insights. The BASICS ministers to Milwaukee and our partners are eager to participate in these efforts and be a part of finding solutions. It takes everyone working together. We cannot overlook our role of empowering those we serve to solve their own problems and make good decisions. As in the example of Nehemiah, all the people dedicated themselves to rebuilding the walls and God was with them:

> O Lord, God of heaven, the great and awesome God, who keeps his covenant of love with those who love Him and obey his commands, let your ear be attentive and your eyes open to hear the prayer your servant is praying before you day and night for your servants, the people of Israel. I confess the sins we Israelites, including myself and my father's house, have committed against you. We have acted very wickedly toward you. We have not obeyed the commands, decrees and laws you gave your servant Moses. Neh. 1:5–7

In the spring of 2016, a group of Sherman Park neighbors held several listening sessions in the local library to brainstorm the issues facing youth and their parents to find solutions to implement. A major crisis often creates an urgent need to change.

In Scripture, Nehemiah has deep concern for the Jewish remnants from Babylon returning to Jerusalem who were in great trouble and disgrace. The walls of the city were broken down, and its gates were burned with fire. When he heard these things, he sat down and wept, mourned, fasted, and prayed to God.

As we attended these listening sessions, we learned we must all work together in making good choices and ultimately love God above all and love our neighbor as ourselves.[1]

If we want God's kingdom to come and his will to be done on

earth as it is in heaven, we have a lot of work to do as a community of faith, hope, and love.

One way to start is letting your love of God to motivate you to obey the Ten Commandments:

And God spoke all these words: I am the Lord your God, who brought you out of Egypt, out of the land of slavery. You shall have no other gods before me. You shall not make for yourself an idol in the form of anything in heaven above or on the earth beneath or in the waters below. You shall not bow down to them or worship them; for I, the Lord your God, am a jealous God, punishing the children of the sin of the fathers to the third and fourth generation of those who hate me, but showing love to a thousand generations of those who love me and keep my commandments. You shall not misuse the name of the Lord your God, for the Lord will not hold anyone guiltless who misuses his name. Remember the Sabbath day by keeping it holy. Six days you shall labor and do all your work, but the seventh day is a Sabbath to the Lord your God. On it you shall not do any work, neither you, nor your son or daughter, or your manservant or maidservant, not your animals, nor the alien within your gates. For in six days the Lord made the heavens and the earth, the sea, and all that is in them, but He rested on the seventh day. Therefore, the Lord blessed the Sabbath day and made it holy. Honor your father and your mother, so that you may live long in the land the Lord your God is giving you. You shall not murder. You shall not commit adultery. You shall not steal. You shall not give false testimony against your neighbor. You shall not covet your neighbor's house. You shall not covet your neighbor's wife, or his manservant or maidservant, his ox or donkey, or anything that belongs to your neighbor. Ex. 20:1–17

If you read what the Scripture says next, it might surprise you:

When the people saw the thunder and lightning and heard the trumpet and saw the mountain in smoke, they trembled with fear. They stayed at a distance and said to Moses, "Speak to us yourself and we will listen. But do not have God speak to us or we will die." Moses said to the people, "Do not be afraid. God has come to test you, so that the fear of God will be with you to keep you from sinning." Ex. 20:18–20

There are times when urban communities face disasters that we hope don't happen but they do, and we must be prepared to respond. Examples of these incidents are riots and drive-by shootings. God has prepared unique individuals from unusual backgrounds to respond to these crises. Here are two stories rarely told about several gangbangers I've met over the years who have survived the gang life and have become believers. They have straightened out their lives after serving their time in prison and now want to give back to the community they've hurt. God has called them to serve as exceptional leaders to do his will in making a difference, bringing God's kingdom to Milwaukee.

RIOT CONTROL
2016

As community leaders, one of the most unwanted news alerts is "Black Man Shot by Police Officer." We all know this is often the spark that is sure to be followed by demonstrations and violence in urban streets.

On August 13, 2016, this happened in Milwaukee in the Sherman Park neighborhood.

Newspaper reporter Aaron Mak of the Journal-Sentinel wrote:

Shots ring out in Milwaukee Street a standoff between police and an angry crowd turned violent Saturday night after police fatally shot an armed man. It wasn't clear if the gun was pointed at the officer. A foot chase, gas station set on fire, firefighters could not for a time get close to the blaze because of gunshots. Later, fires were started at businesses—a BMO Bank, Beauty Supply Company and Auto Parts Stores.[2]

While the demonstrations and violence were occurring, BASICS and GENESIS street chaplains were on the streets urging the youth and gangbangers to stay away to stop the violence immediately. Many of the young people were coming to the scene because it was something fun to do as suggested by the mass media messages. It was like a call to rumble urged-on by imported agitators from other cities from as far away as Chicago. The rock and brick-throwing and fires are typical of what is encouraged by the agitators at these events. ABC News reported: "Some of the protesters used social media to encourage others to participate in the demonstration. Protests turned violent. The Revolutionary Communist Party confirmed that some of its members were among the protesters and that they traveled to Milwaukee to support a revolution but did not intend to incite violence."

Several of our BASICS and GENESIS street chaplains talked to agitators who claimed to be community organizers from Chicago and that they were paid to come to Milwaukee and stir-up violence. The inciters were telling protesters to start fires and turn over cars. In the *Chicago Tribune*, chief of the MPD Edward Flynn was reported to have praised faith and community leaders for their efforts in curbing the violence and assigned blame of the riots to members of the Revolutionary Communist Party—they organized additional protesters, which turned the initial protests violent. There were over thirty instances of gun fire on Sunday with over forty arrests during the three-day period of unrest.

The BASICS and GENESIS street chaplains, residents, and people of faith were actively organizing teams to pray. They stood in circles, held hands, and prayed for peace. When the police came to clear the areas in Sherman Park, they asked to stay and pray. The prayers continued, and the violence subsided. The agitators were escorted out of the area. I believe the relationship of the faith community, Parklawn Assembly of God church members, pastors, and our local police and sheriffs contributed to reducing the escalation of violence and the return to peace. The gangs miraculously stayed away from the demonstrations and told our street chaplains of their anger in seeing outsiders destroying their neighborhoods.

During the following days and weeks, many projects were started to address and solve the problems and bring unity to the Sherman Park community and beyond. Parklawn Assembly of God Church has been at the center of these efforts to heal the damage caused by the violence. Sunday morning at 8 a.m., Sherman Park residents and volunteers from the metro gathered to pray and clean up the streets—a major display of unity, compassion, and love for our neighbors. Good can come out of evil. Praise the Lord!

Street Chaplains, By Frank Woods

The day started with my wife and I preparing for a renewal of marriage vows ceremony between dear friends in Christ in Pewaukee, Winsconson. Upon our return home after a glorious occasion, we were bombarded with chaos from throughout the area as disorder, anger, and frustration seemed to reach its peak. It was a response to recent police shootings. Tension between law enforcement and civilians began to thicken; this unrest was its culmination.

Our home in Sherman Park is just blocks away from where scenes of violence were plastered all over international news platforms. What seemed to be the acts of rebellion and criminality actually stemmed from a series of events brought about early on by community disunity caused by the many unanswered cries for help from our community's invisible people.

The lights of fire trucks and police cruisers, sirens, roadblocks, and smoke with a stench of burning vehicles came from a BP gas station located on Sherman Blvd, a block and a half away from our residence. Something indeed was in the air, as the whole neighborhood seemed to be thrust into scenes only witnessed on world news footage of what happens in third-world countries where corruption is expected.

The following day, sounds of screams, shouts, and moans of a broken community continued, beckoning my attention and the local church as it was a Sunday, the Lord's day. As a part of the leadership in a small congregation amongst the many storefront churches in the inner city, I found myself in a dilemma: whether to continue as usual or run to the aid of the lost, contrite, and brokenhearted people on the streets. I did the latter. As my family and I drove through the neighborhood surrounding ground zero, we were horrified to find out that the damage done exceeded what had been reported through various news outlets.

As a pastor, I felt compelled to serve our community in some way, so we contacted other ministers in the inner city to set up an outreach post on the street with resources to meet with and serve the people roaming the streets. A marvelous group of brothers and sisters responded including Dan Quakkelaar, Rob and Sharon Honey, Lavoris Agee, Richard and Aurelia Brown. In faith, hope, and love, we prayed for and listened to our afraid and hurting neighbors. Multiple ministries eventually joined us: The Captive Project, BASICS, Parklawn Assemblies of God Church, Friend of Sinners Church, and so many others. We all descended on the area to serve through speaking about God's love and praying for peace.

Because of the massive media coverage, many concluded that our Christian outreach setup was only there to receive camera time, and that we were disingenuous. This was far from our intent and, as an urban outreach ministry working only in the parks, we decided to expand this initiative into the streets in ongoing events called the "flash church" held at random inner-city street locations. This has evolved into what is now the "Annual NYEO" (New Year's Eve Outreach) event. This commitment has been consistent every year since as a platform to testify to the unity in the body of Christ locally, and to debunk previously held beliefs concerning the local church and our concern for our neighbors.

December 31, 2017, update:

This yea"s annual NYEO event began a day before the actual event with the team covering the neighborhood in prayer for God to bring out all those he appointed by placing a hedge of protection around his faithful servants.

Arriving at 9:30 a.m. on New Year's Day, I was met with an overwhelming feeling of inadequacy concerning the lost souls who lack hope. I prayed that those who I had reached out to concerning this event would show up. Weathermen predicted with accuracy negative five degrees for the day. Many volunteers came down with the flu, and I became very uneasy.

At 10 a.m. God's servants from different churches and ministries arrived to work together. By design we focused on three different stations. The first was the green trailer equipped with clothing, Bibles, and soup. The next was the hot drinks station surrounded by warm invitations to the grounds with one-on-one Gospel invitations. And third, the One Way Out of the Pit Grill attracted more than hungry stomachs, because we wanted to feed the souls of the whole persons.

Since the unrest of 2015, many Sherman Park residents believed that the church would vanish with the TV cameras. But God displayed his faithfulness by declaring, "I was always a part of the community!" Many donations from the body of Christ showered love on participants through their time, talents, treasures, touch, and tears.

Burleigh and 35th Street is one of the highest traffic areas of the city during this season. God drew attention to the Spirit-filled preaching of his Word, and those who drove by marveled at the stop light when they saw what was going on in the middle of winter in Milwaukee. Many effective and valued gifts were distributed that cold day like socks, hats, and gloves. I was personally blessed that day when my younger brother Aaron joined us to support our ministry. Just as Moses was sent his brother, Aaron to speak, I was sent mine!

During the outreach, a group of ten preteens came to investigate our event, and they encountered my brother. To his surprise, he noticed that all of them were without socks. Cut to his heart, he tearfully beckoned them over and invited them to put on free socks. Filled with emotion, he wept as he helped put socks on such cold feet and wrestled with his feeling of thankfulness with the overabundance of things many take for granted. God is at work in Sherman Park! Praise the Lord![3]

–Frank Woods, Pastor, GENESIS Street Chaplain

Being the father of five sons, I was frequently impressed with how smart they thought their dad became when they reached the age of twenty-five years old. Working with gang youth in the city, they also seemed to respect me as an old man with gray hair. Some even referred to me as Moses.

Respect is an important value in the gang culture where the slightest show of disrespect could be fatal. During the past twenty-five years working on the streets, I've met a fairly large number of impressive men who have aged-out of the gang life and have become respected returning citizens in the community.

Scientists have found through MRI studies that the male brain doesn't mature until age twenty five while females mature at age twenty one. Psychologists have found that men become emotionally mature at forty three—eleven years after women who mature at thirty two.

Adolescents and young adults are much more sensitive to peer pressure and risk-taking, breaking rules, ignoring consequences until they reach thirty years old. At eighteen, they are normally not ready to live in an adult world.

Instability in childhood also has a great impact on the development process affecting the ability to plan, organize, behave, and control themselves. The legal age should probably be twenty five instead of eighteen or twenty one. Obviously, older men have matured and have learned the consequences of bad decisions and can be valuable mentors and coaches for the young men who didn't have fathers to teach them.

This may help to understand and explain, but not excuse, the behavior of youth in the inner-city gang world, which results in drive-by shootings, gang wars, stealing cars, disregarding laws, drugs, and disrespect for authority. These are some of the actions we demand be stopped!

One of these senior men and two of his friends had survived the dangerous gang life, served their time in prison, were no longer on parole, were in legitimate careers, and had become respected business leaders in the community. It was not surprising that each one of them had become believers in Jesus Christ and were committed to giving back by impacting the lives of young gang-bangers to stop them from doing what they had done.

One of these returning citizens became a dear friend who God led to help form the GENESIS Ministry in Milwaukee. He and his two friends had a vision to stop the killing in the city. Each of them was respected by the gangs because they were vetted and understood the gang culture.

They were committed to giving them alternatives to incarceration. Stop the shootings and killings. Get legitimate jobs for the gangbangers. Get them food, clothing, shelter, healthcare, and drug treatment as needed. Give them respect for life, themselves, their family, and even their enemies. Help them choose alternatives to incarceration. Get trained in job skills to support themselves in a career.

Providing guidance and opportunities to change lives while holding participants accountable and teaching them how to live could be the key to bringing transformation in Milwaukee and beyond.

This vision aligned beautifully with the GENESIS mission, vision, passion, and action. We decided to quietly move ahead praying and watching to see how God would work to provide the resources to make it happen.

Specific activity areas we were led to pursue were:

- Auto businesses: sales, repair, detailing, transport
- Food businesses: pick up, delivery
- Communication businesses: TV, radio, media, movies
- Housing: restoration, repair, maintenance

This vision and plan are still being developed and the infrastructure is being implemented under the radar without fanfare and as God directs. Pray for God to lead his people to respond to this vision, his way.

FRONT ROW SEATS
2017–19

When I ask people why they won't go to church, one of the main reasons I hear is they have been hurt by someone who claims to be a Christian. They won't have anything to do with hypocrites! It's interesting that when Christ was in his ministry on earth, he spent a significant part of his time in synagogues telling the Jewish leaders they were hypocrites. Does this issue require our attention today, especially when church attendance is dropping in America? What actions can we take to reverse this image of Christ's Church? How can we help people who have been hurt by Christians?

Gary and Laurie Hendrickson, the new co-presidents of BASICS, are addressing the issue of reconciliation with training classes and seminars called Front Row Seats and Sharpening Your Interpersonal Skills. Their intent is to provide sound, biblical, and practical training to believers in peer-to-peer environments that build bridges of understanding and reconciliation within the Christian communities. Paul writes:

> Therefore, if anyone is in Christ, he is a new creation, the old is gone, the new has come! All this is from God who reconciled us to himself through Christ and gave us the ministry of reconciliation: that God was reconciling the world to himself in Christ, not counting men's sin against them. And He has committed to us the message of reconciliation. We are therefore Christ's ambassadors, as though God were making his appeal through us. We implore you on Christ's behalf: Be reconciled to God. God made him who had no sin to be sin for us, so that in Him we might become the righteousness of God. 2 Cor. 5:17–21

Front Row Seat begins with eight panelists of differing ethnic backgrounds sharing experiences and tackling tough questions. Then during lunch, all attendees have an opportunity to be a part of the dialog in table groups.

Facing one another, they share and listen to racism's impact on their lives through stories. Our goal is to foster new understandings that break down walls that divide not only our city but the church as well.

Front Row Seat at Southbrook Church in Franklin, Wisconsin, is a suburban church where both urban and suburban participants learn from each other the skills of sharing the gifts and fruits of the Holy Spirit. In Galatians, Paul writes:

> *But the fruit of the Spirit is love, joy, peace, patience, goodness, faithfulness, gentleness and self-control. Against such things there is no law. Those who belong to Christ Jesus have crucified the sinful nature with its passions and desires. Since we live by the Spirit, let us keep in step with the Spirit. Let us not become conceited, provoking and envying each other.* Gal. 5:22–23

A diverse group of eighty panelists and participants, representing over twenty-four churches in the metro gathered at Southbrook Church in Franklin for an honest conversation about our experiences with race. Front Row Seat is an event BASICS initiated to invite followers of Christ to live out his commandment to love others in practical and relational ways.

We prayed that this interactive dialog would bring understanding to the unique experiences of race, from either side of the aisle. Peter wrote:

> *Finally, all of you should be of one mind. Sympathize with each other. Love each other as brothers and sisters. Be tenderhearted, and keep a humble attitude.* 1 Pet. 3:8 NLT

Our goal for Front Row Seat was to bridge the divide that separates not only our culture, but the Church as well, to build compassion for one another, unity as one body, one family—one human race under Christ![4]

Another BASICS initiative started by the Hendricksons is called Sharpening Your Interpersonal Skills (SYIS) Workshops. This is a five-day intensive faith-based workshop for anyone who works with others and facing the day-to-day challenges inherent with personal interactions.

Subjects covered include:

- Loving Listening: skills for ministering more effectively by listening well
- Advise and Problem Solving: the role of giving advice and steps involved in helping others solve problems
- Confronting: biblical guidelines and skills for confronting and responding when confronted
- Conflict Resolution: biblical ground rules for both you and others for resolving
- Community: what destroys community as well as the attitudes and skills to build it up
- Stress: its impact on you and on others, including strategies for how to manage stress well
- Suffering Loss: the grief process and ways to help others who have suffered loss

MARKETPLACE IMPACT
2017–19

Marketplace Ministry is a relatively new approach to evangelizing our society and seems to make sense, but it will involve major changes in the attitudes of Christians about their daily lifestyles. The basic idea is that believers should be active in evangelism whenever and wherever God places them.

That means seven days a week, twenty-four hours a day rather than just going to a church and Bible studies a few hours each week. This involves important decisions on how we spend our personal, work, and play time, and that also brings up several practical and ethical issues relating to who we serve.

When Jesus sent out his disciples, he sent them two-by-two with specific instructions. Could this be done today in our current culture? Christians have been marginalized by media and politicians, and most of us have endured silently without saying anything. We stay in our comfort zone. Are we afraid? God tells us repeatedly in Scripture: *"Do not be afraid!"*

Reaching out to our neighbors is relatively easy to do, but we seldom do it. Talking to our coworkers about our faith is probably more difficult and is done on our employer's time (which is unwise), but we can work in a loving and caring spirit with integrity. What is your area of influence in your marketplace?

The late Dr. Bill Bright, founder of Campus Crusade, developed the concept of Seven Mountains of Influence as we consider working in the marketplace and making a difference for our coworkers. God places us uniquely where he wants us to show and tell others about our relationship to him. I've expanded on Dr. Bright's mountains listed below as fields of service in our society. Where are you working?

- Arts and Entertainment
- Business and Industry
- Communications and Media
- Denominations and Religion
- Education and Learning
- Finance and Investments
- Government and Regulation
- Health and Wellness
- Information and Technology
- Justice, Legal and Enforcement

Are you part of bringing the Kingdom of God to our world? Being a good friend may be the best way to start. It may also help lead you to do his work to show and tell about his love! Your faith, hope, and love may bring hope to your friend, which may lead them to faith in your Lord and Savior. This may be your God-given task of building God's kingdom using your time, talents, treasure, touch, and tears in worship of him.

Wouldn't it be great if doing God's work in a loving and caring way was the way to connect with others as partners to make a difference? So often the opposite happens in relationships with those who don't believe in Jesus.

SUCCESSION TO SUCCESS
2017

Has God put you in a position of leadership? The test is whether or not you have any followers. If you do, you are a leader and have a tremendous opportunity to serve those followers to the best of your abilities. Most leaders in the secular world don't think this way, but being a servant leader will open many doors to success! I know this from experience during my entire working career. Most workers love having a good and caring advocate, mentor, coach, or boss who helps them become successful, which makes you successful. Try it. You'll be surprised at the results.

The challenging opportunity in the inner-city neighborhoods of poverty and crime is to find good servant leaders who are strong, brave, smart, skilled in leadership, and who have followers who need direction. There have been a multitude of efforts in the city to control the hoods, stop crime, and control all the related problems that surround the deteriorating conditions that have continued far too long.

In a conversation I had with a pastor in one of the most dangerous hoods, we were talking about the tremendous amounts of money spent to stop crime and eliminate poverty in his neighborhood. He was desperate to find solutions. That Sunday, as he was entering his church, he was grazed by a bullet inches from his left eye. His cry to me was, "This has got to stop!"

BASICS had been helping him renovate his old church building by restoring the basement and putting in a computer center for youth to get them off the streets and teach them valuable skills. He had observed that when gunshots were fired in previous summers, the children would run and hide.

But that summer, they would just stand and watch. Many of them were convinced that they would never reach the age of eighteen; they had lost hope in the future and consequently lost any desire to live. Their only desire was to join the gang and get a gun, so they could be in control.

The pastor pointed out that the youth in his neighborhood were controlled by a strong, brave, smart, and skilled gang leader who was eager to protect his territory and his gang so they could continue the illegitimate businesses they had developed. We brainstormed. What if the gang leader could start constructive, legitimate businesses for youth that would rescue and restore the neighborhood, giving appropriate work and income to these developing young citizens and build hope for the future. This was way out-of-the-box thinking, but it is much more constructive than the gang prevailing in the hood.

As servant-leader pastors of churches in the hood, should we be doing what Jesus did—living close to the people, healing their sick, casting out evil spirits, and changing the attitudes to loving and caring for those who don't know Jesus? That is hard to do when the majority of pastors of inner-city churches have moved away from the neighborhoods where their church is located, and they no longer know their church neighbors. The Genesis Lighthouse movement is taking gang leaders who have aged-out of the gangs and become believers in Jesus Christ with training to be servant leaders to transform gang houses into lighthouses for truth by bringing faith, hope, and love back into the hood—building neighborhoods again.

What will it take to transform the lives of gangbangers and their leaders to become followers of Jesus Christ, who was the perfect servant leader even though there were still people who hated him and wanted to kill him? But Jesus did what God told him to do: *"It is not the healthy who need a doctor, but the sick. But go and learn what this means: 'I desire mercy, not sacrifice.' For I have not come to call the righteous, but sinners"* (Matt. 9:12–13).

What is God telling us to do? The Genesis team is being formed to build an infrastructure of Christian resources throughout Milwaukee to use the prayer, care, share, prepare model of evangelism to bring God's kingdom to our city. Could this be a strategy for transformed gang leaders to change their hoods into neighborhoods where our love of God, our neighbors, and ourselves is demonstrated? This is what is beginning to happen in the GENESIS project.

WORKING WITH WEALTH
2005–2019

As CEO of a nonprofit organization, searching for and obtaining funds is a difficult and constant challenge—probably the most demanding and frustrating part of the work. Building the bridge to Milwaukee generosity is linking to the soul of the city and its passion to bring the resources to make the city great. God's way is to show his love for his creation through people of faith who love and know him and worship him for what he has done for us. Jesus taught:

> *Then the King will say to those on his right, "Come, you who are blessed by my Father; take your inheritance, the kingdom prepared for you since the creation of the world. For I was hungry and you gave me something to eat, I was thirsty and you gave me something to drink, I was a stranger and you invited me in, I needed clothes and you clothed me, I was sick and you looked after me, I was in prison and you came to visit me."* Matt. 25:34–36

Generosity is demonstrated by God's people through volunteering and contributions of time, talents, treasure, touch, and tears. His work is to love God, neighbors, and self.

Two concerns have dominated my prayers when seeking God's direction: How to make the needs of the poor and disenfranchised people in Milwaukee known? And how to find or build the resources required to help them?

Many of the men and women on the BASICS advisory board were also active in the National Christian Foundation Wisconsin (NCF WI), and it occurred to us that this could form a very natural and valuable partnership to unite servants with people of wealth. So with Linda Maris, a gifted and professional executive director, we decided to organize an annual symposium for community leaders to present a State of the City report on what God was doing in Milwaukee through the faith community.

In January of 2010, BASICS and NCF WI sponsored the first annual State of Milwaukee Symposium on Poverty at Heartlove Place on Martin Luther King Jr. Drive. The purpose was to inform not to raise funds. The symposium has grown and continues to this day under the capable leadership of the NCF WI team. Linda Maris gives an extensive description in the section below of the many things this team does.

THE NATIONAL CHRISTIAN FOUNDATION WISCONSIN 2010 BY LINDA MARIS

I have been blessed to walk with many saints. Saints usually do not boldly declare that they are a saint. To do so would be seen as boastful and contrary to the common idea that a saint is righteous or virtuous. I used to think of saints as only those who were holy and those who sacrificed their lives for God, like the disciples and the martyrs of the early church. Or those individuals canonized by the Catholic Church for their life of devotion and miracles they performed. My definition of a saint used to be narrow, and it set a high standard.

My journey with The National Christian Foundation (NCF) Wisconsin (NCF WI) started January 1, 2009. I was beyond ecstatic to have been called to serve and could not have envisioned what transformation God had planned. It is through my work at

NCF where I was brought into community with the saints in Milwaukee.

God's Word clarifies that a saint is not one who is free from sin. We are holy in God's eyes only through belief in Jesus and his sacrifice (Heb. 10:10). In his letters, Paul refers to saints as those faithful, sanctified, and called in Christ Jesus (Eph. 1:1, 1 Cor. 1:2, Ro. 1:7). Saints are believers who stay the course, grow spiritually, and follow God's will. Saints are those ordinary men and women who are led by the Holy Spirit and who God works through.

I have been blessed to walk with many saints, and most of them are from Milwaukee. I am blessed not only because of who they are but because I experience God at work through these ordinary, yet incredible, individuals. It has been an amazing privilege to walk with the saints in Milwaukee. Individuals who do not fear, who live with intention, who give sacrificially of their life and resources, who risk being safe and comfortable, who love their neighbors, who quit lucrative jobs, who move into diverse neighborhoods, who trust in God to provide, who give up their plans and follow God and say, *"Thy will be done Lord, not my will be done"* (Matt. 6:10). These saints are my mentors and teachers. They make my life rich and give me faith and hope in what I cannot see.

Life Purpose

How I came to NCF WI is an unlikely story. It is more accurate to state that I was called to the foundation because it was not my plan. And my story is not unusual in the NCF network of almost three hundred individuals. I share a little piece of my path because it is a story of God's extravagant generosity in my life.

My story gets interesting in 1996. I was a wife, a mother of three small children, and a practicing lawyer. On Friday, December 13, 1996, I was in a car accident just three blocks from home. In the ambulance, I remember thinking that I must have suffered a bad case of whiplash and, with Christmas around the corner, I just did not have time for that!

I have a vivid memory of being in the Xray room when

everyone started to unexpectedly scurry about. Xrays revealed that I had fractured my neck at C-1 and C-2 vertebras (the top ones, closest to my skull). Christopher Reeves suffered from the same injury just a year prior, and it was fresh in everyone's memory. The difference was that, miraculously, my spinal column was not severed. I later learned that I have an unusually large spinal column.

The second miracle came a few hours later. I was being wheeled to my room at Froedtert Hospital in Milwaukee. I was alone at that moment and in pain. I was laying on the gurney and could see a sign that read Spinal Cord Trauma Unit and realized the seriousness of my injury. I don't know if the transport man saw my fear, but he said in a deep voice, "Honey, most people believe that Friday the 13th is an unlucky day but, for you, it is the luckiest day of your life. You will walk out of here one day, but most people in this unit don't."

I never saw him again but call him my angel because God used him to deliver a powerful message. I experienced the type of faith mentioned in the book of Hebrews, *"Now faith is being sure of what we hope for and certain of what we do not see"* (Heb. 11:1). In that instant all was well in my soul. Before I could even develop a bitter heart, it set my mind and my heart on God's overwhelming grace. I was filled with gratitude.

In the years to follow, I thought a lot about the reason for my accident and set out on a journey to find a purpose for my life. Jeremiah writes:

> For I know the plans I have for you, declares the Lord, plans to prosper you and not to harm you, plans to give you hope and a future. Then you will call upon me and come and pray to me, and I will listen to you. You will seek me and find me when you seek me with all your heart. Jer. 29:11–13

I realized my legal work was a career path and not a calling. In 1996 there was not an abundance of resources to help define a person's purpose. But God provided opportunity and experience, and I patiently waited. I prayed, "Send me Lord." Had I ventured off with my own plan, I would have missed what God had planned. I now wake up every morning with purpose where I can integrate my faith, legal knowledge, and leadership training.

The National Christian Foundation Wisconsin History

In 2020 the community will celebrate the twentieth anniversary of NCF WI (first organized in Wisconsin as the Christian Stewardship Foundation). We are thankful to the six visionary families who came together out of the realization that Christians could have a greater impact on the Kingdom of God if they had knowledge about how to make wise, charitable gifts. The vision of the first Board of Directors was to transform Milwaukee and expand the reach of the Kingdom of God through biblical generosity.

In the first year and a half of operations, NCF WI donors directed forty-five grants to charities. As of 2019 NCF WI helps facilitate around four thousand donor-directed grants annually to local, national, and international charities that help those in need and share the good news of Jesus. Today we serve over four hundred and fifty families, businesses, ministries, and churches as part of the NCF WI family. [5]

NCF is national in scope, Christian in focus, and a foundation in purpose. We provide grants recommended by donors to other charities. Our capacity to serve and to have such impact in Wisconsin with a small staff of three is credited to our affiliation with The National Christian Foundation (based in Atlanta and founded in 1982). NCF has twenty-six locations in the US, is currently the eighth-largest charity in the country, and the largest Christian grant-maker in the world. Our vision is "Every person reached and restored with the love of Christ." We accomplish this through our ministry to families, our ministry to ministries and by impacting causes locally and globally.

A Ministry

Studies say that the number one thing people trust more than God is money. That is a big burden to carry. No wonder the Bible has a lot to say about money, wealth, greed, contentment, and other topics on our financial and spiritual lives. In fact, the Bible talks about money more than love, hope, or the Kingdom of God. Think of NCF this way: Many people have a financial strategy but not a giving strategy, and they are wasting opportunity and spending too much on taxes. NCF helps people create a giving strategy so they can be wise stewards of all they have, and experience the joy of greater generosity. The psalmist writes, *"The earth is the Lord's, and everything in it, the world, and all who live in it"* (Ps. 24:1).

NCF is best known for our Giving Fund (Donor Advised Fund) which is like a charitable checking account. Individuals, businesses and organizations can open a Giving Fund at no cost and with no required minimum balance. Deposits into the Giving Fund are tax deductible at the time of the gift. Donors have the option to invest the charitable dollars that are in the fund, and the earnings are tax free. Donors retain the right to recommend grants to their church and favorite charities on their timetable. All of this can be done quickly and efficiently online. A Giving Fund is often an excellent, low-cost alternative to a private foundation.

Ministry to Ministries

NCF WI is a "phone a friend." Many churches and ministries do not have the budget or expertise to advance charitable giving strategies with donors or to accept gifts of appreciated assets like stock or real estate. Once we helped a ministry accept a silo of grain! Part of our ministry is to actively teach on gift-planning strategies to church and ministry boards, staff, and donors. There are strategies that open opportunities for gifts during life, gifts that produce income, and gifts at death. Ministries and churches can benefit from an NCF Giving Fund to accept online donations or stock and mutual fund gifts.

Local Impact

NCF WI has the privilege of convening leaders in Milwaukee to celebrate and accelerate both generosity and the Gospel Movement. We explore how to best communicate (celebrate) to a diverse faith community and how to build unity to serve together (accelerate) to better the city. Much of the community knows of NCF WI because of a signature event called the State of Milwaukee Symposium on Poverty held annually the last Tuesday in January. The symposium was started after the 2010 census to start a conversation around the complex issue of poverty. It would not have been possible without the partnership of BASICS in Milwaukee, for which NCF WI and the community are humbly grateful. The event now convenes an average of three to four hundred individuals to learn about the complex issues in our community and to encourage action and collaboration. The community will celebrate the tenth anniversary of the symposium in 2020.

The local impact of NCF WI is significant as we continue to build a more generous community. NCF WI celebrates the milestone of granting one hundred million dollars locally and globally. Through NCF we daily witness God at work through acts of generosity: hearts transformed, families healed, ministries opened, buildings purchased, neighborhoods changed, communities strengthened, education provided, relationships established, needs met, purpose found, employment secured, and love shared.

Transformation Through Generosity

The most recognizable heart transformation comes from the story of Scrooge. His physical appearance even changed when he embraced generosity. Generosity may start small with one giver and one receiver, but it has the capacity to ripple out to others and to the community. Generosity is powerful and life changing because it is love in action.

NCF embraces generosity through our mantra, Love Gives.

Because everything we are and everything we have is Gods. Love permeates all that we do. John writes:

> *Dear friends, let us love one another, for love comes from God. Everyone who loves has been born of God and knows God. Whoever does not love does not know God, because God is love.No one has ever seen God; but if we love one another, God lives in us and his love is made complete in us."* 1 John 4:7–8, 12

Loving and giving go hand in hand. God's love for us changes everything. Love gives mercy, forgiveness, selflessly, generously, always.

–Linda Maris, The National Christian Foundation Wisconsin, President

------

NCF WI represents financial wealth of the faith community and provides great ways to maximize investments in community improvements in God's ways. Other ways of doing God's work through generosity is to provide food, clothing, shelter, healing, and possibly even jobs for the unemployed. There are many ways to give of our time, talents, treasures, touch, tears—showing and telling God's love. God's Holy Spirit and the examples of Jesus gives us unlimited ways to serve him. Praise the Lord.[6]

---

1. Here is a list of circumstances and conditions that exist in many homes of poverty and crime, both urban, suburban and rural, which by-and-large must be changed by parents cooperating with government programs and laws:
   Money spent on cigarettes and drugs
   Substance abuse in the home
   Unhealthy air quality
   Toxins—mold and lead poisoning
   Unsafe drinking water
   Sewer back-up and resulting pollution.
   Filthy and hazardous living conditions.
   Disrespect for and lack of protection of life
   Not showing, teaching ,and demonstrating the value of prayer
   Not ensuring health, love and care within the home

Immoral, irresponsible and indecent lifestyles of adults

Lack of adequate and healthy – nutritious food

Abusive language and bullying

Violent and inappropriate TV, Movies, Games, Music, etc.

Access to weapons of violence

Not stopping gang immorality and crime

Allowing children to stay home from school

Not insisting on students doing their homework and not attending parent-teacher conferences

Lack of respect for authority

Not teaching children about God, prayer, the Ten Commandments, and love

2. Associated Press, "Milwaukee Crowd Turns Violent After Police Fatally Shoot Armed Man," *U.S. News*, Aug. 13, 2016.

3. What did we Learn About Sherman Park?

There remains a strong racial divide in the city of Milwaukee and we must work diligently to bring unity and respect for everyone.

The residents in Sherman Park are very respectful of their neighbors and proud of their community.

The faith community is active and strong in Sherman Park.

The Milwaukee Police Department and the Milwaukee County Sheriff's Department were very disciplined and controlled in a very difficult situation. They responded very admirably.

The mayor and local assembly leaders communicated effectively with parents and youth giving good directions to calm the situation.

The local media was careful not to escalate the anger of citizens by telling the truth when known and not spreading rumors.

The Sherman Park community will become even better in the future because they are more united as a result of the riot.

4. Some feedback from attendees about their experiences at Front Row Seat:

"Panelists discussions were helpful. They encouraged us to be uncomfortable in a conversation to get to know someone's story that has impacted their life."

"The discussions about racism we all talk about having do not have to be confrontational, negative, and debilitating"

"I loved hearing the panelists talk. I found out I still have a long way to go with my learning."

5. *Do not store up for yourselves treasures on earth where moth and rust destroy, and where thieves break in and steal. But store up for yourselves treasures in heaven, where moth and rust do not destroy, and where thieves do not break in and steal. For where your treasure is, there your heart will be also.* Matt. 6:19–21

In everything I did, I showed you that by this kind of hard work we must help the weak, remembering the words the Lord Jesus himself said: "It is more blessed to give than to receive." Acts 20:35

Command those who are rich in this present world not to be arrogant not to put their hope in wealth which is so uncertain, but to put their hope in God, who richly provides us with everything for our enjoyment. Command them to do good, to be rich in good deeds, and to be generous and willing to share. In this way they will lay up treasure for themselves as a firm foundation for the coming age, so that they may take hold of the life that is truly life. 1 Tim. 6:17–19

6. *When you reap the harvest of your land, do not reap to the very edges of your field or gather the gleanings of your harvest. Do not go over your vineyard a second time or pick up the grapes that have fallen. Leave them for the poor and the alien. I am the Lord your God.* Leviticus 19:9–10

Is it not to share your food with the hungry and to provide the poor wanderer with shelter—when you see the naked, to clothe him, and not turn away from your own flesh and blood? Isaiah 58:7

CITY TRANSFORMATION

2018

"If my people, who are called by my name, will humble themselves and pray and seek my face and turn from their wicked ways, then will I hear from heaven and will forgive their sin and will heal their land."
2 Chronicles. 7:14

What: What God is doing today in Milwaukee.
So what: Get involved.
Now what: Just Do It! Don't Do Nothing!

Milwaukee has frequently been ranked as one of the most segregated cities in America. Unfortunately, this fault has impacted the family of faith also even though there have been many prayers for unity. God's people seek his blessings, but it comes with work on our part as well.

In 2013 Minister Greg Lewis, inspired by Dr. Rev. Donnie Sims and other senior pastors in the inner city of Milwaukee, organized Pastors United. The membership today is over five hundred church leaders. It was a special blessing that Mark Mallwitz and I were invited to become members of such a valuable initiative. We both felt strongly that God was at work to bring unity to his church in Milwaukee.[1]

For four years as an active attender at the weekly Wednesday morning meetings, I listened intently and gained valuable insights into the intensely critical issues facing our inner-city people. As an active student of the many cultures within the human race and family of faith in Milwaukee, I've learned the importance of listening and empathizing with the deep sensitivities and hurts that have led to the devastating segregation dividing our city.

There are numerous, major practical issues demanding solutions if unity in the churches is to ever happen; but before discussing that, one fact must be understood: we are all brothers and sisters in Christ serving our Lord together in Milwaukee. We all pray fervently, love God, and love our families. But we often face insurmountable problems that are difficult to correct without prayer, love, and the resources to heal them.

The Pastors United leaders have identified the strategic problems to be addressed with committees assigned to each and reviewed at each meeting.[2] A typical Pastors United agenda includes these priorities:

- Family structure
- Health and wellness
- Crime, incarceration, and safety
- Economic and employment development
- Education
- Civic engagement[3]

My son is one of the pastors in Pastors United. It is my great honor to begin this chapter with a testimony of God's work in my oldest son's life as God led him to respond to a call to serve in Milwaukee's inner city:

A Message from Dan Quakkelaar

As the oldest of Arn Quakkelaar's five sons, I share with my brothers a unique perspective on his life and his influence. One of my earliest memories is sitting on my father's shoulders, wrapping my arms around his head. It must have been after a hard day's work, because I remember feeling his five o'clock shadow whiskers on my little arms and having my hands removed from in front of his eyes.

In short, my father lifted me up, and gave me his perspective on the world. He gave me a view I did not otherwise have. Much more than this physical perspective, he gave me a philosophical perspective on life as I grew up.

My dad discipled me. He showed me how to faithfully love a woman, my mother. He showed me how to work hard and provide for his family. He showed me the loving guidance of a father for his children, filled with rules, yes, but also filled with grace. He lived out his faith before me. My parents laugh now when I say that I never heard them argue. They assured me they did, but they must have done it in a way that was clothed in grace and mercy and love, because I don't remember a harsh word ever between them.

So it was no surprise when in his mid-fifties my father left his lucrative position and bright future with Rockwell in order to serve the Lord in the inner city of Milwaukee. His philosophy was simple—he wanted to bridge the gap between the church in the city and the church in the suburbs. Now, there are Black, White, Asian, and Hispanic churches in both of those places, but my dad concentrated on one of the most difficult places of pain in our nation, which is the Black-White divide in the church.

We can never expect to bridge that gap in our society if we cannot bridge it in the church. Dr. Martin Luther King Jr. famously said that 11 a.m. on Sunday morning is the most segregated time in America. No one disputes the statement, and it is repeated so often it has unfortunately become a cliché. It is indeed a great shame to the church and requires our repentance.

The question is, who is the one who should repent for this community sin? Often White people say, "I never owned slaves," or "I am not prejudiced." I embrace such statements because I see that they are either true, or at the very least they are aspirations.

Yet in our society, bias and prejudice still exists in ways that mere changes in the law cannot redress. A White man and a Black man walk into a store, and the security officer follows the Black man around. Why is that? A White man and a Black man call to interview for a job, and the Black man is rejected, and the White man is accepted. Why is that?

These and other injustices happen because our national racist past, like a boulder thrown into a lake, ripples into our present whether we like it or not. Who repents for this? What does repentance even look like, when it comes to this kind of national sin?

In Scripture, culpability for sin and the need for repentance at a national level is common. The entire world was judged at the time of the flood. Everyone at the tower of Babel was judged. All of Egypt was judged in the plagues. All of the first wilderness generation was judged before entering the promised land. All of Canaan was judged as Israel entered the land to wipe out entire people groups. All of Israel was judged and sent into exile. All of Assyria was judged and destroyed. Judah was judged and sent into exile.

But we see repentance also. Leaders arose in the Holy Land during the time of the judges who repented and led Israel into repentance. Jonah prophesied against Nineveh in Assyria, and Nineveh was spared because of the repentance of the King. Even Daniel repented for the nation of Israel, for sins he did not commit, but on behalf of his people.[4]

The question is, what does repentance look like in America today for our racism? In Nineveh, it looked like sackcloth and ashes. For Daniel it was regular prayer three times a day. But often what I have seen in America is not repentance but defensiveness. Despite the evidence that Whites have privileges in our society not afforded to Blacks, we deny it. We point to changes in the law to establish our innocence, but we don't deal with the changes that must happen in our hearts.

True repentance is a change in direction. It's not mere confession and the changing of a few rules. It's manifested in friendships, advocacy, celebration together, intermarriage, and honoring one another. We see each other's failings and are willing to acknowledge them to one another. We see each other's successes and find joy in honoring one another for those successes. We place our faith in each other. This is what true repentance produces when reconciliation is needed.

My brothers of African descent should feel that honor if for no other reason that the important role Africa played in the original growth and organization of the church. American Christians have had to bow to the accusation of being a "White man's religion." Nothing could be further from the truth. In fact Christian orthodoxy was established largely in Africa. You can confirm it simply by looking through the list of African church fathers: Origen, Cyprian, Clement of Alexandria, Tertullian, Pachomius, Athanasius, and Augustine. Leaders in the Protestant Reformation looked to these men for guidance in understanding the Gospel and orthodoxy.

Scripture gives significant roles to African men and women. Moses married a woman from Cush (Africa). The original elder board in Antioch that sent Paul and Barnabas on their first missionary journey was composed of two Africans and a man that had been in the courts of Herod. These three initiated the spread of the Gospel to Europe! Later, after Muslims swept through northern Africa wiping out the Christian nations there, it was Europeans who returned the favor by bringing the Gospel back to Africa shortly after the Reformation.

The point is, Europeans and Africans have a long heritage of loving and helping one another. There is also a sordid truth among Europeans of race-based chattel slavery. It is important that we work together. The segregation we see today, the psychological segregation we live out, is an evil and satanic thing. It leads us apart, not together.

Real repentance looks like that early elder board in Antioch. It brings us together in support of one another. Someone, or perhaps many, must rise up and change our direction. The Assyrian King of Nineveh decreed sorrow and change.

We need someone to do the same for the Christian church today. The role that Arn Quakkelaar took models the kind of repentance that is needed. Men and women of character and courage must rise up to bridge the gap in godly ways. When that happens, it takes on a look that is uncommon and distinctly Christian. It is one of Gospel redemption. It is one that understands spiritual gifting. When God provides his church with gifts, he does it without showing favoritism. My dad understands that this gifting will be displayed in men and women of every skin color and ethnic background. When we see that, we celebrate that it is God who is working—not the White community or the Black community. It is a distinctly Christian reality grounded in redemption and the Gospel.

The bottom line is that mercy goes both ways, and partnerships are always reciprocal. A White man seeking racial reconciliation must first find a Black man who is willing to mentor him. The White man must submit to his brother, knowing that it is the Lord who is working in and through his Black brother. There is a godly, mutual humility we express toward one another. None of us should expect any privileges other than what the Gospel provides. We are all sinners saved by his grace, and we are exalted as we humble ourselves.

This is what my dad did. He went into churches and asked pastors and ministry leaders in the inner city to teach him about the community they lived in and what resources were needed. This former International Vice President at Rockwell International humbly went to inner-city pastors and asked to be discipled by them. That's what reconciliation looks like. Oh, to have faithful men and women in every city willing to reconcile with their brothers and sisters.

I watched this process from afar. In the 1990s I was working on my MBA at Cardinal Stritch University, building a career as a marketer. I pursued my career as I had seen my father do in his youth. I knew that my dad had left the business world and was entering ministry full-time. Quite frankly, as my dad was forming BASICS, I had little understanding what he was doing. I was afraid of the city. I was upset when he would go downtown to dangerous neighborhoods late at night because a friend had gone back on drugs and his wife was calling for help. I told him he was taking unnecessary risks.

When the BASICS model was described to me, I didn't understand it at all. I remember asking my dad why people would give him money so he could give it to other ministries? Why wouldn't they skip the middleman and send it directly to the ministry? It made no sense to me.

He was so gracious and patient with me and kept describing some of the ministries he was working with and how he was helping people live out their calling. I didn't get it. I donated to BASICS because it was my dad, and I knew his character and faith. I believed it must be right, but I continued to try and figure out why this highly intelligent and successful man would think that what appeared to be a hair-brained scheme would ever work.

One day I was listening to the Harvard Business Review podcast. The topic was angel investors and venture capitalism. It was aimed at entrepreneurs who needed investment money. But I was struck by what the podcast said: it wasn't the money that was the most important thing. It was the counseling. It was the administration. It was the contacts and networking that an entrepreneur must have to take his or her idea and turn it into a stable organization that can succeed.

It was then that the light went on in my mind. I finally understood BASICS as venture capitalism for ministries. These new or struggling ministries were cash-starved, but that was not their greatest need. It was the need for counseling, administration, contacts, networking, legal help, websites, help with social media, help with setting up their 501(c)(3), help just answering the phone consistently! And yes, donations too. Ministry entrepreneurs did not have the help they needed to transform our inner cities, and the gulf between the city and the suburbs not only crippled our inner-city servants of the kingdom, but it deprived suburban servants from being able to contribute their gifts for the transformation of our nation.

This is the model necessary for reconciliation, and ultimately true repentance for the sins of our nation's past and present. This revelation changed everything for me. I suddenly understood the importance of the model my father created. This model is scalable and powerful. It is the kind of parachurch (my dad dislikes that word and prefers outreach ministry) organization that is largely missing or misunderstood or dismissed in our nation.

The concept of parachurch requires some explanation in relation to the model my dad has put together. I don't believe in parachurch. Neither does my dad. When Jesus prayed for us, it wasn't for parachurch organizations that do the work that the church should be doing. This is not a parachurch mission. God works through his Church. Organizations like BASICS must be held as mere servants of the Church, the body of Christ.

I say this because the temptation will exist to get inspired, call the elders together, fund a BASICS-like organization, and sit back with joy knowing that we are doing what God has asked us to do.

You would be wrong. BASICS requires boots on the ground from your church. By all means, fund organizations like BASICS. It's more important to send real, live people who develop real, live relationships and real, live love for each other.

This is where we must go. My father is nearing the end of his life. His day is coming to a close. His proverbial final five o'clock shadow has emerged. In a very real way, I'm still sitting on my father's shoulders, feeling the stubble on my arms. I went on to become an ordained pastor in the Presbyterian Church in America (PCA). I am currently planting Friend of Sinners Church in the inner city of Milwaukee. Our church vision is to live out the life-perspective we see in Jesus, who is the Friend of Sinners. We strive to gather together as the Body of Christ, to go into places in our city where the Gospel is desperately needed, to grow in the love and knowledge of him, and in our unity with one another. In short, we are working to live out the vision God gave to my father over twenty years ago. I hope the same for you, and your city.

–Dan Quakkelaar, Pastor, Friend of Sinners Church

CHURCH PLANTING
2013–2020

Over the past ten years God has been calling a large number of pastors to start churches in the Milwaukee area, particularly focused on the inner city. BASICS has been receiving phone calls from many of these church planters asking for information on the demographics and details of Milwaukee, resulting in over twenty-five meetings with these leaders.

In response to these discussions, Mark Mallwitz and I decided it would be a good opportunity to meet with all of them together to pray for Milwaukee revival and to get to know each other. It would also be helpful for them to begin working together in selecting their target areas so as not to compete but complement each other in their efforts. The meeting was inspiring and developed a cama-raderie that continues to this day.

The immediate result of the meeting identified target areas uniquely surrounding the inner city while also identifying established inner-city churches we knew that would welcome part-nering with them in each target area.[5]

Power and Unity in Jesus by Mark Mallwitz

On Sunday, October 4, 1997, I experienced one of the most powerful and unifying gatherings in my life. The take-away for me is just as powerful twenty-plus years later as it was on that beautiful day in Washington, DC on the Mall.

Stand in the Gap was a sacred assembly of over eight-hundred thousand men who were simply coming together to pray for our nation. Men were coming from all over the United States and around the world to cry out to Almighty God.

During one of the times of prayer, Max Lucado came to the microphone and asked the men to shout the name of their church or denomination on the count of three. The sound of all those different names was like a lot of noise with seemingly no purpose or benefit to all of us listening to it.

Then he came back to the microphone again and asked the men to shout the name of Jesus on the count of three. The power, the unity, and the blessing of all these men shouting "Jesus!" at the same time made the ground shake and rumble under our feet, John writes, *"My prayer is not for them alone. I pray also for those who will believe in me through their message, that all of them may be one; Father, just as you are in me and I am in you. May they also be in us so that the world may believe that you have sent me"* (John 17:21–22).

The Body of Christ lifting up the name of Jesus in one voice reminded me that he is the only one who has the ultimate power and when we focus on his name, we can become one like Jesus prayed for all believers.

–Mark Mallwitz, BASICS - Minister to Milwaukee

MINISTRY LEADERS SUCCESSION
2008–2019

Attempts to unify the pastors and ministry leaders in the community of faith have brought many church leaders together, but our efforts must be directed and blessed by the Holy Spirit, God's way! As I look over the past twenty-five years, it would be difficult to impossible to list all the efforts that have been made to unite and build up the leadership of the faith community. It is evident to me that selecting the leaders is not my work but God's.

The concept of developing church and ministry leaders starts with discipleship. It starts with preparing believers to be disciples as Jesus did: he lived with them, he knew them intimately, he respected them, he served them, he taught them, and even when they abandoned him, he loved them even to death. Jesus taught:

You know that those who are regarded as rulers of the Gentiles lord it over them, and their high officials exercise authority over them. Not so with you. Instead, whoever wants to become great

among you must be your servant, and whoever wants to be first must be slave of all. For even the Son of Man did not come to be served, but to serve, and to give his life as a ransom for many.
Mark 6:42–45

At a gathering of inner-city pastors and ministry leaders, we were praying and celebrating communion at the Italian Community Center in downtown Milwaukee. At the conclusion of our prayer time, Linda Maris, executive of the National Christian Foundation-Wisconsin suggested Pastor Julius Malone, senior pastor of the New Testament Church, and I bless the leaders who were there by demonstrating what Jesus did for his disciples—washing their feet.

It was a great blessing and honor to perform such a great demonstration of love and unity for our brothers and sisters in Christ serving together in Milwaukee. I will always remember that event because both Pastor Malone and I had recently experienced significant health problems, and it was very difficult and painful for us to bow on our knees to wash everyone's feet (my spine at the lower back was disintegrating, virtually broken, and I was losing two inches of my height). It served as a reminder of the excruciating pain Jesus suffered for me when he was crucified.

This event also signified the importance of preparing successors in ministry as Jesus did while on earth. Jesus worked with his disciples for three years to prepare them for what was to come. God calls and choses the men and women he wants to become leaders in his kingdom, just as he chose Joshua to succeed Moses to lead his people out of the wilderness. Our work as leaders is to teach those individuals God leads to us to serve them to the very best of our ability as models of encouragement, inspiration, and authority.

Over the years, I've observed many pastors and ministry leaders who, for various reasons and circumstances, have dropped out of ministry or were removed from ministry. Jesus was led into the wilderness for forty days and nights to be tested by the devil directly, and he overcame the test. Leaders today will also be tested in many ways to prove their strength and readiness for the work

God plans for them. But they can also be tempted by evil and fail like Judas, which led to his death. The lesson for us is that we must continually guard ourselves from being led into temptation and avoid the sins that will destroy us.

A constant prayer life is what Jesus taught us by his example when he went to the mountainside to pray. We must do the same.

CHOOSE LEADERS TO FOLLOW
2018

As God chose Joshua to follow Moses and Elisha to follow Elijah, God is still in control of leadership succession today. We must pray for wisdom and discernment to find the persons God is preparing for positions of leadership in building his kingdom. We will never know or understand God's way or plan—we watch and pray.

When Mark Mallwitz was injured in an auto accident resulting in years of debilitating health problems, he was no longer able to carry on the leadership of BASICS after I became emeritus of BASICS. Mark and I fasted and prayed together to seek God's direction in choosing our successors. God led us to a couple serving as ministers to Milwaukee who were uniquely prepared and skilled to serve together as co-presidents of BASICS.

Gary and Laurie Hendrickson's Story

It was a midweek, hot summer day that was moving toward early evening. The smell of oppression was in the air. Driving up 27th Street, I saw men and boys sitting on porches trying to catch a breeze with the hazed, glazed look of those gripped by substance abuse. The young women were starting to come out dressed for an evening's work.

I said to myself, "Lord, this is not what I had planned for this season of my life." I heard a quiet response in my heart: "Yah, it's so much more fun, isn't it?"

Growing up in rural Muskego, an area seventeen miles southwest of Milwaukee, I never saw any neighbors or schoolmates different from me. We lived on a winding, tree-covered drive that led past our place. Our closest neighbors were the cows and the pigs of the farm next door. We were bused to local schools, and later (Laurie) a Catholic School in Waukesha where the cost of busing was actually more than the cost of tuition. Everyone in my community looked like me. The goal was to own a home, have nice vacations, and live a comfortable life. We were told, "Never go east of 68th Street because bad things happen there."

A December 2018 report published by the Brookings Institute shows Greater Milwaukee as the single most segregated metropolitan area in the entire United States. Nearly 80 percent of the residents live in neighborhoods comprised of people who have the same skin color.

It is undeniable that there are divisions within the human race that separate not only our cultures but the churches as well. The problem is that, in the divide, we lose the richness and blessings that come from sharing our unique experiences with God—stories of his faithfulness and diverse expressions of the gifts he activates within us.

After over thirty years of serving in the local, rural church first as volunteers, then as staff, and then as minister of groups and guests, there were the beginnings of unrest in my spirit. We had seen God do amazing and life-transforming works through our local church: people reconciled to God and to one another, marriages turned around, families reunited, and supportive communities built.

With all of the wonder we were seeing God do, it was easy to think that we had everything dialed-in and knew how to "do" ministry. But it began to feel as though the walls were closing in on us. Systems of ministry were becoming more important than taking the risk of listening to the Holy Spirit. I began to sense God calling me to step out of the boat, to take risks and learn to trust in him.

When our church hosted a whitewater-rafting trip, I decided

this would be a good first step in learning how to trust and physically take risks. I hit a small waterfall and flipped myself and the canoe into the rapids. I was pulled under the water and almost drowned after the third time. I prayed a simple desperate prayer: "Thy will be done." I popped up out of the raging waters, coughing and sputtering. Things in my heart were beginning to change.

During this time several churches had joined together to host the class Perspectives On The World Christian Movement. It outlines God's perspectives on reaching his people, and that he will go to the ends of the earth in whatever way necessary to reach and gather-up his beloved Church to himself. God was working in my heart.

A close friend of mine had just returned from a short-term foreign mission trip to Rwanda and learned about the 1994 Genocide in Eastern Africa. It was one kingdom, one people, one language, but outside forces stirred-up dissension and division resulting in the mass murders of over one million men, women, and children in just one hundred days. The United Nations ignored the situation thinking, "This is a problem between two tribes, and we have no business getting involved. Let them work it out themselves."

By serving in Rwanda as a minority within a majority Black African culture, I was able to see firsthand the gruesome aftermath of what evil division can do. What breaks my heart is recalling that every government on the planet ignored their cries for help and abandoned them during the mass killing spree, leaving innocent people to be slaughtered. I was convicted with a personal question: Is this how my people treat minorities in my own city of Milwaukee? That question challenged me to search how we treat our neighbors of a different culture and how can we align our actions with what Jesus teaches us and what the Holy Spirit empowers us to do in loving our neighbors.

Together, Gary and I began our ministry journey. Our season in a local rural church came to a painful end and we asked, "Lord, can you use us outside of our comfort zone?" As we looked at the cultures around us in the city and suburbs, we asked God, "What would you have us do to serve in your kingdom of Milwaukee?" We found that many churches struggled with differences and divisions among their own members and a great need for healing from deep wounds and hurts caused by Christian brothers and sisters.

We were led to attend the State of Milwaukee Symposium sponsored by BASICS and the National Christian Foundation in January of 2012 where we were introduced to Mark Mallwitz, then president of BASICS. He talked about the reality of segregation, divisions, and God's vision for churches and ministries working together to build the kingdom of Jesus Christ in our city. We knew immediately God was calling us to whatever we could to work toward a mission of unity with BASICS.

BASICS is a ministry hub of the faith community, linking urban and suburban resources within churches and outreach ministries providing a bridge to many opportunities that build relationships with our neighbors. The gifts of suburban organization and finance combined with wisdom and faith of the urban community result in an infrastructure of cooperation and communication that are part of God's kingdom. Our pastor, Michael Harden, reminds us that "Faith developed through struggle is different than faith developed from knowledge."

Mark and Arn have been patient and gentle mentors, helping us to learn how to reach hurting people in the city. They have learned the Euro-American values of process and projects along with the African, Asian, and Hispanic values of relationships and cultural knowledge. They are the keys to a symphonic harmony that takes many years of preparation, practice, and direction to be successful. Building relationships could be our primary project.

Known for innovative ministries and projects, BASICS has always been about building relationships and uniting urban-suburban resources. The projects have been the vehicle for working alongside each other. As we continue that legacy, we are becoming laser focused on healing the cultural divides in metro-Milwaukee through fervent prayer, practical acts of care, loving compassion, sharing the good news of the sacrificial love of Jesus, and preparing believers to make disciples of Christ.

Our commitment and plan for the future is simply to teach:

Racial recognition

Practical skills for healthy, relational living

Connecting people in deeper ways with God and one another.

God has led us to do this through several vehicles all designed to strengthen churches and introduce people into deeper relationships with God and their neighbors, no matter where they are on their spiritual journey.

In addition to bringing the hope of Jesus Christ through friendship, prayer, projects, donations of food, clothing, household goods, and friendship, we will come alongside the local church and ministries to bring practical training sessions called Front Row Seat and Practical Skills for Healthy Relationships. When brothers and sisters in Christ treat one another as gifted children of God with unfathomable value, worth, and respect made in the image of God, the world will be attracted to the God who created them. *"So then we pursue the things which make for peace and the building up of one another"* (Rom. 14:19). Christ's Church will become an unstoppable force in transforming lives and cultures.

–Gary and Laurie Hendrickson, Co-Presidents, BASICS in Milwaukee, Inc.

The new co-presidents of BASICS are addressing the issue of racial and relational reconciliation through events and workshops geared toward uniting God's people through healthy relationships and conversations. Front Row Seat: Dialogues for Understanding Racism Together was written by Gary and Laurie, and it specifically relates to the issues from a Milwaukee perspective. Sharpening Your Interpersonal Skills is a curriculum written by International Training Partners, Inc., a global network of facilitators and trainers serving together in an informal partnership to provide practical, interactive, biblical training in interpersonal relationships. Both provide sound, biblical, and practical training for believers in peer-to-peer environments that build bridges of under-standing and reconciliation within the Christian community.

Many of these cross-cultural relationships are beginning to go deep. We find we are better together! As we build relationships, we are able to join hearts and souls to overcome the challenges of the city. We pray differently, behave differently, and make different life choices. And Christ is glorified in all.

---

1. The Mission of Pastors United:

   Our mission as an organization of pastors and faith leaders committed to seeking God for guidance is to organize and mobilize for solutions to the social, economic and spiritual problems facing our community.

   The Vision Statement:

   Our vision is to impact the lives of and empower the thousands of people living in our local communities who are disenfranchised due to poverty and inequality and the lack of education, opportunity and hope.

   The leadership of Pastors Unite:

   The Board Officers:

   Minister Greg Lewis, First Vice President

   Pastor Mose Fuller, Second Vice President

   Bishop Warren Kirkendoll, Secretary

   Dr. Pat Robinson, Treasurer

   Board Members:

   Bishop Nathaniel Stampely

   Dr./Rev. Donnie Sims

   Pastor Kenneth Bonner

   Elder Annette Lewis

   Elder Malcolm Hunt

   Pastor Patrice Woods

   Advisors:

   Nathan Conyers

   Rochelle Landingham

   Ms. Shawn Green-Smith

   Dr. Andrew Calhoun

   Apostle Curtis Robinson

2. Note: As a member of Rotary International, we memorized and practiced a Decision-making four-way test of the things we think, say or do:

   Is it the truth?

   Is it fair to all concerned?

   Will it bring good will and better friendships? and

   Will it be beneficial to all concerned?

   Wouldn't it be great if everyone in the world would adopt this practice! It would bring harmony to all our lives!

3. In my listening notes taken during the meetings, I listed some of the characteristic needs and obstacles that must be overcome:

   Overcome despair, apathy, lack of hope

A resource infrastructure for cooperation and coordination
Need for money and resources
Church partnerships – urban with suburban
Ethics and honesty in business matters
Unselfish control of money
Relationships of trust
Commitments and promises kept
Obeying the rule of law
Communications and understanding with empathy
Respect for authority: teachers, pastors, police, politicians, youth, gangs, and God
Have tolerance and forgiveness to love our neighbors

4. Daniel 9
5. Here are some of the pastors and their new churches resulting from God's call to serve in Milwaukee:
   Dan and Emili Parmalee and Paul Stevens, Epikos Church
   Dan and Shereen Quakkelaar, Friend of Sinners Church
   Joshua and Emily Waldoch, The Way Church
   Bill Oliverio, Immanuel Church
   Jason Butler, Transformation City Church
   Tyler Loomis, City Brook Church
   Randy and Sarah Knie, Brew City Church
   Ricardo Valadez, Brookside Baptist Church
   Tommy Orlando, Mercy Hill Church
   Mark Weight, The Ridge Church
   Tony Bleything, Christ Redeemer Church
   Pete Ziolkowski, Imago Dei Church
   Matt Berry, Legacy Christian Church
   Elie Hasbani, Ethnos Church

WHAT'S NEXT?

2020

He who has begun a good work in you will complete it until the Day of Jesus Christ.
Philippians 1:6

What: Jesus is coming back.
So what: Get back to the BASICS of what God expects from us.
Now what: Be ready!

I found two men in the Bible I wanted to be like early in my life—Enoch and King David. Enoch walked with God, and King David was a man after God's own heart. Little did I know at the time, but I was choosing life. That decision has stayed with me throughout the years and has governed many of my life decisions. Writing this book has brought me closer to God than I ever imagined, and has been a driving force in writing this book. My heartfelt desire is to help everyone know the joy of being a child of God. It hurts me deeply when I see people suffering from the consequences of poverty and crime, and I know it hurts our Creator. My urgent prayer is that you reflect on your life and experiences to discern how much God loves you and has a purpose and plan for your life. I pray you choose life.

To test myself on how I'm doing on the road to a life of love, I ask myself critical questions by placing myself in the "I" statements or in the blank spaces below where the Apostle Paul shows us the most excellent way in 1 Corinthians 13:1–8:

> *If I speak in the tongues of men and angels, but have not love, I am only a resounding gong or a clanging cymbal. If I have the gift of prophecy and can fathom all mysteries and all knowledge, and if I have a faith that can move mountains, but have not love, I am nothing. If I give all I possess to the poor and surrender my body to the flames, but have not love, I gain nothing. __ is patient, __ is kind, __ does not envy, __ does not boast, __ is not proud. __ is not rude, __ is not self-seeking __ is not easily angered, __ keeps no record of wrongs. __ does not delight in evil but rejoices with the truth. __ always protects, __ always trusts, __ always hopes, __ always perseveres.__ never fails. And now these three remain; faith, hope, and love. But the greatest of these is love.*

I continually fail in every category! But praise God for his forgiveness through my Lord Jesus Christ!

Believing in Jesus Christ as the Son of God is a big decision and does not bring an easy life. I've experienced many painful, physical problems common to mankind, but when I think about what my Lord Jesus Christ suffered for me in dying a cruel death so that I could be forgiven and walk with God, I'm blessed! I pray you may be blessed by my story of what God has done in my life and be encouraged to live close to him. I'm ending my story of how God has led me to worship him by doing his work in Milwaukee.

God has led me to write this book for the purpose of *informing* you of God's reality in creating you for a purpose, to *inspire* you to not only believe that he is your God, but that he calls you to serve him wherever he has placed you in this world, and to *invite* you to love him above all and love your neighbor as yourself.

Has God touched your heart in some way? Has he challenged you to serve him in a specific way or ministry? Has he called you to love him and to build a special loving relationship with him? Are you ready to work with him and for him in his work? My prayer is that you can answer *yes!* to these questions.

God may be challenging you to begin by making a spiritual timeline of your walk with God to see how God has called and prepared you to serve him. Has he assigned you to a specific area of work or service in the marketplace? Do you sense God's presence and passion to just do it for him? However God is at work in your life, *"He who has begun a good work in you will complete it until the day of Jesus Christ"* (Phil. 1:6). Let us praise God for giving us the opportunity to do his work, his way, for his glory.

APPENDIX 1

My study of scripture uncovered valuable insights to leading God's way:

- "Be shepherds *of God's flock that is under your care, serving* as overseers—*not because you must, but* because you are willing, *as God wants you to be,* not greedy *for money, but* eager to serve; not lording it over *those entrusted to you, but* being examples *to the flock. And when the Chief Shepherd appears, you will receive the crown of glory that will never fade away."* (Emphasis mine) 1 Peter 5:2–4
- "*He* tends *his flock* like a shepherd: *He gathers the lambs in his arms and carries them* close to his heart; *he* gently leads *those that have young."* (Emphasis mine.) Isaiah 40:11
- "*The watchman opens the gate for him, and the sheep listen to his voice. He* calls his own *sheep* by name *and* leads them *out ... I am the Good Shepherd. The good shepherd lays down his life for the sheep ... I am the good shepherd;* I know my sheep *and* my sheep know me— *just as the Father knows me and I know the Father – and I lay down my life for the sheep. I have* other sheep *that are not of this sheep pen. I* must bring them also.

> *They too will listen to my voice, and there shall be one flock and one shepherd."* (Emphasis mine) John 10:3–4, 11, 14–16

- "Keep watch over yourselves *and all* the flock *of which the Holy Spirit has made you overseers.* Be shepherds of the church of God *which He bought with His own blood."* (Emphasis mine) Acts 20:28.
- Knowing God created man to work, and as God gave Adam directions on taking care of the Garden of Eden (Genesis 2:15), so too must leaders be responsible to lead others to do the work as servants to the Lord.

Scriptures that help me understand *God's design for work* are also very helpful:

- Six days *do your* work, *but on the* seventh day do not work, *so that you may* be refreshed. Exodus 23:12
- *"Then I realized that it is good and proper for a man to eat and drink, and to* find satisfaction *in his toilsome labor under the sun* during the few days of life God has given *him—for this is his lot. Moreover, when God gives any man wealth and possessions, and enables him to enjoy them, to accept his lot and* be happy in his work— *this is* a gift of God."* Ecclesiastes 5:18–19
- *"A curse on him who is lax in doing the Lord's work!"* Jeremiah 48:10
- *"Whatever you do, do it with all your heart, as working for the Lord, not for men, since you know that you will receive an inheritance from the Lord as a reward. It is the Lord Christ you are serving."* Colossians 3:23
- *"Devote yourselves to prayer, being watchful and thankful. Pray for us, too, that God may open a door for our message, so that we may proclaim the mystery of Christ, for which I am in chains. Pray that I may proclaim it clearly, as I should. Be wise in the way you act toward outsiders, make the most of every*

opportunity. Let your conversation be always full of grace, seasoned with salt, so that you may know how to answer everyone." Colossians 4:1–6

- *"Now we ask you, brothers, to respect those who work hard among you, who are over you in the Lord and who admonish you. Hold them in the highest regard in love because of their work. And we urge you, brothers, warn those who are idle, encourage the timid, help the weak, be patient with everyone. Make sure that nobody pays back wrong for wrong, but always try to be kind to each other and to everyone else."* 1 Thessalonians 5:12–15
- *'God is not unjust; he will not forget your work and the love you have shown him as you have helped his people and continue to help them."* Hebrews 6:10

APPENDIX 2

The following community justice centers throughout our community provide care and hope for the people of Milwaukee.

The Next Door Foundation is one of the first examples of a community justice center and was founded in 1969 by Our Savior's Lutheran Church as a church-based youth ministry outreach program. Its focus quickly expanded in response to the needs of neighborhood children and youth of families in poverty. By 1995,the ministry grew to a staff of over ninety members, mostly volunteers, and was serving over three thousand children, youth, and families of all faiths.

In 1989 the Helwig Family Foundation generously donated their headquarters building in Metcalfe Park to the Next Door Community Center. The primary goal was to enhance the quality of life for inner-city families through programs that educate, nurture, and enrich them by following healthy lifestyles. Major financial support was provided by Ernst & Young LLP, Johnson Controls, Inc. and Plastikoil Plus, Inc.

Since 198, the Running Rebels Community Organization has been dedicated to developing Milwaukee's youth to become responsible and successful citizens. The mission of Running Rebels has been to provide programs that assist Milwaukee's youth mentally, physically, and spiritually. The executive director, Victor Barnett, has made an outstanding contribution to bringing long-lasting changes in the lives of countless young people in the Harambee Neighborhood where he has served for many years.

In 1993 after several years of research and preparation, a similar concept was developed by a prominent Christian leader who initiated the Building Lives Project to establish a Transition Campus Community. The plan was dedicated to people who have low incomes. He felt God's call to enable disadvantaged persons and families to develop the skills necessary to build healthy, contributing, self-sufficient lifestyles. The proposal was presented to several large churches in Milwaukee but was not implemented due to lack of support and funding. The originator took the project to another major city in a neighboring state. He sensed that his plan was not aligned with God's plan for Milwaukee at that time.

In 1999 Heartlove Place was established as a nonprofit organization through the ministry of a group of dedicated individuals of faith who recognized the huge challenges facing Milwaukee's low-income residents. Broken families, unemployment, lack of education, increasing crime and teen pregnancies were significantly impacting the quality of life in the inner city. To overcome these challenges, the leadership of Heartlove Place relied upon Christian principles and teaching to uplift individuals and communities within their target area on North Martin Luther King Jr. Drive.

The mission of Heartlove Place is to reach out to the community with hearts of love; to teach, encourage, and support families through programs and services centered in Christian values. Heartlove Place connects communities through Christ to empower individuals, motivate families, and build stronger neighborhoods. We integrate the ideals of self-help, motivation, and empowerment with physical and spiritual support in order to do more than just provide a service or render a program. Heartlove Place is a conduit for the kind of lasting change needed to profoundly impact lives. The vision of building a community transformed by Christian values entails a few core areas of focus.

The core areas of focus entail a spiritual development component of connecting families with Christ. It also entails educational development—supporting families through training and self-improvement. There is also creative development aspect of connecting people with their purpose. And finally an emphasis on social development by connecting families to healthy life choices.

The goals of Heartlove Place are to provide services and programming to all community residents who request them, encourage collaboration between public and private agencies to supply needed services, strengthen families through education, quality services, and access to resources and illustrate compassion through Christian principles without passing judgment. They do this through offering a Family Resource Center, job training, and food services.

In 2008 the Zilber Foundation announced the ten-year Zilber Neighborhood Initiative and selected several Milwaukee neighborhoods for targeted investment. Since then, residents, nonprofit leaders, educators, and business owners in Lindsay Heights, Clarke Square, and Layton Boulevard West have come together to envision the future of their neighborhoods and take action. This is an excellent example of a well-planned and well-funded urban initiative.

In 2019 the board of directors committed to continuing to invest in the Zilber Neighborhood Initiative for five more years. Going forward, the foundation will work in partnership with neighborhood organizations and resident leaders to focus on addressing

Attempts to reduce crime and poverty through community justice centers have resulted in some improvements over the years. The Mobile Command Centers came and went over a two-year period with limited results. And even the Homeless Outreach Team program continues with some positive change in attitudes toward the homeless. But we still continue the relentless search for the best ways to reduce crime and bring peace and love to our neighborhoods by doing God's work his way.

Over the past twenty years, numerous Christian volunteers have been led to BASICS with desires to serve God as ministers to Milwaukee but not knowing precisely what God was calling them to do. It seemed appropriate to give them an opportunity to work with experienced ministers as volunterns (volunteer interns) for a period of time to learn what inner-city ministry would be like by working as a partner with someone who has been there, done that. This approach has led to many creative ways to implement the prayer (networking), care (compassion), share (evangelism), prepare (discipling) strategy.

APPENDIX 3

Here is the five-stage process of transformation for GENESIS residents.

In Prison, Phase 1: Choices (six to twelve months)

- Introduction to the Genesis program
- Chapel services
- Life studies
- Mentoring
- Bible studies
- Assessment of needs
- Establish a life plan
- Commitment to a new life
- Write and submit application letter and form
- Interview
- Enrollment in the program
- Meet the GENESIS team at the gate upon release.

———

Welcome Center, Phase 2: Lighthouse (two to four weeks)

- Trip to Parole Agent if required

- Tour of the city and welcome center
- Lunch with team, family, and friends (as appropriate)
- Interview with mentor
- Program orientation
- Life plan review and implementation plan
- Biblical class work and link with church and pastor
- Counseling as required
- Daily routine plan and rules
- Free time policies and procedures
- Chores and work plan
- Group and social dynamics review
- Personal development plan
- Graduation

———

Work, Phase 3: Career (twelve to twenty-six weeks)

- Work performance discovery
- Life skills assessment
- Family relations assessment
- Work discipline and ethic review
- Explore and exercise spiritual gifts and talents
- Responsibility and accountability management
- Person relationships review
- Personal development review and graduation
- Graduation

———

Wealth, Phase 4: Independence (thirty-six to forty-eight weeks)

- Independence discovery
- Progress review and assessment
- Employment review
- Life plan review

- Financial assessment
- Housing review
- Family and friend status review
- Christian ministry and mission assessment
- Life plan review
- Graduation

———

Giving Back, Phase 5: Worship

- Community engagement
- Self-assessment and relationship with the Lord
- Mentoring/coaching others
- United family relationships
- Serve in ministry
- At peace with God

APPENDIX 4

In attempting to discern the Master's plan for our lives and the work we do, it must be driven from what God tells us in his word. Here are key verses we found to help us know his design for our work:

- *"Let us make man in our image, in our likeness, and let them rule over the fish of the sea and the birds of the air, over the livestock, over all the earth, and over all the creatures that move along the ground."* Genesis. 1:26
- *"The Lord God took the man and put him in the Garden of Eden to work it and take care of it."* Genesis. 2:15
- *"Whatever you do, work at it with all your heart as working for the Lord, not for men, since you know that you will receive an inheritance from the Lord as a reward. It is the Lord Christ you are serving."* Colossians 3:23–24
- *"The Spirit searches all things, even the deep things of God. For who among men knows the thoughts of a man except the man's spirit within him? In the same way no one knows the thoughts of God except the Spirit of God. We have not received the spirit of the world but the Spirit who is from God, that we may understand what*

> God has freely given us. This is what we speak, not in words taught us by human wisdom but in words taught by the Spirit, expressing truths in spiritual words." 1 Corinthians 2:9–13

- "Then the King will say to those on his right, "Come, you who are blessed by my Father: take your inheritance, the kingdom prepared for you since the creation of the world. For I was hungry and you gave me something to eat, I was thirsty and you gave me something to drink, I was a stranger and you invited me in, I needed clothes and you clothed me, I was sick and you looked after me, I was in prison and you came to visit me." Matthew 26:34–36

- "I will tell of the kindness of the Lord, the deeds for which He is to be praised, according to all the Lord has done for us." Isaiah 63:7

- "Is not this the kind of fast I have chosen: to loose the chains of injustice and untie the cords of the yoke, to set the oppressed free? Is it not to share your food with the hungry and to provide the poor wanderer with shelter – when you see the naked, to clothe him, and not to turn away from your own flesh and blood?" Isaiah 58: 6–7

- "May the favor of the Lord our God rest upon us; establish the work of our hands for us—yes, establish the work of our hands." Psalm 90:17

- "Commit to the Lord whatever you do, and He will establish your plans." Proverbs 16:3

———

Here's a scriptural summary of what I have found as the basic patterns of life to follow in being part of the family of faith

Obey God's Commandments, Always!

- "Love the Lord your God with all your heart and with

all your soul and with all your mind. This is the first
and greatest commandment. And the second is like it:
Love your neighbor as yourself." Matthew 22:38–40

- "May my heart be blameless toward your decrees, that I
  may not be put to shame." Psalm 119:86
- "Your commands make me wiser than my enemies, for
  they are ever with me." Psalm 119:98
- "Trouble and distress have come upon me, but your
  commands are my delight." Psalm 119:143
- "My son, do not forget my teaching. But keep my
  commands in your heart, for they will prolong your life
  many years and bring you prosperity." Proverbs 3:1–2
- "O Lord, the great and awesome God, who keeps His
  covenant of love with all who love Him and obey his
  commands." Daniel 9:4
- "Whoever has my commands and obeys them, he is the
  one who loves Me. He who loves Me will be loved by my
  Father and I too will love him and show myself to him."
  John 14:21
- "This is love for God; to obey His commands. And His
  commands are not burdensome, for everyone born of
  God overcomes the world." 1 John 5:3–5

Study God's Word, Daily!

- "How can a young man keep his way pure? By living
  according to His word. I seek you with all my heart; Do
  not let me stray from your commands. I have hidden
  your word in my heart that I may not sin against you."
  Psalm 119:9–11
- "Your word is a lamp to my feet and a light for my
  path." Psalm 119:105
- "Take the helmet of salvation and the sword of the
  Spirit, which is the word of God." Ephesians 6:17

- *"Do your best to present yourself to God as one approved, a workman who does not need to be ashamed and who correctly handles the word of truth."* 2 Timothy 2:15
- *"For the word of God is living and active, sharper than any double-edged sword, it penetrates even to dividing soul and spirit joints and marrow; it judges the thoughts and attitudes of the heart."* Hebrews 4:12
- *"Do not merely listen to the word, and so deceive yourself. Do what it says."* James 1:22
- *"And now, O Israel, what does the Lord your God ask of you but to fear the Lord your God, to walk in all His ways, to love him, to serve the Lord your God with all your heart and with all your soul, and to observe the Lord's commands and decrees that I am giving to you today for your own good."* Deuteronomy 10:12–13

True Fasting

Isaiah 58:6–12

Is this not the kind of fasting I have chosen:
To loose the chains of injustice and untie the cords of the yoke,
To set the oppressed free and break every yoke?
Is it not to share your food with the hungry and to provide the poor wanderer with shelter
When you see the naked, clothe him,
And not to turn away from your own flesh and blood?
Then your light will break forth like the dawn, and your healing will quickly appear;
Then your righteousness will go before you, and the glory of the Lord will be your rear guard.

Then you will call, and the Lord will answer; you will cry for help, and he will say: "Here am I."

If you go away with the yoke of oppression, with the pointing finger and malicious talk, and if you spend yourselves in behalf of the hungry and satisfy the needs of the oppressed, then your light will rise in the darkness, and your night will become like the noonday.

The Lord will guide you always;

He will satisfy your needs in a scorched land and will strengthen your frame.

You will be like a well-watered garden, like a spring whose waters never fail.

Your people will rebuild the ancient ruins and will raise up the age-old foundations;

You will be called Repairers of Broken Walls, Restorer of Streets with dwellings.

Lead us Not into Temptation

Luke 11:1–4

Lord, teach us to pray, just as John taught his disciples. He said to them, "When you pray, say:

Father, hallowed be your name,

Your kingdom come,

Give us each day our daily bread.

Forgive us our sins, for we also forgive everyone who sins against us.

And lead us not into temptation."

Deliver us From Evil (The Lord's Prayer)

Our Father, who art in heaven. Hallowed be thy name.

Thy kingdom come,
Thy will be done on earth as it is in heaven.
Give us this day our daily bread,
And forgive us our trespasses as we forgive those who trespass against us.
Lead us not into temptation, but deliver us from evil.
For Thine is the Kingdom, the Power, and the Glory Forever. Amen!

———

Well Done, Good and Faithful Servant!

APPENDIX 5

"We Comin 4 Ya!"

by Lawrence Winters, Cedric Jiles, and T'Angelo Mosley

Check it, Christ was no respecter of persons
He got it in on the streets putting work in
He lived perfect and preached with a purpose
first sin separated; Christ had to purchase
So, He came to seek and to save the blind and depraved, the weak
and the lame
Lepers, mutes, the poor and sick man He preached to prostitutes
and arrogant rich men
He welcomed insults, addressed the hecklers and wasn't above
eating with tax collectors
He took several sinners from various backgrounds cowards turn
into warriors, that never back down
I pray the fallen will embrace The Rock, cuz it ain't the healthy,
but the sick that needed a doctor

[Yeah, you know what I'm saying. That's what we gotta do. We
gotta get out the four walls of these churches. It's time to get after
these people, they need us. They dying without us, yo. Let's go
get 'em!]

Chorus
If you in them streets We coming 4 ya!
And life got you beat We coming 4 ya!
The dough boy in the trap We coming 4 ya!
These youth getting laid flat We thinking 4 ya!
The prostitutes and the homeless We coming 4 ya!
We trying to show you what hope is We coming 4 ya!
Lost souls can be changed We coming 4 ya!
Cuz Jesus Christ came to save We coming 4 ya!

You can't hide man, you see me looking at cha you want me to boost ya sales like interruptions
Taking all the sales from any direction and at the same time you don't let no one detect ya
You gonna work the corner, til the corner get cha working for them thangs you know you can't take 'em witcha
So, what you gonna do, when the death hit cha even with the bling, them gates ya still won't enta
It's been a long night, and ya tired right can't even remember the last time you had a bite
You hate life, you hate the strife and some even might say you hate Christ
Cause things ain't right, you blame Him right what kinda god would let a man live his life
In the world that hates men, a world full of sin by which we've been condemned, until we hate sin
And fall in love with Him, who loves all men gave His life for them, so they can be with Him.

—Chorus—

Listen, what can separate cha from the love of Christ??? His love and sacrifice price to save yo life
God speaks and make the heaven and earth shake setting the captives free from the bondages of sin, it's a prison break

You been a victim of what's common to man what's common to man is having nothing in common with Him
Not common to Him, is man just be conforming to sin sin get a grip on man and man just be gone with the wind
A vicious cycle, but see they think it's tight though when they walking around on egg shells, life is a tight rope
They full of false hope, lights dim, no vision nowhere near, seeking the Lord of provision, for their children
They offspring, yeah man, but all their offering is the awful things, that they see the hard knocks life bring
I preach the gospel, good news to the poor good news to the poor, is that you ain't gotta be poor no more
Poor spiritually, (what) poor physically (yeah) socially, mental, financial, resist the enemy
Man, cause was meant to be sin is the only reason that you ain't got nothing, man and sure you want something
Envision that drive as a gift from God just to drive you to Him, just to seek His heart

—Chorus—

APPENDIX 6

This painting (reproduced in black and white here) was the result of a special project for a men's conference at Elmbrook Church. I was one of six men chosen to paint a picture showing our life's story and then give a five-minute verbal testimony of our lives.

We met one evening in an Art Shop in downtown Waukesha where we were given a brief introduction and lesson on painting with acrylics. The painting was to be completed in thirty minutes.

With a little coaching from our instructor, we finished and each gave our testimonies in preparation for repeating the same at the conference.

My painting displays various significant experiences in my life by showing a skyline of Milwaukee and buildings from left to right starting with the Allen-Bradley clock tower and Hoan Bridge. Then in the background you can see Elmbrook Church behind the Calatrava Art Museum. The tower in the center represents Johnson Controls Headquarters with a large church and steeple with house tops leading to a prison on the far right. This is the story of the major stages of my career and ministry to bring unity in the faith community of Metropolitan Milwaukee.

TO FOLLOW ALONG

Please check in and follow along with Arn's work at:

DoingGodsWorkMKE.com

ABOUT WHITE BLACKBIRD BOOKS

White blackbirds are extremely rare, but they are real. They are blackbirds that have turned white over the years as their feathers have come in and out over and over again. They are a redemptive picture of something you would never expect to see but that has slowly come into existence over time.

There is plenty of hurt and brokenness in the world. There is the hopelessness that comes in the midst of lost jobs, lost health, lost homes, lost marriages, lost children, lost parents, lost dreams, loss.

But there also are many white blackbirds. There are healed marriages, children who come home, friends who are reconciled. There are hurts healed, children fostered and adopted, communities restored. Some would call these events entirely natural, but really they are unexpected miracles.

The books in this series are not commentaries, nor are they meant to be the final word. Rather, they are a collage of biblical truth applied to current times and places. The authors share their poverty and trust the Lord to use their words to strengthen and encourage his people. Consider these books as entries into the discussion.

May this series help you in your quest to know Christ as he is found in the Gospel through the Scriptures. May you look for and even expect the rare white blackbirds of God's redemption through Christ in your midst. May you be thankful when you look down and see your feathers have turned. May you also rejoice when you see that others have been unexpectedly transformed by Jesus.

Made in the USA
Columbia, SC
22 December 2019